The Audio Effects Workshop

Geoffrey Francis

Course Technology PTR
A part of Cengage Learning

COURSE TECHNOLOGY
CENGAGE Learning™

Australia • Brazil • Japan • Korea • Mexico • Singapore • Spain • United Kingdom • United States

COURSE TECHNOLOGY
CENGAGE Learning

The Audio Effects Workshop

Geoffrey Francis

Publisher and General Manager,
 Course Technology PTR: Stacy L. Hiquet

Associate Director of Marketing: Sarah Panella

Manager of Editorial Services: Heather Talbot

Marketing Manager: Mark Hughes

Executive Editor: Mark Garvey

Project Editor/Copy Editor: Cathleen D. Small

Technical Reviewer: Tom Jacobs

Interior Layout Tech: MPS Limited,
 A Macmillan Company

Cover Designer: Mike Tanamachi

DVD-ROM Producer: Brandon Penticuff

Indexer: Katherine Stimson

Proofreader: Melba Hopper

For product information and technology assistance, contact us at
Cengage Learning Customer & Sales Support, 1-800-354-9706

For permission to use material from this text or product, submit all requests online at **cengage.com/permissions**

Further permissions questions can be emailed to
permissionrequest@cengage.com

All trademarks are the property of their respective owners.

All images © Geoffrey Francis unless otherwise noted.

Library of Congress Control Number: 2010922080

ISBN-13: 978-1-4354-5614-3
ISBN-10: 1-4354-5614-9

Course Technology, a part of Cengage Learning
20 Channel Center Street
Boston, MA 02210
USA

Cengage Learning is a leading provider of customized learning solutions with office locations around the globe, including Singapore, the United Kingdom, Australia, Mexico, Brazil, and Japan. Locate your local office at: **international. cengage.com/region**

Cengage Learning products are represented in Canada by Nelson Education, Ltd.

For your lifelong learning solutions, visit **courseptr.com**

Visit our corporate website at **cengage.com**

Printed in the United States of America
1 2 3 4 5 6 7 12 11 10

Acknowledgments

Thanks to Mark Garvey (as ever!) for his professionalism and for the assistance he has given me in the preparation of this book, especially with regard to tying up loose ends and magically making obstacles disappear!

Thanks to Tom Jacobs for his diligent, conscientious, and proactive approach to the role of technical editor. His ideas and suggestions have always been constructive, supportive, and helpful. The project has undoubtedly benefited significantly from not only his sound experience and solid knowledge, but also from his flashes of inspiration.

A special thank you to Peter Hicks, Annie Parsell, Mathew Woolley, Louise Bell, Sue Dilley, and Fred Pribac, whose musical talents are showcased in the sample audio files that are used on the DVD that accompanies this book to demonstrate and illustrate many of the practical examples and exercises.

Finally, a special thank you to Cathleen Small for her (as ever) encouraging, good-humored, and patient way of going about her task as editor. Explaining technical terms and communicating concepts that are sometimes quite complex is never easy. Thanks in no small measure to Cathleen, I hope we have succeeded!

About the Author

Geoffrey Francis is a seasoned veteran of recording (both analog and digital) with more than 20 years of experience. He graduated from Sydney's Professional Audio School in 1991 and rapidly discovered that this represented the beginning, not the end, of the learning process. He has built and successfully run his own studios in a variety of diverse environments, from the bustle and bright lights of Sydney to the calm and tranquility of the Tasmanian bush.

Over the years he has used a number of software packages in his studios. He is the author of *Home Recording for Beginners* and *REAPER Power!,* as well as other REAPER documentation, including *Up and Running* (the official REAPER User Guide) and *ReaMix—Breaking the Barriers with REAPER.*

Contents

Chapter 3
Introducing Audio Effects

Chapter 4
Shaping the Waves: Equalization

Chapter 5
Shutting the Gate: Noise Gates

Chapter 6
Changing Dynamics: Compressors and More   121

Chapter 7
Playing with Time: Delay and Chorus   163

Chapter 8
The Fourth Dimension: Reverb   185

Chapter 9
Time Modulation, Pitch Shifting, and More   215

Chapter 10
Channel FX: Auto-Pan, De-Essers, De-Poppers, and More   241

Chapter 15
Multiband Compressors, Mastering Limiters, and More   307

Chapter 16
Where To From Here?   325

Index   333

Introduction

The topic of audio effects is one that probably excites more passion, more discussion, and more controversy than almost any other aspect of recording and especially mixing. Yet even after reading never-ending streams of magazine articles and participating in any number of discussions in an ever-expanding range of Internet audio forums, it remains a subject that for too many people is shrouded in mystery, myth, and confusion. All of this can be made worse by extravagant advertising claims that will often present this or that piece of software as the silver bullet that will fix all your problems. Used wisely, audio effects can play an important part in adding color, life, and clarity to a good mix. Used badly, they can and will spoil it. That's where the idea of this book came to be born.

All too often, the root of the problem isn't that it's difficult to get answers to your questions. You can jump onto any Internet audio forum and ask a question such as, "Which is the best VST reverb plug-in?" or "Can anybody recommend a good software compressor?" and I can guarantee that very quickly you'll be inundated with friendly and well-intentioned responses—probably more of them than you can handle.

No, the root of the problem all too often is that *you're not asking the right questions*! Even ignoring for the moment some of the dubious assumptions implied in those questions (for example, can there really be such a thing as a single "best" reverb plug-in?), there really is very little point in asking questions like these if you don't yet have an understanding of some of the core concepts that determine exactly what these effects are. For example:

- What is it that you are aiming to achieve with this sound?

- What exactly is the purpose of this particular type of effect?

- What can it do—and what can't it do? What are its strengths and limitations?

- When should and when shouldn't I use it? *And, most important of all...*

- How does it interact with, act upon, and modify or change the characteristics, color, or sound of my recorded material?

Until you understand and can answer the last of these questions, you can't really obtain meaningful answers to all of the others. That's why in many ways the most important chapter of this book is Chapter 2, which deals with understanding the nature of sound and how the human ear perceives it. After that, we'll go on to explore the nature of all of the most commonly used types of audio effects, such as noise gates, EQ, compressors, reverb, and much more, as well as some less commonly used ones. We'll also look at how various combinations of these effects can be made to work together for you, rather than against each other.

To do this, we'll work through a series of targeted exercises and examples, using a series of audio files that you can find on the DVD that accompanies this book. You can do this using your own host DAW and either the plug-ins supplied with that, favorites from your own collection, or any of a number of freeware plug-ins that you'll find listed in Chapter 1. All of these project files have been recorded acoustically to capture real performances by real musicians. This is the kind of music that can often pose the greatest challenge to the audio engineer, and where the use of audio effects needs to be applied the most carefully. No matter how different the genres of music that you are producing may be, you should still be able to learn from these examples. The core underlying principles are exactly the same.

That's what makes this book different. You might have read dozens of articles already about EQ, reverb, compression, and so on, but perhaps you never really got beyond the stage of only vaguely understanding them. This experience will change that, because it gives you the opportunity to turn your own computer into a sound laboratory that will enable you to learn by experimenting, applying techniques, and *listening*. By doing this, you will grow to understand exactly what these various audio effects do, as well as the purpose of each of their parameter controls and how to set them.

As for those questions about which piece of software will give you the best reverb or the best compression, the short answer is that most often it depends on what you are trying to do at the time. More importantly, it's something that once you understand how they work, you'll be able to work out for yourself.

Whom This Book Is For

The Audio Effects Workshop is designed to help just about anyone who ever needs to become involved in recording and especially post-production. Having said that, let me qualify that statement in the following ways.

- If you're a musician with a fairly modest home studio setup who wants to record your own demos for yourself or your band and ultimately perhaps progress to producing a CD to a standard suitable for public release (perhaps to sell at your gigs), then this book could have been written especially with you in mind.

- If you have absolutely no experience with recording whatsoever, then this book isn't the place to begin. There are quite a number of very important aspects to recording, editing, and mixing that you really need to come to grips with before you start thinking about using audio effects. My earlier book, *Home Recording for Beginners* (Course Technology PTR, 2009), would be a good place to start.

- If you've already taken a few—perhaps quite a few—steps into the world of recording, and you want to improve your knowledge and skills to the point where you might eventually be able to offer a commercial service, then you should definitely benefit from this book. If you have no real experience or understanding of audio effects at this stage, that will be no barrier to learning. If, on the other hand, you already have a basic understanding of the purpose of some of the more popular audio effects, then that should serve as a good foundation. However, be warned that you may find yourself abandoning some of those preconceived ideas along the way!

What You'll Need to Have Already

You'll need to have access to a PC or Mac with any digital audio workstation (DAW) program that is capable of importing WAV files into a project and running audio effects. These effects can be native to the DAW itself, or they can be third-party VST, DirectX, or RTAS plug-ins, or some combination of these. Examples of software that easily meets these criteria are (in alphabetical order) Ableton Live, Cubase, Digital Performer, Logic, Podium, Pro Tools, REAPER, Samplitude, and SONAR. This list, of course, is not exhaustive—in fact, almost any serious DAW that you are likely to be using will probably be up to the job.

You will also, of course, need to have your program set up to enable the playback of recorded material, through speakers, headphones, or ideally both.

You'll also need to be able to find your way around at least the very basic functions of your DAW. I'll explain more about this in Chapter 1, but in brief, I really am talking about fairly basic tasks. The fact that you've read this far suggests that it's unlikely you'll find these a problem.

What You'll Find in This Book

In *The Audio Effects Workshop,* you'll first develop knowledge of the nature of sound and of how the human ear receives it and perceives it. I'm not talking about memorizing and being able to recite a whole heap of technical terms or mathematical formulas here; rather, I'm talking about understanding the crucial role that both the musician's and the listener's immediate environments will have in shaping the way the sound of an instrument or voice is perceived and heard. Getting on top of this issue is the key to then being able to understand how the various audio effects that are at your disposal can be used to modify that sound.

You'll be introduced to various audio effects and will use a carefully chosen selection of audio files from the supplied DVD to explore, examine, and learn what each does, how it works, and the role of each of its various parameter controls on its own and in combination with the other parameter controls. You'll find that some of this sample material has been well recorded, some of it intentionally less so. The effects that you'll be learning about will include (but not be limited to) noise gates, EQ, compressors, expanders, limiters, chorus, delay, reverb, modulators, stereo imaging, and stereo panning. You'll also be introduced to a number of analysis tools and will develop an understanding of just how useful and important these can be.

You'll then take the crucial next steps, learning how these different effects behave in combination with each other. We'll look at what works well together and how. In this context, you'll be introduced to concepts such as serial and parallel effects (FX) processing and shown how you can use these to your advantage.

Please also note that the topic of working with synthesizers (hardware and software) is outside the scope of this book. The main reason for this is that different synthesizers are so different in their design, construction, controls, and interface that giving any useful general advice in this area is practically impossible. What you won't find here, either, is a simple "one size fits all" answer to the question of when you should and when you should not use audio effects. That's because there is no such answer. What you will gain, however, is the confidence and ability to be able to answer that question yourself in each situation that arises.

DVD-ROM Downloads

If you purchased an ebook version of this book, and the book had a companion DVD-ROM, we will mail you a copy of the disc. Please send ptrsupplements@cengage.com the title of the book, the ISBN, your name, address, and phone number. Thank you.

1 Before You Begin

The purpose of this chapter is to make sure that you have everything set up correctly and that you are ready and able to proceed with the material in the chapters that follow. In particular, you'll need to pay attention to the following:

- Your DAW and hardware setup
- The terms and terminology used throughout this book
- Core DAW tasks and functions
- Creating the sample projects and importing the media files
- Installing FX plug-ins onto your computer
- Making these plug-ins available to your DAW

DAW and Hardware Setup

Before you do anything else, please make sure that your DAW software has been installed and set up correctly so it's ready for you to work through the examples and exercises that will be presented throughout this book. There are two main areas to which you may need to pay special attention—these are the installation of audio effects and the enabling of hardware outputs.

Installing Audio FX

Most audio software is supplied with a collection of effects and plug-ins, either native to the host program or supplied by one or more third parties. In some cases, however, by default these are not automatically all installed with the program. It might be worth your while to check your install program again to make sure that you have selected any option or options that may be required to install any plug-ins that you are likely to need. Figure 1.1 shows an example of this, using SONAR 6. (Notice where the mouse cursor is pointing.) In this example, the fact that the item Audio Plugins is not checked indicates that some of the available items are not selected by default. Most other DAWs include a similar option at some time during the install process.

In most cases, if you missed this option during your original install, you can run the install program again, selecting only those options that you missed before, without

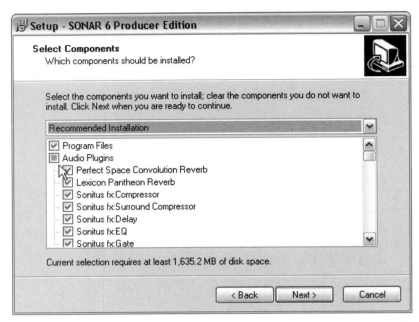

Figure 1.1   Installing the audio effects supplied with your DAW.

having to reinstall the whole program. You should check the documentation supplied with your DAW for more information about this.

Enabling Hardware Outputs

Most of the time, you will likely want to use speakers when you are playing back and listening to your audio material. However, there will be quite a few times (during some of the examples) when you might prefer to use headphones. If your soundcard has two or more pairs of audio outputs, then you should in most cases be able to set this up to enable you to switch output between the different pairs from within your DAW. The "heavyweight" DAW programs (including Ableton Live, Cubase, Digital Performer, Logic, Podium, Pro Tools, REAPER, Samplitude, and SONAR) let you install and use multiple outputs. This usually involves initially using an audio preferences or settings screen, accessed by some command such as Options > Preferences > Audio, Options > Audio Preferences, Edit > Preferences > Audio, File > Preferences, or perhaps something else (depending on which program you are using). Figure 1.2 shows an example of this, again using SONAR.

Once you have set up your multiple outputs, switching between them is usually achieved quite simply by one or two mouse clicks somewhere on your DAW screen, usually in the mixer or master track. You should consult the documentation supplied with your DAW software to check how this is done.

Some budget shareware programs do not have this capability. If you are using one of these—or if you prefer not to make these changes within your DAW's window—you

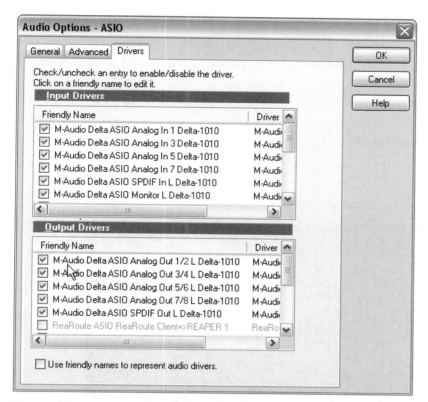

Figure 1.2   An example of setting up a DAW to allow multiple pairs of audio outputs to be used. Typically, you will need to select which drivers—usually paired—you wish to use.

may need to physically disconnect and connect various pieces of equipment at different times to be able to switch between speakers and headphones.

DAWs and Terminology

Most DAWs share a good number of core functions in common. For example, they all allow you to record audio, save it, and play it back. They all have a view that displays your various tracks and recorded items in line and another that displays a virtual mixing desk. Unfortunately, they do not always use the same words to describe either the actions that you are taking or the various elements of the environment within which you are working.

For example, the virtual mixing desk is referred to in some programs as a *console,* in another as *Session view,* and in others as just the *mixer.* The files that you use to save your projects are variously called *sessions, projects, project files,* or just plain *files* by various programs. In each case, these different terms refer to something that is essentially the same thing in all programs. Layout, design, and other details will vary, as will some of the features and capabilities, but the primary reasons for its existence will in every case be the same.

In a book like this, it is necessary to settle on one set of terms and to use it consistently throughout, rather than risk confusing you by using different terms to describe the same thing at different times. Figure 1.3 shows a slight variation of REAPER's default interface. Please take the time to study the various elements identified there and to familiarize yourself with the terms that I have used, as these are the words that I will be using throughout this book. You may need to relate these back to the language with which you are familiar from your own DAW before continuing.

Figure 1.3   One example of a DAW screen. Notice the terms that are used here to describe the different elements.

Table 1.1 summarizes these terms and gives an explanation of each.

Core DAW Tasks and Functions

There is absolutely no point in trying to use audio effects with your recorded material until you have mastered at least some of the basic functions and controls of your DAW software. Each program will have its own distinct characteristics, but at an absolute minimum, you should make sure that you are comfortable with all of the following before you proceed much further.

- Installing and setting up your DAW.
- Opening and closing the program.
- Creating and saving project files.

Table 1.1 Summary of DAW Descriptive Terms Used in This Book

Term	Explanation
Project file	Any DAW program uses a number of files and different types of files for any number of purposes. The project file contains all of the information and material related to any recording project. It is the file that you open in order to work on your project and that you save and close at the end of your work session. In the example in Figure 1.3, a project file called Mud Sliding is open. You can see that among other things, this project contains seven tracks. Other terms used to describe the project file include *project definition file* and just *file*.
Menu	This is displayed (in this example) immediately below the project file name and contains a number of commands that you can use when working with your project.
Toolbar	Displayed immediately below the menu, this contains a number of icons (in this example, 14). These are used for executing certain commands or for accessing various settings screens.
Track view	Occupying (in this case) about half the DAW window, this displays a project's recorded tracks as a series of lanes. Terms used to describe this Track view in some DAWs include *Edit view, Main view, Arrange window,* and *Arrangement view.*
Track controls	To the left of each track, there is a panel that holds a number of buttons and faders that are used to manage the audio on that particular track. Some software may include here items that other programs do not have, but typically these will include pan and volume faders, as well as solo, mute, and record arm buttons.
Media items	Each track shown here contains one recorded media item. Typically, these will together be a series of WAV, AIF, or MP3 files or material recorded in some other format. These are known by a number of different terms in different DAWs—for example, *audio items* or *waveforms.* In this book, we will be addressing audio effects and audio items, but not MIDI items.
Transport bar	This resembles (at least loosely) the controls that you will find on an old-fashioned cassette recorder. Its uses include playing, pausing, stopping, and rewinding your recorded material.
Play cursor	This is a vertical line that indicates the point at which playback was last stopped and from where it will next commence. During playback, the play cursor will normally move across the screen from left to right. In this example, the play cursor is located at 1:36.000 (1 minute 36 seconds). If you look on the timeline (just above the media items), you can see a small triangle attached to a vertical line, which in this case indicates the position of the play cursor.

(Continued)

Term	Explanation
Clock	This displays clearly the current position of the play cursor. The clock is usually known as . . . the clock! If your DAW does not show a clock, check out what other means are available for reading the current play cursor position.
Mixer view	The Mixer view is loosely modeled on a traditional mixing desk. In Figure 1.3, it occupies approximately the bottom 40 percent of the DAW window, with one strip shown for each track and (right) a master control. Among other things, the mixer should include VU meters (or similar) for each track. These meters display a visual indication of the volume of each track as it is played. Many DAWs also offer you the option of displaying VU meters in Track view. Other terms sometimes used to describe this view include *console* and *Session view.*
Master	The master is the place where the mixed output of the various tracks ends up. In fact, the output of the master is what you hear when you play back your project. The master is also sometimes referred to as the *master track* or *master bus.* In some DAWs, this master is contained within a separate view.
FX bins	The FX bin is where a track's audio effects are inserted and managed. FX bins are likely to be found in the mixer strips, the track controls panes, or both. In this example, the FX bins are displayed in the mixer strips, and Tracks 1, 2, 4, 5, and 7 have all had FX inserted. These individual FX are often referred to as *plug-ins.* Other names that you may have encountered for FX bins include *FX windows, FX channels, device chains,* and *FX trays.*

■ Closing and opening project files.

■ Recording audio items.

■ Importing media items (for example, WAV or AIF files) into a project as new tracks.

■ Changing the order in which the tracks appear. (In most cases this can be done by dragging and dropping.)

■ Using the main controls on the transport bar, especially Play, Stop, Pause (if available), and Rewind.

■ Using the following track controls: volume, pan, solo, and mute. In addition, make sure you know how to apply the mute and solo controls to more than one track at a time.

■ Familiarity at least at a basic level with the concept of a master track or bus and what its role is.

- Inserting audio effects (FX plug-ins) into a track's FX bin.

- Toggling on and off a plug-in's bypass.

- Removing plug-ins from a track's FX bin.

- How your DAW works with third-party effects, including VST effects (see below).

- How your DAW uses effects busses (see below).

- How to create and use a submix (see below).

- How your DAW handles automation, and especially FX parameter automation (see below).

Of course, the capabilities of your DAW program will extend well beyond those items listed above. Beyond these, there are doubtless many other tasks that you will need to master. These are likely to include editing your recorded material, creating loops, and so on. The bulleted list above is confined solely to those aspects that you will need to understand before you can start to benefit from this book, not everything you will ever need to know about recording and post-production work!

Third-Party Effects, Busses, Submixes, and Parameter Automation

Throughout this book you'll encounter numerous examples that use various VST effects (plug-ins). In some cases, you will probably want to test out their various settings using an equivalent effect of your own, perhaps using those supplied with your DAW. However, there may also be occasions when you will wish to try out the examples using the exact same effects as used in the examples themselves. Especially for less experienced users, this can be a good way to build confidence. To do this, not only will you need to install the plug-ins onto your computer, you will also need to make sure that your DAW recognizes them and is able to use them.

Later in the book, we'll get to some examples that use busses and automation. An understanding of busses and FX parameter automation isn't essential before you can set about learning what the various types of audio effects are, what they do, their underlying principles, and so on. Nevertheless, if you are to put this knowledge to its best possible use, you will at some time need to come to grips with effects busses and automation. It's worth taking a moment or two even now to look at each of these topics at least in overview.

Third-Party VST Effects

Toward the end of this chapter, I'll deal with some of the issues involved in installing VST plug-ins onto your computer. Before that, however, you'll need to check on just how your DAW program accesses and uses them once they have been installed.

With some programs, you need to identify and locate the directory that you need to use for third-party VST plug-ins before you install them. With others, you should first install them onto your computer and then tell your DAW program where it can find them. Usually this is done somewhere in your preferences settings. Before you start installing any third-party VST plug-ins, you should find out exactly how your DAW program handles these issues.

Some programs allow you to specify any number of directories; others (like the example shown in Figure 1.4) allow you to specify only one directory. If this is the case, you can of course still create as many subdirectories as you wish within this directory.

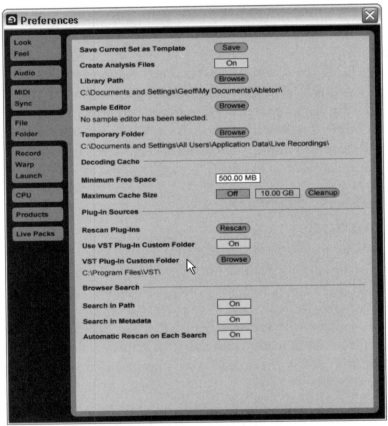

Figure 1.4   An example of specifying where your VST plug-ins are stored, in this case C:\Program Files\VST. This example shows the relevant page of Ableton Live's preferences settings. The setting is indicated by the position of the mouse cursor.

After you have specified your preferences, the DAW will need to scan your VST folder before it is able to use their contents. With some programs this is done automatically, with others you have to give some command to make this happen, and with others you may need to close and reopen the program. This is another area where you will need to consult your software's documentation.

You may come across types of plug-ins other than VST. For example, Windows software can also use DirectX plug-ins, and Pro Tools uses RTAS. For the most part, however, installation of these plug-ins is simpler than it is for VST. In most cases the program will automatically recognize them without much intervention on your part. You should check your DAW's documentation for more information about this.

A Word about Plug-In Formats   You've probably already seen terms such as VST and DX used in connection with various audio plug-ins. These terms simply refer to different formats.

The VST (Virtual Studio) format was developed by Steinberg for use with its Cubase and Nuendo programs. DX (DirectX) is an alternate format developed by Microsoft. Today, most Windows-based DAWs can use plug-ins in both these formats. Some VST plug-ins are also available for use on the Mac.

AU is a format designed for use with the Mac OS series computers, and as such is recognized as standard by most Mac DAW software. RTAS is a proprietary format developed by Digidesign, specifically for use with Pro Tools.

Working with Effects Busses

More often than not, you will want to insert your various effects (such as noise gates and EQ) directly into a track's FX bin. However, there will also be times when you are likely to want to use an effects bus instead. An effects bus (sometimes spelled *buss*) is a device for allowing more than one track to use the same audio effect (or effects) at the same time. This concept is illustrated in Figure 1.5. Typically (but not exclusively), this is often used for adding reverb to a number of tracks. The use of an effects bus can bring

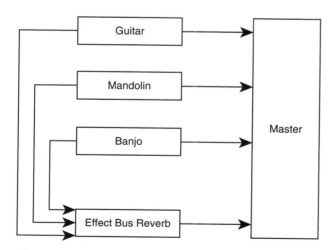

Figure 1.5   This illustrates the concept of an effects bus. In this example, we have three vocal harmony tracks. Rather than add the same reverb effect separately to each of the three tracks, we have chosen to use an effects bus to enable all three tracks to share a single reverb instance. For each track, a send is used to connect the track to the effects bus. Notice that each track's pre-reverb (dry) signal is also sent directly to the master, where it is mixed with the output of the reverb bus.

several advantages, not the least of which is that it is relatively economical in the use it makes of your computer's CPU.

Unfortunately, the method required to set up and use busses varies considerably between different DAWs. Some programs come with a number of busses (typically two to four) automatically created for you every time you make a new project file. With others you have to add these busses yourself. With some you need to modify an ordinary track's properties to use it as a bus. In every case, you will need to know how to create sends that will route the audio signal from your individual tracks to the bus.

You won't need to start using busses until we get to Chapter 6, "Changing Dynamics: Compressors and More," or Chapter 8, "The Fourth Dimension: Reverb." Before then, you should take the time to find out how your particular DAW uses effects busses. Effects busses are also sometimes known as *auxiliary busses* or *aux busses*.

Using Submixes

There will be times when you will want to apply the same audio effect (or several effects) to a whole group of tracks. This might happen, for example, with an entire drum kit or a group of backing vocals. In these circumstances, you will need to create a submix. With a submix, the output of the individual tracks does not go directly to the master. Instead, it goes to the submix, where it is processed in some way. The output of the submix then goes to the master. Figure 1.6 illustrates this concept. The individual track controls (such as volume and pan) together determine the blend of output from the individual tracks that is sent to the stereo submix.

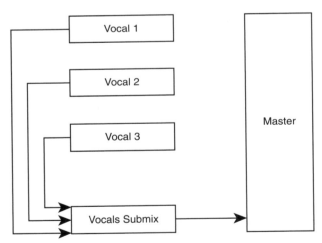

Figure 1.6   This illustrates the concept of a submix. In this example, we have three guitar tracks. A guitars submix is created, and the output of each of the three individual tracks is sent to that rather than directly to the master.

With a submix (unlike an effects bus), the signal from the individual tracks is sent only to the submix and not directly to the master. Most DAW software programs use a bus to create such a submix. One notable exception is REAPER, which uses track folders. Make sure you are conversant with how to create submixes using your DAW program.

FX Parameter Automation

If you are using any of the "heavyweight" programs that I referred to earlier, you will find that they have some automation process(es) that allow you to record and replay changes to various parameters in real time. Very often this feature is used to raise and lower the volume of various tracks at different times during a song or to adjust the panning (perhaps to help highlight a particular instrument that is being featured on a lead break). Most DAWs store and use the recorded automation data in the form of envelopes.

Most good DAW software also lets you automate changes to your various FX parameters in a similar way. You won't need to do this before we get to Chapter 11, "Harnessing the Power of Automation," where you will see how powerful this technique can be. You should therefore make sure that you understand how to create, edit, modify, disable/enable, and delete automation envelopes for your various tracks using your DAW software.

Creating the Sample Project Files

On the DVD that accompanies this book, you'll find five sets of WAV files, one set for each of five sample projects that you will be using from time to time in the various examples and exercises that will be presented to you. Setting these up will take you a little while, but be patient and persevere. You will later find that the effort has been well worth it.

First, copy the entire folder called Audio Effects Projects from the DVD to a suitable location on your hard disk. If you have more than one hard disk, use a disk other than the one where your programs are stored. Assuming that you have copied this folder to a D: drive, you will now have the following directory structure:

D:\Audio Effects Projects

D:\Audio Effects Projects\AloneAgain

D:\Audio Effects Projects\FoggyDesperation

D:\Audio Effects Projects\LyingBack

D:\Audio Effects Projects\MudSliding

D:\Audio Effects Projects\Whiskey

Each of the five lowest-level folders (AloneAgain, FoggyDesperation, LyingBack, MudSliding, and Whiskey) contains the WAV files that are required for one of the five projects. In the case of LyingBack, these are 16-bit WAV files. All of the other projects use 24-bit WAV files.

All major PC (Windows)-based hosts are capable of importing WAV files, as are the most popular Mac-based programs (Pro Tools, Logic, Digital Performer, and so on). In the unlikely event that you are using a DAW that cannot read WAV files, you should take whatever steps are necessary to convert these files to your required format. Shortly, I'll say a little more about each of these projects, but before that you should use your DAW software to initially create one project file for each of these projects.

Because every DAW handles this task slightly differently, the instructions that follow should be regarded as guidelines only. Follow them as closely as you can with regard to your own DAW.

1. Open your DAW program.

2. Check (possibly within the program's Options or Preferences settings) how your program stores imported media items. In some cases it may make new copies of these as they are imported and store them with the project file. In other cases, it will use the original imported files themselves and leave them at their original location. It is possible that within your Preferences settings (or elsewhere), you can specify which of these you prefer. In any event, take the time to understand just how your imported files are handled.

3. Check (possibly within the program's Options or Preferences settings) how your program interprets the media format of imported items. In some cases it will retain the original format (in this case, WAV); in others it will automatically convert them to some other default format (such as AIF format). Some programs offer you the choice. Any of these possible outcomes will allow you to work through the examples in this book, but you should be aware of which of these scenarios will apply to you.

4. For each of the five sample projects, you will need to create a project file. Call these five files Alone00, Foggy00, Lying00, Mud00, and Whisky00, respectively. Note that some DAWs require you to name the file when you first create it, others when you first save it.

5. In each case, import into the project all of the WAV files required for that project. Most DAW programs allow you to do this either by using some command from the menu (such as Insert > Media File or File > Insert Media) or by dragging and dropping from a Media Explorer window (which of course might go by some other name) or even from Windows Explorer.

6. In each case, after importing the tracks, rearrange them into an order that makes sense to you. For example, you might want to put all vocal tracks (where they exist) together. You probably will want to put your drum tracks (kick, snare, overhead, and so on) together. Figure 1.7 shows an example of a reasonably sensible track order for one of the projects.

Figure 1.7   An example of how your arrangement might look for one of your projects—Foggy00—after importing the media items and putting the tracks into some logical order. This example uses REAPER, but you could use any DAW.

7.   Don't forget to save your project files when finished in every case!

8.   As a precaution against accidentally playing back your projects too loudly, perhaps clipping or even damaging your audio equipment, you might wish to consider inserting a simple limiter in the master of each of your sample projects. You'll learn more about the ins and outs of limiters elsewhere in this book (especially in Chapters 6 and 15). For the time being, if you're not sure how to do this, refer to the instructions at the end of this chapter in the section, "Using the JS Plug-Ins."

Your projects are now ready for you to begin! For the time being, leave each track's control settings at their defaults. For example, by default every track will be panned dead center with a volume setting of 0 dB. We'll get around to doing something about this in Chapter 2, "Sound: Its Characteristics and Its Qualities." Meanwhile, here is a brief overview of each of these projects.

The Sample Project Files   The five sample project files used for the various examples in this book have been selected primarily in order to help you learn about the use of audio effects. They employ a selection of five different musical genres, but with a little imagination and creativity on your part, the lessons that you can expect to learn by exploring them should readily be able to be applied to most, if not all, other styles of music besides these.

Alone Again is an instrumental country/rock tune featuring the electric guitar. Its purpose is primarily to help you understand the use of delay and guitar effects (from Chapter 7 onward).

Foggy Desperation is a pop/rock song that consists of 11 tracks, including lead and harmony vocals (both male), acoustic and electric guitars, electric bass, and a drum kit. Performed by Peter Hicks. Words and music by Peter Hicks, copyright 2008.

Lying Back is a bluegrass/pop song made up of nine tracks, including a lead vocal, two female and one male backing vocals, banjos, acoustic double bass, guitar, and mandolin. Performed by Coyote Serenade. Words and Music by Peter Hicks and Geoffrey Francis, copyright 2004.

Mud Sliding is an instrumental blues arrangement whose seven tracks include a resonator guitar, harmonica, various percussion items, and a room microphone. Performed by Peter Hicks and the Bad Licks. Music by Peter Hicks, copyright 2005.

Now Is the Time for Whiskey is a country/pop song. It includes both female and male lead vocals, vocal harmonies, guitars, and a sakuhachi. Performed by Twice Bitten, words and music by Anne Parsell and Mathew Woolley, copyright 2009.

Installing FX Plug-Ins onto Your Computer

The DVD that accompanies this book includes a collection of Windows VST plug-ins (ReaPlugs). These include various EQ plug-ins, noise gates, compressors, delay and chorus plug-ins, and much more. Several of these plug-ins are used in a number of the examples that are presented throughout this book. You don't have to use these exact same plug-ins when you work through the examples, but you might find it helpful, especially at first.

A number of other quality freeware plug-ins that are not included on the DVD are also used in some of the examples. Again, you don't need to employ these if you already have others that you prefer, but it might be useful to have at least some of these at your fingertips. For your convenience, there follows shortly a summary table that lists these plug-ins, what they are, and where you should be able to find them.

The Plug-Ins Supplied on the DVD

The Effects folder of your DVD contains a file called reaplugs20-install.exe. These are versions of the plug-ins normally packaged and included with REAPER, adapted to make it possible for you to use them with any other Windows DAW that accepts third-party VST plug-ins.

Of course, if the DAW that you are using is REAPER, then you will not need to install these plug-ins from the DVD, because they will already have been installed on your system when you installed REAPER. If you are a REAPER user, please also note that you will not need to use the VST plug-in ReaJS, as the JS plug-ins can be inserted directly into your tracks' and items' FX bins.

Otherwise, you should run the file reaplugs20-install.exe and follow the onscreen prompts to install the software into your VST plug-ins folder. Its directory structure should be similar to that shown in Figure 1.8. Please note that because of possible late changes to the content of this package, the content of your ReaPlugs folder might not be exactly identical to that shown in Figure 1.8. This will not matter. Also, note that at the time of writing, this plug-in set is available for use with Windows only; no OS X version is available.

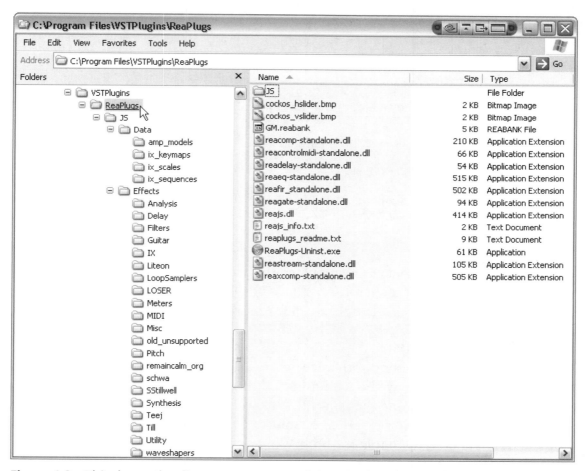

Figure 1.8   This shows the directory structure of the ReaPlugs series of plug-ins. Extract the file reaplugs.zip directly to your VST plug-ins folder to ensure that this structure is maintained.

When you next open your DAW program, provided you have already specified the location of your VST directory, these plug-ins should now be available to you. You can check this by using whatever method is used in your DAW to add VST plug-ins to your tracks. Figure 1.9 shows this being done in Cubase SX. You can see that the various ReaPlug items have been recognized by the program, are listed on the menu, and are available for use.

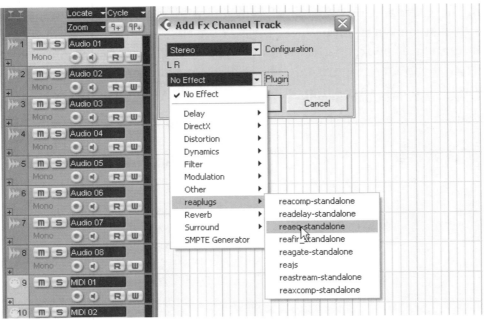

Figure 1.9 Checking that your ReaPlugs have been successfully installed and are available for use. In this example, the host DAW is Cubase SX.

If the ReaPlugs are not displayed as available within your DAW's VST menu, it may be necessary to tell it to rescan the directory. You will need to consult the program's documentation and/or Preferences settings screen for more information about this.

Other VST Effects Plug-Ins

Table 1.2 summarizes a number of other freeware and donation-ware plug-ins you can download and install if you wish. A number of these are used in various examples throughout this book. If you find them useful, please consider making a donation where this is requested on the author's webpage. Some are available for use with Windows only; others have versions available for both Windows and OS X.

At the time of writing, all of these links have been tested and the downloads found to be free of any viruses, spyware, or malware. You are nevertheless strongly advised to run reliable anti-virus security software when downloading anything from the Internet. Also, please remember that like all URLs on Linux servers, the addresses shown here are case-sensitive.

Table 1.2 Some Freeware VST Plug-Ins Worth Considering

Item	Comments
VST MultiInspectorFree	This handy analytical tool helps you to identify the frequency range and patterns of different instruments and voices and to compare them to each other. www.vertexdsp.com/products_multiinspectorfree.html
Blue Cat Freeware Bundle	Some great stuff here, including chorus and EQ plug-ins, but especially useful for its FreqAnalyst Spectrum Analyzer. Available for Mac and PC. www.bluecataudio.com/Products/Bundle_FreewarePack
Kjaerhus Classic Series	You could fork out a lot of money for plug-ins not as good as these. This comprehensive set includes a compressor, limiter, EQ, chorus, delay, and much more. However, it's the Kjaerhus Classsic Reverb that merits a special mention. www.kjaerhusaudio.com/classic-series.php
Voxengo Free Series	Along with Kjaerhus, Voxengo plug-ins are respected and used by many of the industry's most experienced and capable audio engineers. You'll find an assortment of first-class freebies, including Voxengo Span, Stereo Touch, and Tube Amp, at www.voxengo.com/products.
KResearch Free Series	These include delay and reverb plug-ins for both the PC and the Mac. Their well-designed interface helps the user to understand the purpose of the different parameter controls. www.kresearch.com/news.html
MDA VST Effects	This huge and comprehensive bundle of some 30 or so VST plug-ins comes in versions for both Windows and OS X. Their value comes from the simplicity of their structure and their plain interface. This can make them a really good learning tool, especially at first, for the less-experienced user. mda.smartelectronix.com
GVST Freeware Effects Package	Another large and comprehensive package of VST plug-ins, this time made available as donation-ware. Some of these you won't use, some you might. It includes pitch correction software and a multiband compressor. www.gvst.co.uk/packages.htm
MeldaProduction Free VST Effects	Some interesting stuff here (PC and Mac): As well as the regulation compressor, limiter, EQ, and so on, you'll find an analyzer, waveshaper, and stereo expander. Definitely worth a look. Donate if you like what you see! www.meldaproduction.com/freevstplugins/mstereoexpander.php
UK-Music	A modest but easy to use collection of plug-ins, including a four-voice stereo chorus. www.uk-music.de

(Continued)

Item	Comments
KarmaFX Plug-Ins Pack	This donation-ware plug-in set doesn't contain a lot, but what it has is good. The reverb plug-in is especially handy as a starting point for those trying to understand more about reverb. karmafx.net.
Magnus Plug-ins	These donation-ware items (Windows VST and OS X) are quite a find. There are only five of them, but the ambience reverb is rather impressive, and the Nyquist EQ boasts an unusual interface that will appeal to many. What's more, the MjCompressor includes an upwards expander. magnus. smartelectronix.com
Geocities Japan	This website showcases a small number of quality hand-picked freeware VST plug-ins, including AutoGate (a noise gate and expander) and LinearPhaseGraphicEQ. www. geocities.jp/webmaster_of_sss/vst/index.html
RhythmLab Mo'Verb	What I especially like about this plug-in is that it is well designed with a clean interface, it's easy to use, and it includes all of the standard parameters and controls that you would expect to find in a quality reverb plug-in. VST donation-ware. www.rhythm-lab.com/plugins
GlaceVerb VST	Definitely worth getting hold of. This is another plug-in that can be used to help you to learn more about reverb. www.topshareware.com/GlaceVerb-download-20202.htm or vst-plugins.homemusician.net/effects/glaceverb.html
HybridReverb	Freeware convolution reverb plug-ins are somewhat thin on the ground, which makes this offering from Christian Borss all the more special. www2.ika.rub.de/HybridReverb2. From the same website, you can also download a complete database of impulse samples.
SIR 1 Impulse Reverb	Impulse reverb creates its effect using a different method from conventional reverb. It uses recorded impulse files, and you can even create and use your own. Several DAW programs, including Logic, REAPER, and SONAR, include at least one impulse reverb plug-in as standard. SIR 1 is a handy freeware item that matches many of their functions. www. knufinke.de/sir/sir1.html
More Reverb Impulse Samples	If you're using an impulse reverb plug-in, you'll need some sample impulse files to go with it. In time, you'll be able to track down everything you'll ever want or need, but the samples available at these sites will be more than enough to get you started: www.rhythminmind.net/presetblog/2009/ 08/lexicon-m200-impulse-set and stash.reaper.fm/tag/ Reverb-Impulses

Installing VST Plug-Ins

Many of these plug-in sets come with their own installation package, in which case you should run the installer, taking care to select your VST plug-ins directory as the destination. Others consist of just a single zip file that contains a number of DLL files. An example of this is the MDA set of plug-ins. Figure 1.10 shows the contents of the downloaded file mda_vst_fx_win.zip displayed using 7-Zip. In this case, you should simply extract the various DLL files to your VST plug-ins directory. For good housekeeping, you should also ensure that each set of plug-ins is kept in a separate folder within this directory.

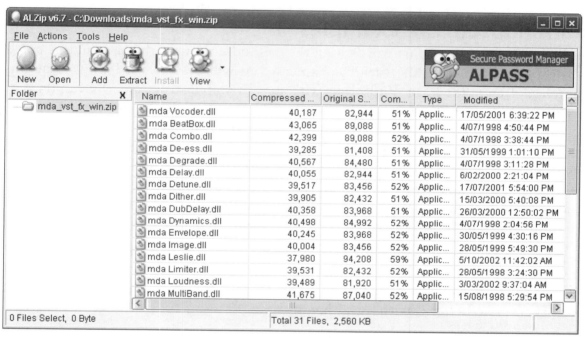

Figure 1.10   An example of using a utility program to display a zip file's contents and to extract them as a series of files. This example uses the program 7-Zip, but you could equally use WinZip, EasyZip, or some other similar program to do this.

A word of caution before we move on: Plug-ins are obviously only of any use when they are put to work inside a host DAW. Herein lies a potential problem. Every plug-in is different, and every DAW is different. It's not unheard of for particular combinations of "this" plug-in with "that" DAW to cause problems. This can lead to unwanted performance issues and even the occasional crash.

A particular plug-in might work perfectly every time in one host, yet cause all sorts of drama in another. If this happens, it doesn't mean necessarily that there's anything inherently wrong with either the plug-in or the host. It just means that they don't work well together. Usually the simplest and best solution is not to use that particular plug-in with that DAW. Find another that does the same thing and use that instead.

Removing VST Plug-Ins

After a while, you'll get to know which plug-ins you like and use and which ones you don't need. When that's the case, consider removing the unwanted plug-ins from your hard drive.

Where these plug-ins were installed simply by extracting the DLL files to your VST plug-ins directory, it should be safe for you to simply delete these files from your hard drive. Where these were installed using some installer program, however, you should check the install program in case it also provides you with an uninstall option. Using this option rather than simply deleting the DLL files should ensure that any unwanted associated entries will also be deleted from your registry.

Learning from the Examples

Finally for this chapter, a last word about the methodology used throughout this book. As you progress through the various chapters, you will be presented with numerous examples, often in the form of tutorials with step-by-step instructions you can try out. As you work through these examples, always try to stay focused not on the example itself, but on the points it is illustrating and on what you can learn from it. For example, you might come across a sample project where the use of reverb parameters is explored with the help of a recorded shakuhachi. You might never have used a shakuhachi, you might never be going to use a shakuhachi, and indeed you might even have absolutely no idea what a shakuhachi is. That doesn't mean you won't be able to learn some valuable lessons that you will be able to apply at some time to your own instruments in your projects.

No matter how well you think you understand the material, it is very important that you find the time to work through the step-by-step tutorials as and when you reach them. There is no better way to learn than by doing!

Using the JS Plug-Ins

If you have correctly installed the various plug-ins supplied on the DVD that accompanies this book, you will now have access to several dozen JS plug-ins. From time to time throughout this book, one or another of these JS plug-ins will be used in some of the examples. These are not VST plug-ins as such, but they can be used with any Windows DAW program that uses VST plug-ins.

If you are using REAPER, you can insert these plug-ins directly into your FX bin. For PC programs other than REAPER, they are loaded into and used in any of your tracks via the VST plug-in ReaJS, also supplied on the DVD. Figure 1.11 shows the ReaJS plug-in inserted into a track in Cubase SX.

ReaJS itself appears at first to be nothing more than an empty shell. Shown also in Figure 1.11 is how, after clicking its Load button, you would go about selecting the JS Utility limiter.

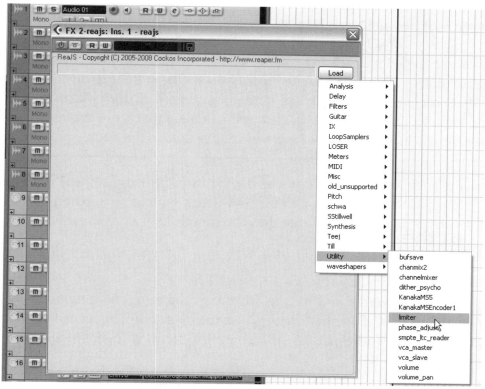

Figure 1.11   The VST plug-in ReaJS as it appears after being inserted into a track's FX bin (in this case, in Cubase SX). The Load button is used to select the required JS effect.

This limiter (see Figure 1.12) has only one control—threshold. When you are using this limiter as a safety device to prevent clipping, you should set this threshold to about −0.5 dB or −1.0 dB.

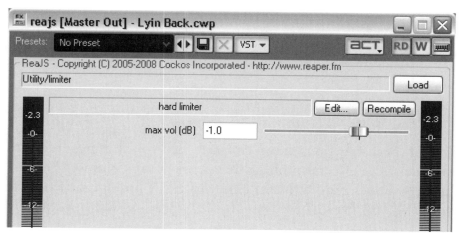

Figure 1.12   The JS Utility/Limiter plug-in inserted into a master track after being loaded into the VST plug-in ReaJS. In this example, the host DAW is SONAR.

JS Splitter, Joiner, Switcher, and Mixer Plug-Ins   As you browse through the various available JS plug-ins, you may notice that several include words such as *splitter, mixer, switcher,* and *joiner* in their names (for example, 3BandSplitter and 3Band-Joiner). These particular plug-ins are designed specifically for use in REAPER, in conjunction with that program's channel splitting and joining capabilities. They facilitate, for example, parallel FX processing on a single track, an option that is not available with most DAW hosts. These plug-ins will therefore not be used in this book.

Users of Mac software such as Logic and Pro Tools will not be able to use ReaJS or any of its associated JS plug-ins. Instead, you should simply use whichever of the plug-ins supplied with your software most closely matches the functionality of that used in the example.

Project Files Log

As this workshop progresses, you'll find yourself opening, changing, making, and saving a fair number of project files. Together, these will give you a complete record of your work. However, this process, and especially the naming system, can get to be a little bewildering at times.

The system used is that each project file you save will use the name of the original project with the tutorial name appended. So, for example, if Tutorial 5.3 were to ask you to save a version of the project called Foggy, then it would suggest that you use the name Foggy53.

To help you keep track of this, a summary table is included at the end of each chapter.

Right now, if you have completed all of the instructions and examples in this chapter, you should have the following project files to work with:

> Alone00
>
> Foggy00
>
> Lying00
>
> Mud00
>
> Whiskey00

If you have completed all of the instructions in this chapter, then you're almost ready to start examining some of the audio effects and how they work. I say "almost" because before that, you will need to understand at least some very basic and important facts about the nature of sound.

2 Sound: Its Characteristics and Its Qualities

Throughout this book you'll be introduced to working with a number of different types of audio effects. The functions, uses, and applications of these different effects will of course vary enormously, yet at the same time they all have one crucial characteristic in common. They all shape, affect, and in some way change the sound of whatever items they are applied to. Put at its simplest, after it has passed through any effect, your audio material will in some way sound different from how it sounded before. Each and every such change will modify the listener's experience, and in particular how she will perceive that sound—for better or for worse.

Figure 2.1 illustrates one example of this concept. In this example, the sound is passed through some audio effect (or series of effects), as a result of which our ears now perceive the sound to be louder.

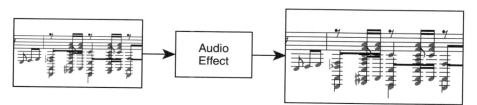

Figure 2.1 Passing music (or any other sound) through some audio effects may result in the sound appearing to be louder. This diagram illustrates this concept.

Figure 2.2 illustrates another example. Think about it for a moment. In this example, some audio effect (or effects) are applied to a piece of music to in some way change its timbre, perhaps to make it sound more mellow. Of course, different effects will alter the original sound in different ways, but the key principle is the same. Do you really know

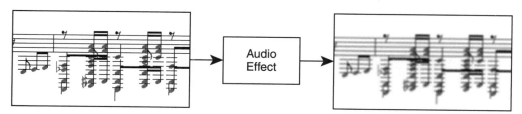

Figure 2.2 Passing music through some audio effects may cause the sound's character to be changed in some way. This diagram illustrates this concept—but don't take it too literally!

and understand just what you're doing to that sound when you slap it through an equalizer, a compressor, a delay unit, or some form of reverb—or some permutation of these?

Put this in the context of a project with maybe 20 or 30 tracks, some with perhaps as many as three (or even more) effects applied, plus perhaps a few more added to the overall mix, and suddenly whatever is going on here starts to get a tad complex—very complex in fact. All sorts and any manner of tricks are being played on the listener's ear at any one time. The goal is to get these to work together, not only to make each and every instrument and vocal track sound its very best, but also to ensure that they sound as good as they can together.

Isn't it strange, then, that people will often try to set about using audio effects in their projects in the hope of achieving these outcomes without first taking the time to understand at least the basics about what sound is and what exactly they are doing to it? To understand this, you'll also need to know something about how sound travels to us, how our ears perceive it, and how eventually our brains interpret all this information. You need to understand some basic information about the nature of sound in general, and recorded sound in particular. Only after getting a grasp of these can you really hope to understand how the appropriate use of audio effects can change the sound of your recorded items to enhance and improve them.

That's what this chapter is about. You won't find any mathematical formulae and equations here, and you'll find that the use of technical terms has been kept to an absolute minimum. To the fullest extent possible, the emphasis will be practical rather than theoretical. You'll need to understand a little theory, but only inasmuch as it will help you with what you are doing and enable you to do it better.

There'll be some practical experiments for you to carry out as part of this learning process. Some of these will be easier to manage if you can get a friend to help you. Failing that, you should be able to get by on your own—it just might not be as much fun!

Introduction

In this chapter, you will examine some fundamentals about sound that will help you to understand how and when you should consider using audio effects and for what purpose. In particular, we'll look at the following:

- The nature of sound
- Characteristics of sound: volume
- Dimensions of sound: frequency
- Dimensions of sound: space and direction
- Dimensions of sound: space and distance

- Sound, time, and the acoustic environment
- Fundamentals and harmonics
- Sounds of musical instruments
- Sounds of the human voice

Understanding Sound

So much has been written on this subject that you could be forgiven for thinking that there isn't anything more that can be said. In many ways you'd be right, but with one important exception. Much, if not most, of the information that is presented in the next few pages will be information with which you may already be more or less familiar. What matters here, though, is understanding how these different pieces of information fit together and how they work together as a whole to produce, shape, and manipulate the sounds we hear. We need to examine this especially in the context of musical instruments and the human voice. When you have grasped this bigger picture, you will have in your hands an important set of keys for being able to use audio effects well.

Let's start by summarizing what we know about sound.

The Nature of Sound

I'm going to make this simple and keep the emphasis solely on those qualities on which you will need to focus when working with sound and audio effects.

You probably already know that our ears receive and perceive sound as a result of pressure exerted on our eardrums—pressure that comes from waves of sound traveling through the air. As to how they travel . . . well, it's likely that at some time you've come across the visual analogy of a succession of waves moving out from the center of a perfectly still pond when a stone or pebble is dropped in the center of it. That's pretty much the way that sound travels, as a succession of waves. It's also just a matter of common sense to add here that in general you would expect that the nearer you are to the source of theses sound waves, the louder you will hear the sound.

Understanding Sound Waves   Sound waves don't only travel through the air. They will also travel through water and through solid matter, such as brick and stone—through anything, in fact, except a vacuum. These sound waves will take on different characteristics as they travel through different media. You probably have already noticed, for example, that certain frequencies penetrate brick walls more successfully than others do. However, for the purpose of this book, whenever I talk about sound waves, their qualities, and their characteristics, I'll be talking about sound waves *as they travel through air*. I'm assuming that you won't be doing too much underwater recording!

I expect that you also have some idea what we're talking about when we use terms such as *pitch* and *frequency*. These are the characteristics that determine the different timbres and qualities of different sounds. It's why, for example, the sound of a violin will always be different from the sound of a cello. Different violins will exhibit individual sound traits different from each other, but they will all still sound like violins, and none will ever sound like a cello. We'll get to why this matters shortly.

Two more dimensions that influence the way we perceive sound are two of the dimensions of space—direction and distance. When your brain combines the different sound images that it receives from your ears, one thing it will attempt to do is to locate the source of that sound. It does this by attempting to coordinate various crucial pieces of information that are somehow contained in the messages with which it is being constantly bombarded. How far away is it? Is it coming farther from the left or the right? Is it stationary or is it moving? Is it moving closer to us, farther from us, or across our path? Is it higher up or lower down?

Finally, the sounds that we hear can seldom (if ever) be considered in isolation, but only ever in the context within which they are created and within which we are listening. That's why when you sing in the shower, you'll sound very different from when you sing in an open space, such as a field. This context can be thought of as being the *immediate environment*.

It isn't entirely as simple as this, but taken together, the four paragraphs that precede this one should supply you with a lot of food for thought. Ultimately, we hear not just with our ears, but also with our brains. To understand audio effects and how they are used, therefore, you will need to understand not only the qualities that shape and determine the actual sounds that our brains hear, but also how the different audio effects that you have at your disposal can fool the brain into thinking it is hearing something different from what is actually there.

It's time now to look at each of these qualities individually in just a little more detail. When you've taken that in, you'll be just about ready to begin.

Volume

At this point there's not a lot that needs to be said about volume. The volume of sound is determined by its sound pressure level, and you probably already know that this is measured in decibels. Because the human ear is sensitive to a very wide range of sound levels, decibels are measured on a logarithmic scale.

Thus, 0 dB is considered to be the low threshold of human hearing, just above total silence. A sound measuring 10 dB (perhaps very quiet breathing) is 10 times as loud as this. A quiet room measuring 20 dB is 10 times as loud again. A quiet voice at a distance of about a meter measures about 40 dB—100 times as loud again, and so on. The greater the sound pressure level, the louder the sound. The louder the sound, the greater the difference between the peaks and troughs of the wave pattern. This is known as its *amplitude,* or to be more precise, its *peak-to-peak amplitude* (see Figure 2.3).

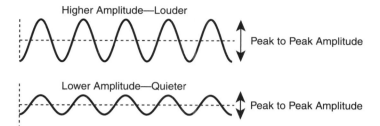

Figure 2.3 The louder the sound, the greater its amplitude.

Just how the decibel scale applies to digital audio is often the cause of confusion. Quite obviously, the 0 dB that you see on your DAW's track or channel meters certainly does not represent the bare threshold of human hearing, so just what is it? To understand the answer, you must first understand that the term dB has no meaning outside of the context in which we place it. In the real world outside, this reference point is set at the threshold of human hearing.

The answer, then, is that the scales you see on your track's meters use a different reference point for displaying sound levels. The 0 dB here represents the maximum level at which you can safely record without creating an unwanted digital effect known as *clipping,* which will irreparably damage the recorded material. The actual sound level of recorded material when it is played back will then be measured relative to this. Figure 2.4 shows an example.

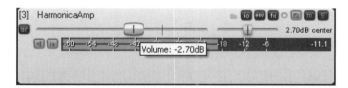

Figure 2.4 A typical volume fader and track meter in a typical DAW. Notice in this example that the fader has been set at −2.70 dB and the meter measures a range of volume from −60 dB up to just above 0 dB. In this case, the current playback level (right) is −11.1 dB. A level of −10 dB on this scale is equivalent to about 110 dB in the outside world—about the same as a very loud rock concert.

During playback, you might on occasion have lifted the volume of individual tracks above this threshold of 0 dB without experiencing any unpleasant consequences. The short answer to this one is that during playback it is the master (where the output of all your tracks is mixed together before being directed to your speakers or headphones or being burnt to CD) that must never be allowed to exceed 0 dB, not the individual tracks themselves.

All of this leads me to make one very important but often overlooked point. *You should think of, and be prepared to use, the volume controls on your tracks and channels as audio effect in its own right.* Yes, really! Usually you have two of these at your fingertips—a gain or trim fader that controls the volume of the audio coming into the track (before you do anything else to it, such as panning or adding compression) and a volume fader as such, which controls the volume going out from the track. Both of these help determine how the track's audio content will ultimately sound. Start thinking about your tracks holistically rather than simply in terms of individual effects.

Where Are My DAW's Track Gain Controls?   Many (but not all) DAW programs include a trim/gain control fader in the track controls area for each track. However, this isn't always the case. With REAPER, for example, you'll need to either add a pre-FX volume envelope or use the individual gain controls on the media item itself.

Frequency

Frequency reflects a sound's pitch and is measured in Hz (hertz) and kHz (kilohertz). The value itself is determined by the number of times the sound's waveform cycle is repeated every second (see Figure 2.5).

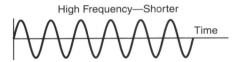

High Frequency—Shorter

Time

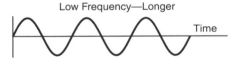

Low Frequency—Longer

Time

Figure 2.5   The shorter the length (duration) of the waveform's cycle, the more times a second it is repeated, and the higher its frequency.

The frequency rage of human hearing is generally considered as being between about 20 Hz and 20,000 Hz (that is, 20 kHz). There's no universally agreed-upon exact standard for the way this rather large range is divided into different bands. Table 2.1 probably makes as much sense as any other that you may have seen. Be aware, however, that the boundaries between the different bands are somewhat arbitrary and should be used as a guide only.

Different instruments tend to cluster around different frequencies or bands of frequencies, and each has its own unique characteristics. I'll have a lot more to say about these later in this chapter, in the section "The Sounds of Musical Instruments."

Table 2.1 Dividing the Frequency Spectrum

Band	Comment
Below 40 Hz: Sub Bass	Very often you'll feel rather than hear these frequencies. This is where you'll find the bottom end of instruments such as the kick drum and the bass guitar.
40 Hz to 200 Hz: Lows	This is the range normally referred to as bass or bottom end. The lower range of frequencies that you'd expect to find in a bass, tenor, or baritone voice as well as a heap of instruments including guitar, cello, piano, accordion, bassoon, trombone, and tuba can all be found here.
200 Hz to 800 Hz: Mids	This is the range where crowd control is most likely to be an issue when you're mixing and looking at how to use some audio effects, especially panning and EQ. It's therefore the territory that's likely to cause you the most headaches. The top end of low instruments (such as bass guitar, double bass, and tuba) lives here, as do the bottom end of higher instruments (such as the mandolin, flute, and trumpet) and some part of just about everything else in between.
800 Hz to 5,000 Hz: High Mids	The first thing you need to understand about the high mids is that the human ear just loves to hear them. If you need to tamper with them, the watch phrase is "handle with care."
5,000 Hz to 8,000 Hz: Highs	This corresponds to the range often known as *treble*. When you get this far up, you're working mostly with an instrument's harmonics rather than its basic sound. Gain here can add brightness or sparkle to a mix.
Above 8,000 Hz: Ultra Highs	This range mainly contains various instruments' late harmonics.

Space and Direction

You're probably already reasonably familiar with your DAW's track pan controls, as you've most likely already used them to some extent. You might also have already discovered how these can be used to position different instruments in various positions between fully left and fully right and how this can create an illusion of different instruments appearing to originate from different positions between the speakers.

With this in mind, there's a rather interesting experiment that I'd like you to perform. The purpose of this experiment is to take an important step toward understanding not only the importance of panning, but also just what it is the listener hears when she recognizes what she believes to be the clean, natural sound of a musical instrument.

It will help if you have a friend (preferably someone who can play an instrument, such as an acoustic guitar) to help you with this. If this isn't possible, don't worry. You can complete this little experiment on your own. In this example, you will begin by creating a new project file and then recording four tracks, one at a time. You'll then examine and analyze what you have recorded.

Tutorial 2.1: Exploring Frequency and Direction

1. Create a new project file and save it with the name AudioExperiment21.

2. In Figure 2.6, the four Xs mark four of the many possible positions where you might wish to place a microphone when recording an acoustic guitar. If you do not have an acoustic guitar on hand, you can use a different instrument of your choosing. You'll just have to interpret the instructions a little more creatively.

Figure 2.6   Four of the many possible places where you can place a microphone to record an acoustic guitar. X marks the spots.

3. Choose a fairly simple, gentle tune. Record about 60 seconds or so of your guitar being played with the microphone about 9 inches from the guitar at any of the four positions shown in Figure 2.6. Use a count-in before you begin recording. The quality of the musicianship will not be an issue here.

4. Using headphones and with the same microphone, overdub (synchronized to the original track) one at a time three more guitar tracks, each time with the microphone 9 inches from the instrument but at a different one of the other three positions marked with an X in Figure 2.6. Record all four tracks as closely as you are able at the same volume. You should end up with something similar to Figure 2.7.

5. Save this work.

6. Now play your recordings back, one track soloed at a time. You should notice that each track sounds distinctly different, despite it being the same guitar and the same microphone.

7. Now comes the really interesting part. Decide upon four different pan positions for your four tracks. For example, you might start with 60% left, 25% left, 25% right, 60% right.

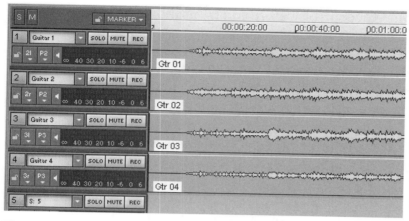

Figure 2.7   The same guitar piece recorded four times, each time on a different track with the microphone in a different position. In this example, this has been done using Samplitude.

8.   Using the same four pan positions, swap the tracks around. For example, if the first track was at 60% left, try moving it to 25% right, and so on. You'll find that you have plenty of permutations to play with.

9.   As you do this, are you finding that some permutations seem to work better than others, producing a better overall sound? Almost certainly this will be the case.

10.   Save your work again. It's time to figure out just what is going on here.

Quite a few things have been going on here, but for now I'd like to focus on just three of these.

■   First, a musical instrument does not produce a single homogenous blend of frequencies that defines its sound. On the contrary, there are different blends of frequencies emanating from every part of the instrument at the same time. This produces a remarkably complex pattern of simultaneous audio streams that our listener absorbs as his ears take them all in. One of the reasons we use audio FX is to re-create this in our recordings, where more often than not all we have is one single audio stream recorded for each instrument, using in each case a single microphone.

■   Second, you have seen how microphone selection, positioning, placement, and distance from the musical instrument are all critical in determining just how the sound of the instrument is recorded. You have also seen how even subtle variations in any of these factors will audibly color and shape the sound that is recorded. *You should therefore regard these as together making up your very first sound effect.* Being able to record the sound as close as possible to how you want it to sound is usually preferable to having to later use audio effects, such as plug-ins, to try to re-create it.

■   Third, panning can change—and in some cases quite dramatically change—the way your music sounds to the listener. In other words, *panning in and of itself and in its own right can be a powerful and important audio effect.* Very often it makes good sound sense to reach for the pan controls before you try grabbing hold of some other effect to achieve the sound you are seeking.

These points will become clearer as you progress through the book. In the section "The Sounds of Musical Instruments," you'll learn more about this, but in short, it can often pay to identify those frequencies where different instruments may be fighting over the same frequencies and to see whether panning might not be the best way to resolve these conflicts. Later in the book we'll look at other possible solutions—for example, in Chapter 4, "Shaping the Waves: Equalization," we'll look at using equalization.

Space and Distance

You already know that the volume at which your ears will hear a musical instrument or human voice will decrease as the source of that instrument or voice becomes more distant. Figure 2.8 illustrates this concept.

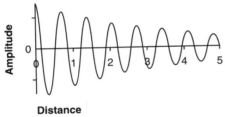

Figure 2.8 The sound that we hear from a musical instrument (or any other source) decreases with distance.

However, that isn't the whole story.

We've already learned that our ears hear some frequencies better than they hear others. In general terms, our ears are far more sensitive to sounds within the range of about 1,000 Hz to 6,000 Hz than they are to sounds outside of this range. You also need to understand that these relationships are not fixed for any and all sound pressure levels. As the volume at which we hear the sound changes, so does the relative ease with which we perceive different frequencies.

Various attempts have been made to measure and plot these relationships, the earliest and still best known of which is the Fletcher-Munson curve. Recording such data accurately, however, is no easy task (in part because of the large number of environmental variables involved), and most experts today would consider the Fletcher-Munson data to be flawed. Rather than continuing to use the term *Fletcher-Munson curve*, the more generic expression *equal loudness contours* is preferred, in particular with reference to the International Organization for Standardization (ISO) 226:2003 model.

You do not need an intricate knowledge of this topic to understand its implications for your audio work. However, if the topic interests you, the website en.wikipedia.org/wiki/Equal-loudness_contour is a good place to start.

The equal loudness curve attempts to display the variation in sound pressure (decibels) required for different frequencies for the listener to perceive the sound at all frequencies to be equal. This perceived loudness level is measured in phons. To take one example (from the graph shown in Figure 2.9), at 80 phons a 20-dB tone would need to be generated at approximately 120 dB for the listener to perceive it to be equal in volume to a 1,000-Hz tone generated at approximately 82 dB.

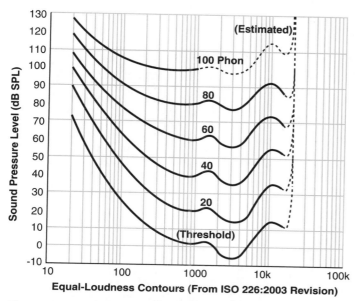

Equal-Loudness Contours (From ISO 226:2003 Revision)

Figure 2.9   The above equal loudness curve shows the levels at which sounds of different frequencies are perceived by the human ear to be equal. For a more detailed explanation, see en.wikipedia.org/wiki/Equal-loudness_contour.

Notice that as the sounds become quieter (or more distant), this variation increases. At 20 phons, for example, a 20-dB tone of approximately 90 dB would be perceived to be equivalent to a 1,000-Hz tone of only about 20 dB. This leads us to an interesting discovery that you can explore in Chapter 4 when we look at equalization. *By making changes to the gain and/or dynamics at certain frequencies of any sound (instrument or vocal), you can make it appear to be coming from a distance closer to or farther away from the listener as you wish.*

Let's not get ahead of ourselves. Before looking at how you can use audio effects such as compression, equalization, reverb, and more to shape and modify sound, it's worth learning at least a little more about the sound frequency patterns produced by different instruments in different situations.

Figure 2.10 shows the frequency ranges of the four guitar tracks on the project Whiskey00, all taken at the same time. Notice how extraordinarily different they all are. Incidentally, the top two are the same guitar with two different microphones, and the bottom two are another guitar, also with two different microphones. From this you can learn a very important lesson. *There is no such thing as a standard or uniform frequency response for any instrument.* Of course, all instruments of a particular type will share certain characteristics in common (and I'll have more to say about that toward the end of this chapter), but each one will also need to be treated individually.

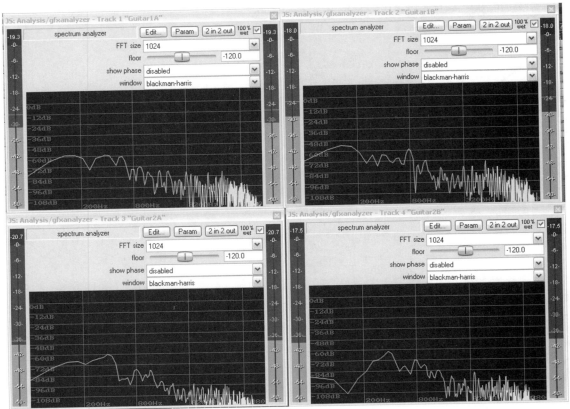

Figure 2.10   Snapshots of the frequency pattern of four acoustic guitar tracks playing together. All four snapshots were taken at exactly the same time, but each is quite different from the others. The plug-in used here is the JS plug-in Analysis/gfxanalyzer supplied with the ReaPlugs on your DVD.

Let's now go one step further than in Tutorial 2.1 and explore these concepts in practice a little more.

Using Mixer Snapshots or File Versions   The exercise that follows (like most of the exercises in this book) will encourage you to explore different settings and different permutations of settings to discover how they can affect the sounds of your audio projects.

Some DAW programs, including Pro Tools, REAPER, and amplitude, allow you to create mixer snapshots on the fly. These enable you quickly and easily to switch between different combinations of track and parameter settings. Others, including

SONAR, allow you to create multiple file versions, which, though a little cumbersome, can be used to similar effect. You're likely to find either of these features helpful when working through these exercises.

You will need to consult your DAW's documentation to see whether it supports mixer snapshots or multiple file versions.

Tutorial 2.2: Exploring Frequency, Direction, and Distance

For the purpose of really understanding the points being made by this exercise, you might find that you will get more out of it if you use headphones as well as monitors when working through the step-by-step examples. The exercise will show how making changes to the volume and pan faders and pan law settings alone can dramatically change the way your tracks will sound.

In giving these examples, I'm not saying that any one of the options presented is inherently any better (or any worse) than any of the other examples given or that it's better or worse than any of the numerous other possibilities that exist—it all depends on what kind of sound you are aiming to achieve. What I *am* hoping to show you is that if there are tracks in your mix that don't sound right, often it will pay to revisit your basic sound controls—pan and volume—before slapping on dollops of some secondary sound effect, such as equalization or compression.

1. Open the project file Whiskey00 and save it with the name Whiskey22.

2. Mute all tracks except the four guitar tracks. If you are able to select a pan law, choose the 0 dB pan law.

3. If your DAW supports mixer snapshots, engage this feature and save each of the scenarios that follow as a separate snapshot. This will make switching between and comparing the different scenarios easier.

4. Leave the four guitar tracks panned dead center with their volume faders at 0 dB. If your software supports mixer snapshots, save this as Snapshot 1. Play the tune. The four tracks will effectively be merged together in such a way as to make it difficult for you to identify their individual characteristics.

5. Now pan Guitar 1A 100% left, Guitar 1B 80% left, Guitar 2B 100% right, and Guitar 2A 80% right. Make this Snapshot 2. You should now hear each of the two instruments quite distinctly—almost as if they don't want to talk to each other!

6. Now pan Guitar 1A 65% left, Guitar 1B 35% left, Guitar 2B 65% right, and Guitar 2A 35% right. Change the volume of 1A and 2B to +2 dB and 2B and 1A to −2 dB. Make this Snapshot 3. You should still be able to hear each of the two instruments quite distinctly, but they should also now appear to be playing together more.

7.   Now try something different. Pan Guitar 1A 80% left, Guitar 1B 80% right, Guitar 2B 25% left, and Guitar 2A 25% right. Leave the volume settings as they were in Snapshot 3. Make this Snapshot 4. You should still hear each of the two instruments quite distinctly, but with the sound of one guitar now entirely wrapped around the other, the sound should appear noticeably more full.

8.   Now for something quite interesting. If your DAW allows you to do this, change the pan law for these tracks (or the whole project) to first −6.0 dB and then +6.0 dB, each time listening to the project. The change in how your material sounds should not be ground-shifting, but it should be noticeable.

9.   Change the pan law back to 0 dB. Switch between the different snapshots as you play the tune, comparing and contrasting the different sounds.

10.   When finished, save the file.

Understanding Pan Laws   Most DAW programs allow you to specify your preferred pan law, either for the whole project or on a track-by-track basis. Pan laws determine the way a mono audio signal is (or is not) attenuated as it is moved across the stereo spread of your mix from left to right (or vice versa).

This is easier to understand if we look at a couple of examples. With a pan law of 0 dB, a track that played back at 0 dB when panned fully to one side would continue to play back at that level as you moved the pan control first to the center and then to the other side. With a pan law of −6.0 dB, however, that same track would be gradually reduced in volume until by the time it reached the center it would play at −6.0 dB. By the time it reached the other side, it would be back up to 0 dB again. Less commonly used, positive pan laws (such as +6.0 dB) would have the opposite effect, actually increasing the volume as it moves toward the center and lowering it as it moves away.

One reason why you need to understand this is simply that many of the actions you take to modify the sound of your tracks with audio effects may produce different results depending on whichever pan law is being used for that track.

Let's take a moment to comprehend and analyze just what's been going on here.

■   First, this example again shows that you should not think of the term *sound effects* as applying only to external equipment and plug-ins. The term legitimately can and should be applied to anything and everything you do that affects the way your recorded media will sound.

■   Second, we started this exercise by examining how very different the frequency responses produced by seemingly similar instruments can be. At the same time, however, their patterns will also reveal many striking similarities. Figure 2.11 shows the same four tracks analyzed together using VST MultiInspectorFree. The picture is not entirely easy to read in places; you might want to consider inserting this plug-in into each of your four guitar tracks in the project WhiskeyPan so you can see it in action for yourself.

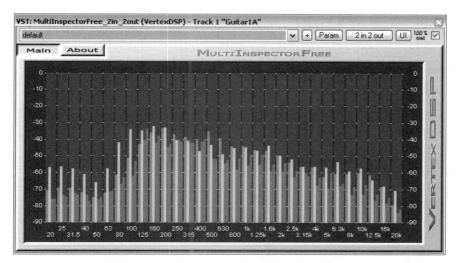

Figure 2.11 The frequency response of the same four tracks, this time analyzed using VST MultiInspectorFree. As you examine this picture, notice not so much how different the four items are, but how similar! Details about how to obtain MultiInspectorFree can be found in Table 1.2 near the end of Chapter 1.

- When you pan similar instruments close together, those frequencies where their volume is quite similar will tend to obscure each other. They will tend to merge into one sound rather than be heard as distinct instruments. In Figure 2.11, for example, this will tend to happen (among other frequencies) on the 315 Hz bar. At the same time, individual instruments will be heard more clearly at those frequencies where they are distinctly louder. In this example, this would be the case with the second (white) bar at frequencies below about 100 Hz and again at frequencies higher than about 5,000 Hz. Within those frequency ranges, this instrument is likely to dominate any of the other three instruments it is panned close to.

- In general, the more similar the frequency range of different tracks, the more likely it is that they will lose their individual clarity as they are panned closer to each other. The more different the frequency range of different tracks, the closer to each other they can be panned while still maintaining their individual clarity. This will be examined in more detail shortly, in the section "The Sounds of Musical Instruments."

- Because of this, different permutations of panning, pan laws, and volume levels will radically affect the way different instruments or even different tracks of the same instrument will sound when played together. You can therefore think of your pan and volume controls together as making up the first and arguably most fundamental sound effect that you will need to use after you have finished recording! This is a theme that will recur throughout this book. For the time being, get into the habit of checking your mixes in mono as well as in stereo. More will be said on this topic later, especially in Chapters 12 and 15.

By now you should be starting to understand that panning isn't just about positioning your instruments and vocals across the left-right spread so that each has a little space to itself. It's also about achieving a balance between preserving each individual track's distinct clarity and helping it to blend in with the mix.

If you think you need to practice this further, use the supplied project files MudSliding00 and FoggyDesperation00. In each case, save the file to a new name (such as MudSliding20) before working on it. Mute all vocal tracks where these are present—we'll come to vocals later in this chapter.

Notice as you're working that you're not looking for the one absolutely definite best solution, because although there will be many panning combinations that just don't work, there will almost certainly be more than one that *does* work. Which of these is best will depend on what you are trying to achieve.

Sound, Time, and the Acoustic Environment

To say that it takes a certain amount of time for the sound of any musical instrument or human voice to reach our ears might at first seem like a statement of the obvious, as is the observation that the more distant the source of the sound, the more time it will take to reach us. Moreover, you've probably already figured it out for yourself that this delay, however short, will play some part in shaping exactly what it is that our ears hear and exactly what messages they send to our brains.

There's another set of variables, however, that needs to be factored in along with this, and together they are tremendously important in determining how we hear sound. These are the variables created by the acoustic qualities of the environment within which you are listening.

Think about it for a moment. An instrumental recital will sound different in a large church than that same recital will sound in a small basement. Both will sound different again if the premises are full of people than they will when the premises are empty. These are just a couple of examples of the numerous different types of environment where music can be presented. And just as every instrument of the same type has its own unique sound, so does every environment. No two churches or basement nightclubs, for example, will ever shape and color sound in *exactly* the same way. What's more, even within the same venue, the person sitting at the front will hear the performance differently from the person sitting at the back.

This brings us into the territory of exploring such phenomena as delay and reverb. This is an area where there is a lot to learn, and for that reason these topics have been left until later in this book. They will be introduced from Chapter 7 onward, by which time you should be in a better position to understand them.

Fundamentals and Harmonics

Each musical note is made up of a combination of its fundamental frequency and a series of harmonics. The fundamental is the note that is initially produced when you (for example) pluck a guitar string or strike a piano key. The harmonics are produced at multiples of the frequency of that fundamental. Indeed, it is the harmonics that primarily enable you to distinguish the sound of one musical instrument from another. Listen carefully the next time you play a single guitar note. You will hear a whole series of other notes coming on top of the original (fundamental) note. It is this combination of notes that, when absorbed and interpreted by our brains, gives the instrument its distinct timbre.

Notice how in Figure 2.11 the volume levels appear to tail off quite significantly at frequencies above about 1,500 Hz. That's because at the higher frequencies you are no longer hearing the fundamentals (the actual notes played by the musician), but only the harmonics. As a rule, these higher frequencies are very important for their role in helping to define and shape the sound of the musical instrument but contribute less to its overall volume.

You do not need to be fully conversant with musical theory to grasp the key facts about harmonics and why they are important. It's probably easier if you start by focusing on the harmonics' relationship to the fundamental—that is, the note originally produced. The second harmonic will be an octave above the fundamental. The third will be an octave and a fifth above the fundamental. The fourth will then be two octaves higher than the fundamental, and so on. Thus, the harmonics will alternate between being a major third and a minor third higher each time. Figure 2.12 illustrates this relationship.

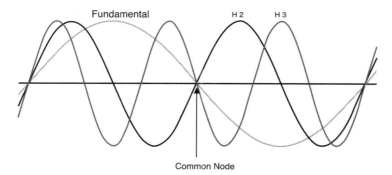

Figure 2.12 A diagrammatic representation of a fundamental note together with its second (H2) and third (H3) harmonics. Notice that because of the relationship that exists between the fundamental and its harmonics, they will all share a series of common nodes.

Let's now take a specific example—say, the single note A4 when it is played on an acoustic guitar. The fundamental will have a frequency of 440 Hz. The second harmonic will therefore be at 880 Hz. The third harmonic will be at 1,230 Hz, and so on. Table 2.2 shows the series of harmonics for this note.

Table 2.2 An Example of a Root Note (Fundamental) and Its Harmonics

Harmonic	Frequency	Pitch
Root (fundamental)	440 Hz	A4
2nd	880 Hz	A5
3rd	1,230 Hz	E
4th	1,760 Hz	A (2nd Octave)
5th	2,200 Hz	C#
6th	2,640 Hz	E
7th	3,080 Hz	G 1/4 flat
8th	3,520 Hz	A (3rd Octave)
9th	3,960 Hz	B
10th	4,400 Hz	C#

Of course, there would be no point in trying to memorize information like this—what matters most is that you understand the bigger picture and what is happening there. Let's relate this information back to the question of how we set about using and applying audio effects. Here are a few points to consider:

■ The wide frequency range covered not only by an instrument's fundamentals but also by the many series of harmonics that it will produce creates the potential for an even greater need to resolve conflict caused by different instruments competing for the same acoustic space.

■ One tool that is available to help resolve these conflicts is the use of panning and volume faders.

■ As you will see in Chapter 4, another powerful tool that can help here is equalization—but don't think that this is the only use for equalization or that using equalization will always be your best solution.

■ Identifying and understanding what is happening to an instrument's sound at different frequencies isn't only important when panning or equalizing. It will come up over and over again—for example, with noise gates (Chapter 5), compression and expansion (Chapter 6), delay (Chapter 7), reverb (Chapter 8), and much more besides.

Working with Sound

Now that you understand more about just what sound is and how your brain perceives it, a useful exercise would be to develop a broad understanding of where some of the different sounds that you are likely to be working with the most sit along the frequency spectrum. You can see that I've given vocals a separate section from musical instruments. This isn't strictly necessary—the main reason for doing this is simply that vocals often require special handling in your mixes and can therefore often be considered as belonging to a separate category of their own.

The Sounds of Musical Instruments

By now you should be starting to at least get an inkling of the complexity of the patterns of sound waves that together make up even the simplest of the music we listen to. You should find useful the information in Tables 2.3 through 2.7. They contain general summary information about the frequency ranges usually associated with different types of instruments. Remember, though, that because every individual instrument is different (and can be played in a number of different styles), you should regard this information as providing you with a general reference starting point and approximate guide only.

Tables 2.3 through 2.7 are generally self-explanatory but require one further comment. The second column in each case gives the frequency range within which you would expect to find the fundamentals for the various instruments. Of course, the lower harmonics of some of the lower fundamentals will also occur within this range. Within the frequency ranges indicated in the third column, however, you can expect to find only harmonics, no fundamentals.

Table 2.3 Approximate Frequency Ranges of Different Percussion Instruments

Instrument	Fundamentals	Harmonics Only
Congas	180 Hz to 1,000 Hz	1,000 Hz to 5,000 Hz
Cymbals	200 Hz to 800 Hz	800 Hz to 15,000 Hz
Kick	50 Hz to 500 Hz	500 Hz to 8,000 Hz
Snare	100 Hz to 250 Hz	250 Hz to 10,000 Hz
Timpani	60 Hz to 700 Hz	700 Hz to 3,000 Hz
Toms	70 Hz to 500 Hz	500 Hz to 7,500 Hz

Table 2.4 Approximate Frequency Ranges of Different Brass Instruments

Instrument	Fundamentals	Harmonics Only
Bass Trombone	50 Hz to 400 Hz	400 Hz to 5,000 Hz
French Horn	60 Hz to 800 Hz	800 Hz to 5,000 Hz
Tenor Trombone	80 Hz to 500 Hz	500 Hz to 5,000 Hz
Trumpet	160 Hz to 1,100 Hz	1,100 Hz to 9,000 Hz
Tuba	30 Hz to 380 Hz	380 Hz to 2,000 Hz

Table 2.5 Approximate Frequency Ranges of Different Woodwind Instruments

Instrument	Fundamentals	Harmonics Only
Bassoon	50 Hz to 650 Hz	650 Hz to 9,000 Hz
Clarinet	140 Hz to 2,100 Hz	2,100 Hz to 14,000 Hz
Flute	250 Hz to 2,200 Hz	2,200 Hz to 15,000 Hz
Oboe	220 Hz to 1,800 Hz	1,800 Hz to 12,000 Hz
Piccolo	600 Hz to 4,000 Hz	4,000 Hz to 16,000 Hz
Sax (Alto)	140 Hz to 750 Hz	750 Hz to 8,000 Hz
Sax (Tenor)	110 Hz to 700 Hz	700 Hz to 8,000 Hz

Table 2.6 Approximate Frequency Ranges of Different String Instruments

Instrument	Fundamentals	Harmonics Only
Banjo	150 Hz to 1,200 Hz	1,200 Hz to 5,000 Hz
Bass	40 Hz to 350 Hz	350 Hz to 6,000 Hz
Cello	65 Hz to 520 Hz	520 Hz to 7,500 Hz
Guitar	80 Hz to 1,200 Hz	1,200 Hz to 5,000 Hz
Harp	30 Hz to 3,000 Hz	3,000 Hz to 6,000 Hz
Mandolin	80 Hz to 1,300 Hz	1,300 Hz to 5,000 Hz
Viola	12 Hz to 1,000 Hz	1,000 Hz to 6,500 Hz
Violin	200 Hz to 1,200 Hz	1,200 Hz to 15,000 Hz

Table 2.7 Approximate Frequency Ranges of Various Other Instruments

Instrument	Fundamentals	Harmonics Only
Accordion	55 Hz to 1,800 Hz	1,800 Hz to 12,000 Hz
Harmonica - C	130 Hz to 1,800 Hz	1,800 Hz to 12,000 Hz
Harpsichord	40 Hz to 1,300 Hz	1,300 Hz to 6,000 Hz
Piano	30 Hz to 4,000 Hz	4,000 Hz to 12,000 Hz
Pipe Organ	20 Hz to 15,000 Hz	

Tables 2.3 through 2.7 tell a story, but only part of the story. In later chapters (especially Chapter 4), we'll break down this information further and see how you can identify (and work with) key frequencies for different instruments.

The Sounds of Vocals

Including harmonics, the frequency range covered by the various types of human voices goes from about 70 Hz up to about 16,000 Hz, with (as you might expect) considerable differences between male and female.

The fundamentals for the different types of voices also vary. A bass vocalist covers a range of approximately 70 Hz to 300 Hz, baritone approximately 90 Hz to 400 Hz, tenor approximately 110 Hz to 440 Hz, alto approximately 140 Hz to 600 Hz, and soprano approximately 180 Hz to 900 Hz.

You should be aware that while the frequency range is extremely important, it is not the only thing that distinguishes one voice type from another. Other factors include:

■ **Vocal weight.** This is the perceived lightness or heaviness of the singing voice.

■ **Vocal tissitura.** Think of this as a subset within the normal range of any vocal type. Each individual will have his (or her) own certain areas within his vocal range where his voice is at its best.

■ **Vocal timbre.** The timbre is what gives each individual voice its own distinct qualities. Qualities that make up the timbre include the use made of vocal range and the voice's envelope (or shape) characteristics, including attack, decay, sustain, and release. This theme will resurface from time to time throughout this book, including in Chapter 6, "Changing Dynamics: Compressors and More," where we will deal with compression.

■ **Vocal registration.** Vocal registration events take place within different pitch ranges. Most commonly used is the chest voice, whereas with training the head voice may also be accessed to produce a resonant sound.

■ **Physical characteristics.** Differences in the physical makeup of different individuals will contribute to different vocal qualities.

This matters because it means that making a vocal track sound just right may often require attention to more than just the frequencies alone. In many respects, however, the same issues that apply when you are balancing instruments also apply when you are balancing vocals. To demonstrate this, I'd like to finish this chapter with another short exercise.

Tutorial 2.3: Exploring Frequency, Direction, and Distance with Vocals

This example uses the four vocal tracks in the project file Lying00, which you should have created during Chapter 1. As you can see from Figure 2.13, there are considerable variations in the frequency ranges of these four voices.

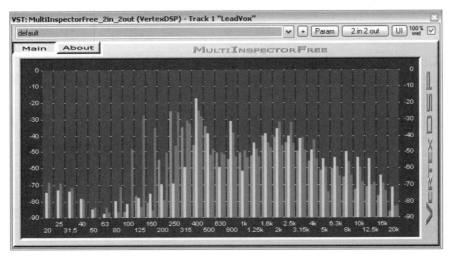

Figure 2.13 VST MultiInspectorFree is used here to compare the frequency patterns of the four voices used in the project Lying00.

Before you begin, be warned that this project has been included largely because of the number of challenges it presents. It won't take you very long to discover that this project was recorded in anything but ideal circumstances. In the examples that follow, you will see that two of the vocal tracks have been recorded separately, as discrete tracks, while the other two (including the lead vocal) have been recorded together along with various instruments, resulting in considerable bleed. Try not to let this get in the way of the points demonstrated by this exercise.

If your DAW software supports mixer snapshots, you will almost certainly want to use them during this exercise. If it does not support this feature, you should still be able to manage without them. Also, if you are able, test the listening examples separately, both through speakers and with headphones.

1. Open the project file Lying00 and save it with the name Lying23. If you are able to select a pan law, select the 0 dB pan law.

2. Loop the section that runs from 2 minutes 25 seconds to 3 minutes 6 seconds. This is the longest passage that features all four vocal tracks.

3. Either solo the four vocal tracks or mute all tracks except these four. Play the song. Because of bleed, you will still hear some of the musical instruments in the background. Try not to be concerned about this.

4. Create the first mixer snapshot. This leaves all four vocal tracks panned dead center. Lower the volume of all four tracks to about −2.9 dB.

5. Play the song. Panning the songs together should help blend them, but because of the variations in the frequency ranges of the different tracks, you should still be able to quite clearly hear four distinct voices.

6. Your second mixer snapshot will allow each individual voice just a little more distinction. Set the LeadVox to 5% right, 0 dB; Bvox1 to 40% left, −1.0 dB; Bvox2 to 40% right, −0.5 dB; and Bvox3 to 24% left, −3.5 dB. Notice how the two female vocals have been panned to opposite sides.

7. A third possible panning option is offered by the third mixer snapshot. This places the females closer together on one side and the males on the other. Set the LeadVox to 15% right, 0 dB; Bvox1 to 40% left and −1.5 dB; Bvox2 to 245% left and −0.3 dB; and Bvox3 to 32% right and −2.5 dB. You should still hear the voices blending together well, this time with a little less individual emphasis.

8. Save the file when you have finished.

The point of this exercise, like most of the exercises throughout this book, is not to determine which of these three arrangements is the best, but rather to help you understand that pursuing different options will give you different outcomes. In every case, it is for you to decide which outcome you prefer!

Project Files Log

If you have completed all of the examples and tutorials in this chapter, you should have created the following files:

Tutorial 2.1: AudioExperiment21

Tutorial 2.2: Whiskey22

Tutorial 2.3: Lying 23

Your complete project file log should now be as follows:

Alone00

AudioExperiment21

Foggy00

Lying00, Lying23

Mud00

Whiskey00, Whiskey22

3 Introducing Audio Effects

By now you should be realizing that the factors that go into creating the musical sounds that your ears receive and transmit to your brain are both large in number and complex in nature. You have also seen how items that you might never have thought of as being audio effects in their own right—items such as a track's volume and pan faders—will nevertheless shape and help determine the sounds you hear. If only for that reason alone, I would argue that these controls should be regarded as primary audio effects.

Of course, very often you will want more than just these. That is where what I call your *secondary audio effects* can come into play. These come in any number of shapes and sizes—equalizers, compressors, delay and chorus units, reverb units, noise gates, and so on. Think of each of these as being a tool. In fact, the analogy of a toolkit isn't a bad one. A carpenter's toolkit might include hammers for banging in nails, saws for cutting through wood, planes for smoothing rough edges, and so on. Each will have its own particular (and usually well-defined) functions, but its real value will come from its role as part of the overall kit. Much the same can be said of the various audio effects you have at your disposal, whether they take the form of software plug-ins, outboard equipment, or some combination of both.

This chapter will provide you with an overview of the main kinds of tools you'd expect to use in your audio effects toolkit. You'll be introduced to each of these individually, along with some very simple and basic examples of how they are used. You'll then be given at least a rudimentary understanding of how they can work together. Subsequent chapters will examine each of these tools (and more) individually and in more depth before returning toward the end of the book to a further examination of how they can be used together.

In this chapter we will look at the following topics:

- Types of audio effects
- Manipulating frequency
- Modifying dynamics
- Playing with time

47

- Combining effects
- Audio signal flow

Preparing the Project File

Before you can do any of this, you will need to prepare a project file that you can use to work through the various examples that will be presented in this chapter. The song *Now Is the Time for Whiskey* makes a good choice, in part because of its simple arrangement. You'll need to create a reasonable mix of this song to give you something to work with. The instructions that follow will give you this mix. Please follow them as closely as you can. They are designed to give you not necessarily the best possible mix for this song, but a mix designed to be used in conjunction with the examples that follow.

Preparation: Creating the Project File

1.   Open the file Whiskey00 and save it as Whiskey30.

2.   Adjust the track controls (volume and pan faders) on the various tracks as follows:

> VocalM: volume 0.00 dB, pan 12% left
>
> VocalF: volume 0.00 dB, pan 12% right
>
> Guitar1A: volume −1.50 dB, pan 60% left
>
> Guitar1B: volume −1.50 dB, pan 40% left
>
> Guitar2A: volume −1.50 dB, pan 40% right
>
> Guitar2B: volume −1.50 dB, pan 60% right
>
> Shakuhachi: volume 0.00 dB, pan center

3.   If you inserted a simple limiter into the master when you created the file Whiskey00, then of course that limiter will still be there in your new file. If you did not do this, insert a limiter now into the master's FX bin and set the maximum volume control to −1.0. If your limiter also includes a threshold control, set it to 0.0 dB. If you wish, use the ReaJS plug-in for this purpose—just load the utility limiter into it, as explained in Chapter 1.

4a.   PC users only: Also in the master FX bin, insert an instance of ReaJS before your limiter. The method for doing this is explained toward the end of Chapter 1. Into this plug-in, load the utility called Volume/Pan. Set the volume to +5.0 dB (this will add a 5-dB gain to the volume of the incoming mix) and specify a pan law of −3.0, as shown in Figure 3.1.

or

4b.   Mac users only: If you can, use whichever method your DAW employs to add a 5-dB gain to the signal coming *into* your master. *This is not the same as increasing the master output.* Also, if you are able, set the pan law for the project to −3.0 dB.

5.   Save the file.

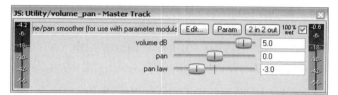

Figure 3.1   The JS Utility Volume/Pan plug-in. It lets you adjust the overall volume and/or panning of the incoming audio on any track, bus, or mix.

Types of Audio Effect

Audio effects do their work by modifying the audio stream in one or more of three ways—manipulating the frequencies of the sound waves, modifying in some way the dynamics of the sound, or making some changes to the way the audio is perceived to interact with time. Most of the plug-ins that you will use for these purposes will tend to work primarily in one or another of these three areas, but there are some that operate in two or more ways at once (see Figure 3.2).

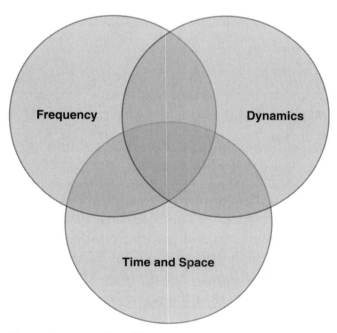

Figure 3.2   Audio effects mostly achieve their results by working in one or more of three areas—modifying the frequency of the sound, changing its dynamics (including volume) in some way, and playing with time and space.

Let's take an initial brief look at each of these in turn:

- **Manipulating frequencies.** Different parts of the frequency range of different instruments and voices emphasize different qualities of the voice or instrument, such as warmth or presence. By manipulating these frequencies, you are able to change the way the voice or instrument will sound.

- **Modifying dynamics.** The dynamic range of a voice or a piece of music is a measure of the difference between the quietest and loudest parts of a voice or instrument during a performance. By making modifications to this range, you are able to make changes to the sound of the voice or instrument.

- **Interacting with time and space.** How a piece of music will sound will be significantly affected by its immediate environment and by the time and journey its sound waves take before they reach our ears. By using audio effects, we are able to re-create for the listener different acoustic environments that make different uses of these variables.

In the three sections that immediately follow this one, we'll look at an example or two in each of these categories. For the time being, don't even try to understand everything there is to know about these effects; we'll return to each of them in much more detail in subsequent chapters. For now, just focus on getting your mind around the bigger picture of where each type of effect fits into the general scheme of things. In particular, I'm hoping this will help you develop an understanding of how what you do with the various controls that you'll find in your various plug-in windows relates to what happens to the sound of your recorded material.

Manipulating Frequencies

By far the most commonly used audio effect for manipulating frequencies is equalization, often known as *EQ*. There are several types of equalizers, and each can be used for any number of tasks. In this section, we'll just look at one or two relatively simple examples.

In this first example, I'll be using a graphic equalizer because its controls are simpler to understand than other types of equalizers, such as the parametric equalizer (which we'll get to in Chapter 4, "Shaping the Waves: Equalization"). You'll see how you can use equalization to roll some of the presence off the vocals and produce a more mellow, laid-back sound. Keep in mind in all of these examples that I'm not saying you would necessarily wish to do this here—that's a matter for your own judgment. The object of the exercise is purely to help you understand what equalization is and how it works.

Tutorial 3.1: Using an Equalizer to Manipulate Frequencies

A graphic equalizer divides the frequency spectrum into a number of bands. Gain faders are used to increase or decrease the volume on any of these bands. Figure 3.3 shows the

KarmaFX 31-Band Equalizer being used for this purpose. At the default setting of Full, the entire frequency spectrum is divided into 31 bands. You'll find download details in Table 1.2 of Chapter 1, or you can use any other graphic equalizer, such as one that might have been included with your DAW program.

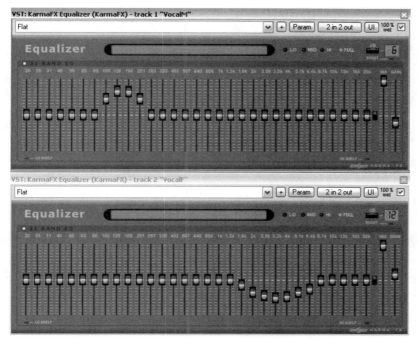

Figure 3.3 This shows a graphic equalizer being used to add more warmth to one vocal track (top) while rolling a little presence off the other (bottom).

1. Open the file Whiskey30. Save it as Whiskey31.

2. Add your preferred graphic equalizer plug-in to both of the vocal tracks.

3. For the male vocal, increase levels between about 100 Hz and 200 Hz, as shown in Figure 3.3 (top). This is not a frequency range that our ears hear especially well, so be prepared to add as much as 5 dB at the peak. To compensate for the extra volume, lower the overall gain control (far right) by about 2.5 dB.

4. For the female vocal, decrease levels by up to 6 dB within the approximate range of 1,500 Hz to 7,500 Hz, as shown in Figure 3.3 (bottom). Because you are working mainly with harmonics here, you will not need to raise the overall gain level (far right) by very much to compensate. Try raising it by about 0.5 dB.

5. Play the song several times, with the equalizers alternately engaged and set to bypass. The difference should be noticeable. This is especially the case if the two tracks are soloed.

6. Save the file.

Take a moment to think about what you have done here.

On the first track, by adding gain at some frequencies and then reducing the overall gain, you have effectively lowered the levels of all frequencies except those at which you added gain. On the second track, you did the opposite: By lowering some frequencies and increasing the overall gain, you have effectively raised levels on all frequencies except those that you specifically lowered.

Notice, too, that the changes you have introduced have not been dramatic. It will often be the case that you will want to use audio effects to bring about subtle rather than dramatic changes to the way your material sounds.

Checkpoint 1

If you feel you'd like to experiment some more with EQ before moving on to the next section, go right ahead (but remember that we will be returning to the subject in depth in Chapter 4).

Save the project file Whiskey31 as Whiskey31Extra. See whether you can use equalization on a couple of the guitar tracks (one of each pair) to make them sound a little brighter. Don't overdo it. If it seems that you're depending too much on trial and error, don't worry. The exercise will serve as a good experience when we examine the frequency spectrum in more detail in Chapter 4.

If after doing this you wish to save your work, please do so. This file will not be required for any future tutorials.

Modifying Dynamics

Widely used for modifying the dynamics of a piece of music is an audio effect called the *compressor*. Compression is quite a complex subject—for now, you'll just scratch the surface to give you a broad-brush understanding of what a compressor is and how it works. The subject will be covered in detail in Chapter 6, "Changing Dynamics: Compressors and More." We will be concentrating mainly on just two of the compressor's many controls—threshold and ratio. Understanding what these two do is a very good starting point when it comes to understanding and using compression.

Tutorial 3.2: Using a Compressor to Modify Dynamics

In this example you'll create a submix for your four guitar tracks and then use a compressor to modify the dynamic range of this submix in order to prevent the loudest notes from jumping out of the mix. (If you're not sure how to create a submix [or if your DAW software doesn't allow this feature], you can still do a variation of this tutorial.

Instead of using a submix, you will need to add a compressor to each of the four individual guitar tracks.)

Figures 3.4 and 3.5 show two ways of creating a submix. Your DAW probably uses one or the other of these methods. Figure 3.4 shows the more commonly used method. In

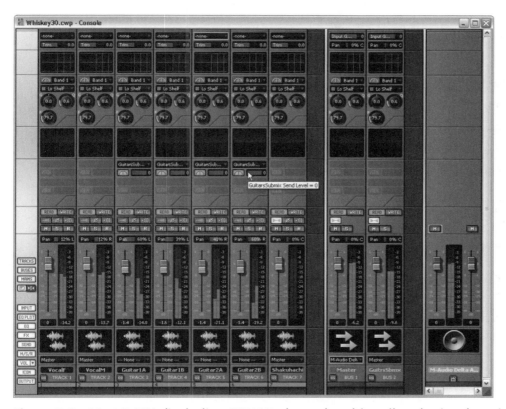

Figure 3.4   Most DAWs (including SONAR, shown here) handle submixes by using busses. In this case, the Guitars Submix bus (together with the master) is shown in a separate section to the right of the tracks.

either event, make sure when you are creating a submix that direct output from the individual tracks to the master is disabled (as explained in the section "Using Submixes" in Chapter 1).

You can see a couple of examples of projects with submixes in different DAW environments in Figures 4.2 and 4.3 (in Chapter 4).

Submix Settings and Levels   When you are setting up a submix, your DAW might require you to specify certain levels and settings for the send. If this is the case with your software, make sure that (for all the examples in this book) in each case you set

Figure 3.5   Not all DAWs use the bus method of handling submixes. Shown here is REAPER, which uses track folders for this purpose. Notice the Guitars Submix folder.

the send level to 0.0 dB and the pan position to center and that you select a Post FX option.

This assumes that your DAW conforms to a standard procedure whereby the volume and pan settings that you specify in a send will be relative to the track's own volume and pan settings. For example, if a volume send level is set at 0.0 dB, then the level actually sent will always be exactly the same as that determined by the track's volume fader. If it is set at, say, −3.0 dB, then it will always be 3.0 dB quieter. You might need to check your DAW's documentation to confirm that it behaves in this way.

We'll then use a compressor's threshold control on the submix to determine the level of volume above which we want to start trimming back the guitar notes, and the ratio control to determine how drastically we want to cut them back.

1.   Open the file Whiskey31. Save it as Whiskey32.

2.   Increase the volume fader on all four guitar tracks to +1.0 dB.

3. Create a submix for these four guitar tracks. Make sure their output goes only to the submix, not directly to the master. Of course, the output from the submix should go to the master.

4. Insert a compressor into the FX bin for your guitar's submix. Figure 3.6 shows ReaComp (one of the VST plug-ins supplied on your DVD) being used for this purpose. You could use another compressor if you wish, but if you use ReaComp for this example at least, you will find it easier to follow the exact instructions.

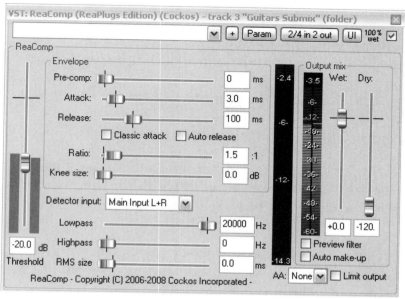

Figure 3.6   This shows a compressor being used to "tame" the peaks on a track or (as in this case) a submix.

5. For now, set the ratio to 1:1. This should be its default level.

6. For now, mute the two vocal tracks. Play the song. Lower the threshold fader on the compressor until its two vertical green VU bars bounce around just above the top of the actual fader. This is likely to be somewhere close to −30.0 dB.

7. Now slowly move the ratio fader all the way from left to right. As you do, you should notice:

  ■ The volume of the guitar mix grows progressively quieter.

  ■ The vertical red bar (left of the output mix VU) becomes taller and more prominent. This is a visual indicator of the amount by which the volume of the compressed signal is being reduced.

  ■ There is a loss of clarity or sparkle in the sound of the guitar mix.

8. Now unmute the vocal tracks.

9. Move the ratio fader back to the left until it reaches 1.5:1. You should now notice that the red bar flashes far less aggressively. This indicates that less compression is being applied. However, the fact that the red bar remains visible all the time indicates that the compression is being applied to the guitar mix all the time.

10. Adjust the threshold setting to −20.0 dB. You should notice the following:

    ■ The red bar now flashes on and off much less aggressively. It is no longer visible all the time. This indicates that only the louder passages are being compressed.

    ■ When it is applied, the amount of reduction is generally in the order of −2.0 dB to −3.0 dB. This suggests that the degree of compression is generally quite subtle.

    ■ The guitars have had their clarity and sparkle restored.

11. Save the file. It's time to see just what exactly has been going on here.

What you have seen is how important it is to get your threshold and ratio settings right when you are using a compressor. Of course the other controls also matter, but if you don't get the threshold and ratio settings right, tweaking with the other controls isn't going to help you.

Take a look at Figure 3.7. This shows a different compressor being used, with settings similar to those that we ended up with in Tutorial 3.2. Look at the diagonal line that goes from bottom left to top right in the graph.

The white dot represents the threshold. As long as the volume of the guitar mix stays below this threshold (in this case, −21.0 dB), no compression will be applied. Look above this threshold on the graph, and you can see two lines—a strong one and a faint one. The faint line indicates what would happen to the signal if the compressor was not applied—for example, if it was set to bypass. The stronger line shows what actually happens to the signal when it exceeds the threshold level. For every 1.5 dB by which the original (dry) audio stream exceeds this threshold, the outgoing (wet) audio stream will be allowed to increase by only 1 dB.

Not understanding how this ratio control works (or at least not using it correctly) is a major cause of compression being applied poorly, especially to acoustic music. Take a look at Figure 3.8.

This shows the result of using four of the many different compression ratios that can be used when compressing an audio signal. These are at 1:1, 2:1, 4:1 and infinity:1. At infinity:1, any signal above the threshold level is just squashed down. What may

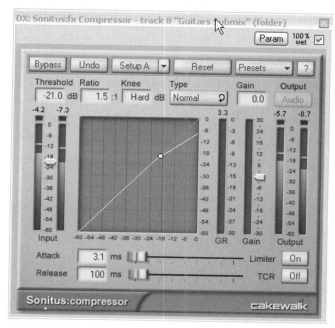

Figure 3.7   This shows a different compressor (Cakewalk's Sonitus compressor) being used with settings similar to those used in the ReaComp.

surprise you is seeing the significance of the amount of compression that is being applied even at seemingly low ratios, such as 2:1 and 4:1. With the ReaComp compressor (and with most others), these levels are positioned quite close to the left of the fader and visually may appear to be quite low. It would be easy for a relatively inexperienced user

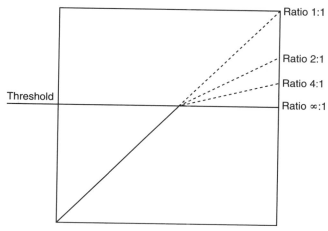

Figure 3.8   This shows how the threshold and ratio settings work together to determine how the dynamics of an audio stream are modified. The compression ratio is applied whenever the volume exceeds the level determined by the threshold setting. As the ratio is increased, so is the degree of compression applied.

to go for an apparent midrange setting with the expectation that this would be a safe bet. In this example, this would result in a compression ratio on the order of 25:1, which for most purposes would be far too heavy.

Figure 3.9 shows the Kjaerhus Audio Classic Compressor. Its design and layout is different again from the others that we have examined, despite offering similar functionality. Notice in this case, however, the setting of 2:1 is placed right in the center of the ratio control. One lesson to be learned here is that it really is important to study the controls of any audio effect that you are going to use. Take the time to understand exactly how they work.

Figure 3.9   This shows another compressor—Kjaerhus Audio Classic Compressor. All three of the compressors that we have looked at are very similar in their functionality but also very different in their visual layout and interface. For download information on the Kjaerhus Classic series, see Table 1.2 in Chapter 1.

Playing with Time

Effects such as delay, chorus, and reverb can be used to great effect in enhancing the sound of your instruments by modifying the way they appear to behave within the context of time and space. I've listed them in that order for a reason: As you go from each one to the next, the issues involved become more complex, and it becomes easier to make your instruments and your mixes sound worse instead of better!

Tutorial 3.3: Using Simple Delay to Create Atmosphere

In this example, we'll be looking at simple delay only. There are some key points about even this simple effect that you need to understand before you'll really be ready to move on to the next level. You'll see how by adding a little delay to an instrument (in this case, our shakuhachi), you can create a moody, haunting effect. The three main issues you will need to understand are the delay length, the amount of feedback added, and the dry/wet mix.

1.   Open the file Whiskey32. Save it as Whiskey33.

2.   Select the Shakuhachi track and add a delay plug-in of your choice to its FX bin. In the example shown in Figure 3.10, the plug-in used is GDelay. You can, of course, use any other delay plug-in of your choice. For this particular example, however, one advantage of GDelay is its simplicity.

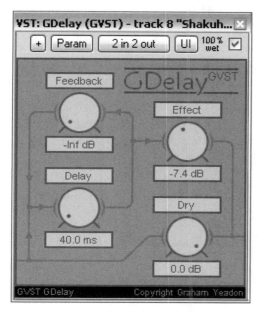

Figure 3.10   This shows simple delay plug-in, GDelay, being used to add some delay to a track. Download information for the GVST set of plug-ins can be found in Table 1.2 in Chapter 1.

3.   The example shows the effect (wet) level set within the range of about −7.0 dB to −10 dB and the dry level set to 0.0 dB. Set your wet/dry controls to values similar to these. (See the upcoming "Delay Parameter Controls" note.)

4.   Loop the passage from about 2 min 56 sec to 3 min 20 sec and play the song. Gradually adjust the delay (length) control all the way up to its maximum setting and then back down to somewhere in the range of 30 ms to 40 ms again. Play the tune with the FX alternately bypassed and engaged to help you notice the difference.

5.   Solo the Shakuhachi track. Gradually increase the feedback up to about −25 dB.

6.   Unsolo the track. By adding delay, you have also increased its overall volume. Pull this back to about −2.0 dB.

7.   Remove the loop. Save the file.

Delay Parameter Controls   It's a common issue with audio software that different products use different terms to describe what is essentially the same phenomenon. For example, the control shown here with the name Delay will on some software be called Length. The control labeled Effect (which determines how much of the delayed signal is added to the mix) is often called Wet. Also, you may find that some delay software might use a single Wet/Dry balance control rather than separate controls for each of these two parameters.

Let's take a look now at what has been going on here.

Figure 3.11 might help you understand how simple delay changes the sound of the music to which it is added. It shows three scenarios. In each of these, no feedback has been added. We'll get to feedback shortly.

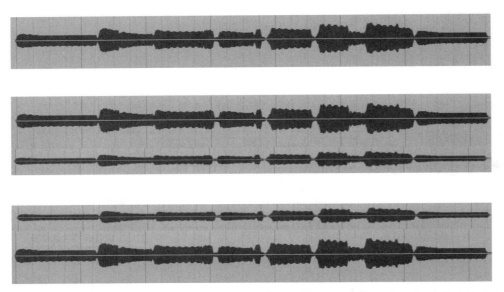

Figure 3.11 A diagrammatic representation of how adding simple delay to a track changes the wave pattern of the track's output.

The first scenario (top) represents the original recording. No delay has yet been added.

In the second scenario (center), delay has been added at a lower volume than the original dry signal. (In Tutorial 3.3 we have taken off about 7.0 dB to 10 dB.) Look at the illustration carefully, and you will see that the delayed signal plays just a very short time after the original. Our ears hear both the original dry and the delayed wet signal being played at the same time, one just a few milliseconds after the other. This pretty much represents what's happening at Step 4 of Tutorial 3.3.

The third scenario (bottom) is one that you have not yet encountered, but it is definitely worth mentioning even this early in your understanding of delay. The only difference between the second and third scenarios is that the relative volume of the dry and wet signals has been reversed. The dry signal has been faded down while the delayed wet signal has been increased back up to 0.0 dB. In Chapter 7, "Playing with Time: Delay and Chorus," you will see that there are actually times when you may wish to do this, but meanwhile it is important that you understand what happens if you do. It's difficult to think of many real-world examples where the volume or strength of a sound will actually increase with distance! Nevertheless, an easy mistake for the novice to make is to create an unrealistic blend of wet and dry signals. As a general rule, you will want to ensure that when used in this way (directly in a track's FX bin), your effect's mix will contain more of the original dry signal than of the delayed wet signal.

The other control that you used in Tutorial 3.3 was feedback. This is harder to describe and harder still to show visually. Figure 3.12 aims to achieve this. It is important that you understand the concept of feedback, not least because understanding how delay feedback works will be a useful step toward later understanding how reverb works.

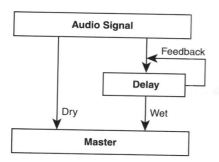

Figure 3.12   A diagrammatic representation of how delay feedback works. A portion of the delay is fed back into itself, resulting in a smoother transition between the original (dry) and the delayed (wet) signal.

Always be careful when using feedback. Start at zero and increase the fader gradually until you achieve the sound you want. You'll find another example of using delay with feedback in Checkpoint 2 at the end of this section.

Take a moment to consider why adding some delay to a track can make it sound more haunting. This effect is created by the blend of the original (dry) signal with the delayed (wet) signal. In part it is due to the relationship that exists between time and distance. The longer a sound takes to reach our ears, the more distant it appears to be. As you have already seen, some frequencies will survive such a journey better than others. By playing with time in this way, you have therefore also played with the blend of frequencies that the ear receives and transmits to the brain.

Checkpoint 2

Here's an optional extra example that will really show you more about how the parameter's delay length, feedback, and effect (wet) output levels modify a track's sound.

Save the file Whiskey33 as Whiskey33Extra. Now add the same delay plug-in as you used before to the female vocal track (after the EQ plug-in that is already there). Set the feedback to 0 dB. Loop the passage that goes from approximately 3 min 20 sec to 4 min 12 sec. Play the song.

Slowly increase the delay length to about 500 ms. You should clearly hear the delayed vocal as a separate audio stream, running about a half second behind the original. As you increase the delay length, the gap between the two audio streams increases accordingly.

Now lower the delay slowly. At some point (probably around 15 ms), you will find that it becomes very difficult to detect that there is a second delayed vocal signal. Instead, the two streams merge inside your brain to sound more like a single fatter vocal. Increase the feedback to about −15 dB. This will have even more the effect of helping the two signals blend together as one.

Now remove the loop and unsolo the female vocal track. Save the file and play the song.

Combining Effects

In Checkpoint 2, you encountered an example where two effects were used on the same track—in this case, both equalization and delay were employed on a female vocal track. This leads us to consider a very important point. The use of more than one effect on a track is not unusual, and you will need to understand not only what individual effects do when used on their own but also how they work together in combination. For this reason, two entire chapters of this book (Chapters 12 and 13) will be devoted to an in-depth examination of this topic. However, some simpler examples will also be introduced in various chapters before those, as this is an issue that realistically cannot be avoided.

Tutorial 3.4: Using Multiple Effects on Tracks

In this tutorial we'll look at another example of compression, this time applied to a vocal submix, in a situation where both of the vocal tracks already have other audio effects applied to them individually.

As you play the song *Now Is the Time for Whiskey,* you will notice that where both voices are singing together, the vocals at present are too loud. There are actually several options available to you for fixing this, each one producing a significantly different sound. In this example we'll look at just two. The first of these uses compression; as for the second . . . well, you'll find out soon enough!

1.   Open the file Whiskey33. Save it as Whiskey34.

2.   Create a submix for the two vocal tracks. Make sure that the output of these two individual tracks is directed to the submix only, and not directly to the master. Of course, the output from the submix should go to the master.

3.   Into the FX bin for your vocal's submix, insert a compressor of your choice. Figure 3.13 shows the MCompressor from Melda being used for this purpose.

Figure 3.13   This example uses a different compressor, the MCompressor from Melda Productions. If you wish to use it, download details can be found in Table 1.2 in Chapter 1. Notice the two white horizontal bars below the graph. The first of these shows the amount of signal reduction being applied at any time; the second shows the volume of the incoming audio signal.

4.   Make sure that you disable the option Maximize Signal Strength to 0 dB. (See the position of the mouse pointer in Figure 3.13.) Leave the other controls at their default settings.

5.   Play the song. Set the threshold at a level that will generally engage the compressor only when both voices are singing. This is likely to be around −24.0 dB.

6.   This time we are going to try a more aggressive threshold setting. Try about 3.7:1. One nice feature of the MCompressor is that the graph gives you clear visual feedback as the song is played.

7.   If you can save this as a mixer snapshot, do so. We're now going to try something else. For this next experiment, you will need to know how your DAW uses automation envelopes. Figure 3.14 shows a volume envelope added to a bus in SONAR.

Figure 3.14 This example shows a volume envelope being used while the compressor in the FX bin is bypassed. The DAW used here is SONAR.

8. Set the FX bin for the vocal submix to bypass.

9. Add a volume envelope to the vocal submix. Play the song, adjusting the envelope so that the volume of the vocals when both voices are singing appears to be about the same as when there is only one. This will probably be somewhere around −4.0 dB or −5.0 dB.

10. Save the file.

11. Now alternate between using the envelope with the compressor bypassed and using the compressor with the envelope bypassed. Can you identify in what ways the two effects differ?

Listen carefully, and you will be able to discern the difference between these two options. For example:

■ With the compressor (rather than the envelope) engaged, the quieter parts of the vocal harmonies are not reduced. This will tend to prevent the odd syllable, word, or phrase from getting lost in the mix.

■ With the envelope rather than the compressor engaged, the dynamics of the original recording are better preserved. This will tend to give you a natural, cleaner sound.

■ Because the compressor restricts the dynamic range of the vocals, you are likely to find that its use will tend to blend the two voices together more, whereas using the envelope is more likely to maintain their distinct clarity.

Which is preferred? That's something you'll have to decide for yourself by listening. Moreover, even ignoring the possibility of using any techniques other than compression or volume envelopes, you still have another option. You can use both a compressor and a volume envelope, but engage each somewhat more gently. This gives you a compromise, which you might (or might not) prefer. What's more—and again, depending on exactly how you want your vocal mix to sound—you could also consider whether using equalization to reduce the level of certain frequencies might have a part to play.

Chaining Audio Effects Keep in mind when you're chaining audio effects that the order in which you place the individual effects matters. For example, if you are adding both equalization and compression to a track, then placing the EQ before the compressor will produce a different outcome from placing it after the compressor.

In that example, if the compressor is placed after the EQ, then the equalization changes that you make by adding or subtracting at certain frequencies will themselves be reshaped by changes that you then make to the track's dynamics. On the other hand, if the EQ comes after the compressor, then equalization will be applied after the changes are made to the track's dynamics. Don't get hung up on this for the moment—just make a mental note of it somewhere!

This theme will be developed and explained more as this book progresses.

Audio Signal Flow

If you are not already familiar with your DAW's audio signal flow, then now is the time to put that right. Figure 3.15 is a simplified diagram that represents a typical order of events in which different activities occur as the signal from your recorded media items is processed during playback.

You will need to check to see whether your DAW program uses this sequence or whether it introduces any significant variation. Typically, controls placed directly on the media items (clips) themselves, such as clip envelopes and/or fades, are processed first, followed by any audio effects that have been placed on the media item directly.

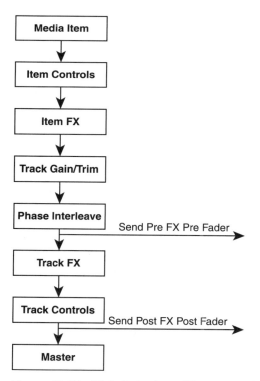

Figure 3.15   This flowchart illustrates the order in which activities typically occur when recorded material is played back in most DAW programs.

After this, any gain added to the track is applied, followed by any phase interleave setting. This is the signal that is sent to auxiliary busses and/or submixes when the pre-FX, pre-fader options are specified. As the signal continues its flow through the track, effects placed in the track's FX bin are then processed, followed by track control settings such as volume, pan, and mute. This is the signal that is sent to the master (if the master send has not been enabled in favor of a submix) and to any busses and/or submix where the post-FX, post-fader option has been specified.

You can see, therefore, that it can make an important difference whether your effects are placed directly on the media items themselves or in the track's FX bin.

Software and Hardware Effects Audio effects can be applied to your recorded material using either software plug-ins (as in the examples that you have encountered so far) or separate pieces of physical equipment connected to your computer, often known as *outboard effects*. The underlying principles that determine how the effect works will be the same in both cases. For example, a software compressor will use the same parameters as an outboard compressor.

It is obviously not possible to distribute a rack full of equipment, such as compressors and reverb and delay units, with this book. For that reason, all of the examples used will employ software effects rather than hardware ones. What you learn from these examples should help you when you are working with both hardware and software effects. You should be aware, however, that using outboard hardware effects can introduce latency issues and that not all DAWs resolve this issue very well.

Before You Move On . . .

In this chapter you've been introduced to some simple examples of the main areas in which audio effects can be used to change the sound of your recorded material—these are frequency, dynamics, and time. Before moving on, try this simple experiment.

If you have completed all of the preceding tutorials, then each of the audio effects that you have used in this project has been applied quite gently—and there have not been very many of them. However, taken together, you might be surprised at just how much difference they have made. Compare how the file Whiskey35 sounds with and without all the effects set to bypass. Most good DAW programs have a single command or control that lets you toggle global FX bypass on and off. If your software lacks this feature, you will need to toggle each item's status individually. You've probably learned more than you realize! Take the time to reflect that:

- Even the simplest effect will often make a substantial difference to the way a track will sound to the listener. You will often find that a little goes a long way.

- Quite often, you may have more than one option available to you when you are aiming to achieve a particular outcome. Understanding the similarities and differences between these options will help you determine which is preferred in a particular situation.

- Don't use artificial effects just because they are there and available. Often the best outcome will be a clean, simple, clear recording.

- Anything that you do with an audio effect on one track will affect not only that track, but also the overall balance and sound of your project. For example, if you use equalization on one instrument to make it sound brighter or more present, then other instruments may by comparison sound less bright or less present as a result. This is not necessarily a good thing or a bad thing—but you need to be aware of it.

- Any audio effect is likely to produce a different outcome when used in combination with another effect (or chain of effects) than it will when used alone.

- There are no rules that state when you should and should not use any particular effect. There are, however, definite laws that determine what will happen when you *do* use them.

Project Files Log

If you have completed all of the examples and tutorials in this chapter, you should have created the following files:

Preparation: Whiskey30

Tutorial 3.1: Whiskey31

Checkpoint 1: Whiskey31Extra (optional)

Tutorial 3.2: Whiskey32

Tutorial 3.3: Whiskey33

Checkpoint 2: Whiskey33Extra (optional)

Tutorial 3.4: Whiskey34

Your complete project file log should now be as follows:

Alone00

AudioExperiment21

Foggy00

Lying00, Lying23

Mud00

Whiskey00, Whiskey22, Whiskey30, Whiskey31, Whiskey32, Whiskey33

4 Shaping the Waves: Equalization

In Chapter 2, you learned about the frequency spectrum and how it is generally divided into a number of bands. In Chapter 3, you were introduced to using equalization to make changes to the volume of a piece of music at specific frequencies or bands of frequencies. In this chapter, you will learn a lot more about equalization and how you can use it.

As you work through this chapter, however, there are two important facts that you should keep in mind. These are:

- Some DAWs include the option to automatically include EQ on every channel in their mixer view. An example of this is Samplitude (see Figure 4.1). In this respect, their graphical user interface (GUI) can be made to resemble an analog mixing desk. At times this can be convenient, but it brings with it the danger that you might think that because it is there, you should be using it. Nothing could be further from the truth. EQ, like any other effect, should be used only if you have a specific reason for doing so.

- Remember what you learned in Chapter 3: Equalization is only part of the story. Don't try to solve all of your problems with equalization. Before applying EQ to any track, make sure that it really is the most appropriate tool for the job. Remember also that quite possibly you may need to use EQ in conjunction with some other audio effect.

In this chapter, we will look at the following topics:

- Analyzing and understanding frequency bands
- Key frequencies for different instruments
- Understanding equalization and the different types of equalizers
- Applying equalization to your tracks
- Bonus EQ plug-ins (overview)

Figure 4.1   Some DAWs provide built-in EQ on every channel strip. Shown here is Samplitude's mixer console, which includes a four-band parametric equalizer on every channel (track).

Preparation

These first two tutorials will enable you to make two of the sample projects—Mud Sliding and Foggy Desperation—ready to be used for trying out the other many examples that follow. For both projects, you will need to create a reasonable quick mix as a starting point. In later tutorials, several of these settings will be changed.

In the case of the project Foggy Desperation, you will need to create a number of submixes. The topic of creating submixes was discussed earlier, in Chapter 3.

Preparation: Creating the Project Files

As in earlier chapters, before attempting the tutorials you will need to create a rough mix for the projects involved. The object of this exercise isn't to create a perfect mix for each of these projects; rather, it is to bring them both to the stage where they are suitable to be used for the other tutorials and examples that follow. In both cases, follow the instructions as closely as you are able.

1. Open the file Mud00 that you created earlier and immediately save it as Mud40.

2. If you are able to choose a pan law, set the pan law of -3.0 dB for this project.

3. Adjust the volume and pan faders for the various tracks as follows:

   Guitar1: volume 0.00 dB, pan 20% left

   Guitar2: volume 0.00 dB, pan 20% right

   HarmonicaAmp: volume -2.1 dB, pan center

   Kick: volume 0.00 dB, pan 30% left

   Snare: volume -2.00 dB, pan 30% right

   PercOhead: volume -20 dB, pan 8% left

   RoomMic: volume -12.6 dB, 8% right

4. Insert the ReaJS effects Utility: Volume/Pan and Utility: Limiter into the master. If you are unsure of how to do this, refer back to the last section of Chapter 1.

5. Set the volume level of the JS Utility Volume/Pan to $+2.0$ dB. If you were unable to set the pan law at Step 2, set the pan law within this plug-in to -3.0 dB. Set the max volume on the limiter to -1.0 dB.

6. Save the file and close it.

7. Open the file Foggy00 and immediately save it as Foggy40.

8. Create the following three submixes, each made up of the tracks specified. In each case, ensure that the output of the individual tracks concerned goes only to the appropriate submix, not directly to the master.

   VoxMix: consisting of VoxLead and VoxHarmony

   GuitarMix: consisting of GuitarAcoustic1, GuitarAcoustic2, and GuitarElectric

   PercussionMix: consisting of Kick, Snare, Ohead1, and Ohead2

9. Notice that the tracks Bass and Mandolin will be output directly to the master without using a submix.

10. If you are able to specify a pan law for this project, select -3.0 dB.

11. Adjust the volume and pan faders for the various tracks and busses as follows:

VoxLead: volume 0.00 dB, pan center.

VoxHarmony: volume −3.00 dB, pan 5% right.

GuitarAcoustic1: volume −5.00 dB, pan 45% right.

GuitarAcoustic2: volume −5.00 dB, pan 45% left.

GuitarElectric: volume −0.75 dB, pan 62% right. If your DAW doesn't allow you to adjust the volume in increments of less than .1 dB, set this to −0.7 dB instead.

Bass: volume: 0.0 dB, pan center.

Mandolin: volume −2.00 dB, pan 62% right.

Kick: volume −4.50 dB, pan 30% right.

Snare: volume −4.50 dB, pan 30% left.

Ohead1: volume: -4.50 dB, pan 80% left.

Ohead2: volume: −4.50 dB, pan 80% right.

VoxMix submix: volume 0.0 dB, pan center.

GuitarsMix submix: volume 0.00 dB, pan center.

PercussionMix submix: volume 0.00 dB, pan center.

12.   Insert the ReaJS effects Utility:Volume/Pan and Utility: Limiter into the master. If you are unsure of how to do this, refer back to the last section of Chapter 1.

13.   Set the volume level of the JS Utility Volume/Pan to +2.0 dB. If you were unable to set the pan law at Step 2, set the pan law within this plug-in to −3.0 dB. Set the max volume on the limiter to −1.0 dB.

14.   Save the file and close it.

Frequency Bands

In Chapter 2, we analyzed the frequency spectrum and divided it into five main bands—bass (bottom end), low mids, mids, high, and ultra high. By increasing or decreasing levels at key frequencies within one or more of these bands, we are able to change the sound of a musical instrument so as to emphasize (or de-emphasize) any particular characteristics. In this section, we're going to start by looking more closely at each of these five bands and then identify possible key frequencies for various musical instruments.

Know Your Frequencies

Table 4.1 identifies some terms that you might be inclined to use to describe the qualities associated with each part of the frequency spectrum, together with some words that might come to mind if you find an instrument or mix either lacking or top-heavy at any part of this spectrum. For example, if an instrument contains too great a level of low

Table 4.1 Commonly Used Terms to Describe Different Sound Bands

Band	Too Little	About Right	Too Much
Bass (40 Hz to 200 Hz)	Anemic, Sparse, Thin	Full, Punchy, Solid	Boomy, Heavy, Rumbly
Low Mids (200 Hz to 800 Hz)	Distant, Empty, Hollow	Fat, Full, Warm	Barelly, Muddy, Tubby
Mids (800 Hz to 5,000 Hz)	Muffled, Stifled, Veiled	Clear, Present, Up Front	Boxy, Honky, Nasal
High (5,000 Hz to 8,000 Hz)	Dull, Foggy, Unclear	Bright, Clear, Live	Piercing, Strident, Tinny
Ultra High (over 8,000 Hz)	Cheap, Flat, Lifeless	Crisp, Gleaming, Sparkling	Brittle, Searing, Sizzly

mids, you might describe its sound as being muddy. If, on the other hand, a mix was lacking in bottom end, you might say it sounded anemic.

Of course, these bands and their descriptions should be considered as generalities. Use them for guidance, but don't let them be your master!

Know Your Instruments

Before getting down to some practical examples that will help you understand more about how equalization works, I'm going to say something about key frequencies. The series of tables in Chapter 2 summarize the frequency ranges of various musical instruments. In this section, more of an emphasis will be placed on the key frequencies of some of those instruments (see Table 4.2).

Key frequencies are those interesting frequencies on any instrument where changes in volume are likely to have the most significant effect on the sound of a recorded instrument as it is played back. Of course, these frequencies will also be influenced by a whole range of other factors, such as microphone selection and placement, the musical genre, and the musician's individual style of playing. For this reason, the tables that follow should be used for general guidance only, not as directives to be slavishly obeyed. Later in this section, you'll be shown how, by using this information as a starting point, you can identify and target the key frequencies on your own individual recordings.

You'll notice that for some instruments, mention is made of *formants*. Formants are those frequencies at which the volume of the instrument can be expected to peak, regardless of the pitch at which the instrument is being played. These formants play an important role in giving the instrument its particular timbre. Where formants have been included in the relevant tables, you are likely to find that these are frequencies to which you may wish to pay particular attention.

Table 4.2 Frequencies of Interest on Various Musical Instruments and Vocals

Instrument	Frequencies
Accordion	Left side fat around 100 to 250 Hz. Right side piercing above 5,000 Hz. Bright (left and right) around 2,500 Hz to 4,000 Hz.
Bass guitar	Full around 40 Hz to 60 Hz. Cut around 300 to 400 Hz if muddy. Attack at 700 Hz to 1,000 Hz. Present at 1,000 Hz to 2,000 Hz. Subtle high harmonics at 5,000 Hz.
Congas	Resonant at 200 Hz to 240 Hz. Muddy around 500 Hz. Present at 4,000 Hz to 5,000 Hz.
Cymbals	Clang around 200 Hz. Present around 3,000 Hz. Shimmer at 7,500 Hz to 12,000 Hz.
Dobro	Full around 300 Hz to 500 Hz. Bite at 1,500 Hz to 2,000 Hz. Bright from 2,500 Hz up to 5,000 Hz.
Guitar (acoustic)	Full around 100 Hz to 300 Hz, but too much in this range will produce a muddy sound. Clarity might be improved by cutting between 1,000 Hz and 3,000 Hz or boosting around 4,000 Hz to 6,000 Hz. Presence up to 5,000 Hz to 7,000 Hz. Sparkle above 8,000 Hz.
Guitar (electric)	Full around 100 to 200 Hz. May be muddy around 200 to 800 Hz. Bite around 2,000 Hz to 3,000 Hz, but too much at 3,000 Hz to 5,000 Hz can cause irritation. Crisp around 5,000 Hz. Presence around 6,000 Hz. Sparkle above 8,000 Hz.
Harmonica	Fat at 250 Hz. Present around 2,500 Hz. Bright and airy above 5,000 Hz.
Harp	Check for pedal noise below about 180 Hz and string twang around 2,000 Hz to 4,500 Hz. Clarity around 5,000 Hz to 7,000 Hz. Air at 7,000 Hz to 10,000 Hz.
Hi-hat	Muddy around 300 to 400 Hz. Sparkling at 10,000 Hz to 12,000 Hz.
Horns	Full at 100 Hz to 200 Hz. Present around 1,000 Hz. Clarity at 5,000 Hz to 7,500 Hz. May be muddy around 500 Hz.
Kick	Punch at 50 Hz to 100 Hz. Full at 100 Hz to 250 Hz. May be muddy around 300 to 400 Hz. Hollow around 400 Hz. Presence at 2,500 Hz to 3,000 Hz. Attack at 3,000 Hz to 5,000 Hz.
Mandolin	Full at 200 Hz to 300 Hz. Clarity from 2,500 Hz to 5,000 Hz. Searing above about 8,000 Hz.
Overheads	Muddy around 300 Hz, possible irritation in midrange. Present at 2,500 Hz to 3,000 Hz. Bright around 6,000 Hz.
Piano	Resonant around 50 Hz. Bottom end 80 Hz to 100 Hz. May be honky around 1,000 Hz. Bite around 3,000 Hz to 5,000 Hz. Present at 5,000 Hz to 6,000 Hz. High harmonics up to 15,000 Hz.

Instrument	Frequencies
Sax (alto)	Honky around 400 Hz. Squawk around 2,000 Hz. Reed buzz at 6,000 Hz to 7,500 Hz.
Sax (tenor)	Honky at 250 Hz to 350 Hz. Squawk around 1,000 Hz. Reed buzz at 5,000 Hz to 6,000 Hz.
Snare	Body at 100 Hz to 120 Hz. Fullness at 120 Hz to 240 Hz. Tingling around 900 Hz. Attack at 2,500 Hz to 4,000 Hz. Crisp at 4,000 Hz to 5,000 Hz.
Steel guitar	Deep at 80 Hz to 240 Hz. Fat at 240 Hz to 750 Hz. Bite at 1,750 Hz to 2,500 Hz.
Toms (floor)	Full at 80 Hz to 120 Hz. Boomy around 300 to 450 Hz. Clarity at 3,000 Hz to 8,000 Hz.
Toms (rack)	Full at 250 Hz to 400 Hz. Attack at 5,000 Hz to 7,000 Hz. Clarity at 7,000 Hz to 8,000 Hz.
Trumpet	Fundamentals around 165 Hz to 1,200 Hz. Formants at 1,000 Hz to 1,500 Hz and 2,000 Hz to 3,000 Hz.
Violin	Full around 180 Hz to 300 Hz. Formants at 300 Hz, 1,000 Hz, and 1,200 Hz. Scratchy around 7,000 Hz to 10,000 Hz.
Vocal (female)	Full at 180 Hz to 270 Hz. Present at 2,000 Hz to 4,000 Hz. Possible sibilance between 4,000 Hz and 9,000 Hz. Air above 10,000 Hz.
Vocal (male)	Full at 100 Hz to 180 Hz. May be boomy at 200 Hz to 300 Hz. Present at 2,000 Hz to 4,000 Hz. Possible sibilance at 4,000 Hz to 9,000 Hz. Air above 10,000 Hz.

In the next section, you'll learn more about the different types of equalizers and how to use them. You'll then go on to apply this knowledge to some of the material in your sample project files.

Understanding Equalization

In Chapter 3 you were introduced to one kind of equalizer, the graphic equalizer. Other methods of equalizing include parametric, semi-parametric, and linear phase. In this section we'll be looking at each of these in turn.

Graphic EQ

The graphic equalizer is in some respects the simplest, because the only action you usually need to take is to increase or lower the gain at certain frequencies. If you want the increase or decrease applied as a series of gentle steps before and after the desired frequency, you can do so by also adjusting the faders before and after this frequency. This is what we did, for example, in Tutorial 3.2 in Chapter 3.

This approach might work well if the changes that you wish to make are simple and premeditated (that is, you are confident before you begin that you know which frequencies you wish to modify). However, it doesn't lend itself too well to experimentation. If, for example, you are searching to find the exact frequency (or range of frequencies) that you want work on in order to make your guitar sound less muddy, then pretty soon your graphic equalizer becomes a rather clumsy tool.

Despite this, graphic equalizers can be handy, especially if their inherent limitations are compensated for to any extent by any clever additional features built into either the design of the particular EQ software or the host DAW within which it is being employed.

One example of a graphic equalizer with an enhanced feature set is the Sony Graphic Equalizer (see Figure 4.2). You can use it in either 10-band mode or 20-band mode (top) and then switch to view your settings in graph format (middle). You can then make adjustments to your equalization settings by clicking and dragging directly on the graph (bottom).

An example where additional functionality comes not from the plug-in itself but from the host program is REAPER.

Figure 4.3 includes three screenshots. The first (left) represents the settings made in Figure 4.2, with the wet/dry mix set to 100% wet (see the mouse pointer) and bypass disabled (indicated by the check mark). This produces exactly the same outcome as you would get if neither of these controls was available. In the second (middle) screenshot, the wet/dry mix has been wound back almost one-third of the way from its six o'clock setting, so that (right) we now have a 68% wet/32% dry mix. This would be the equivalent to restoring each of the individual faders 32% of the way back toward its default 0-dB level. Notice also that in the third instance (right), we are also able to use the small check box to toggle bypass on and off. You are able to err on the side of overdoing the EQ in your initial settings and then experiment by winding it back until you get the level just about right.

The combination of these two features clearly makes the plug-in much more useful and more usable. Of course, this functionality can (within that particular host) be applied to any and every plug-in you ever use. Therefore, you should definitely make sure you familiarize yourself with whatever extra tools, tricks, and techniques your DAW makes available to you when working with plug-ins. It's possible that there might be more there than you had realized.

Parametric EQ

Time to take a deep breath. The parametric equalizer is without doubt the type of tool that you will use the most when you are equalizing your tracks. There's also quite a lot to know about it.

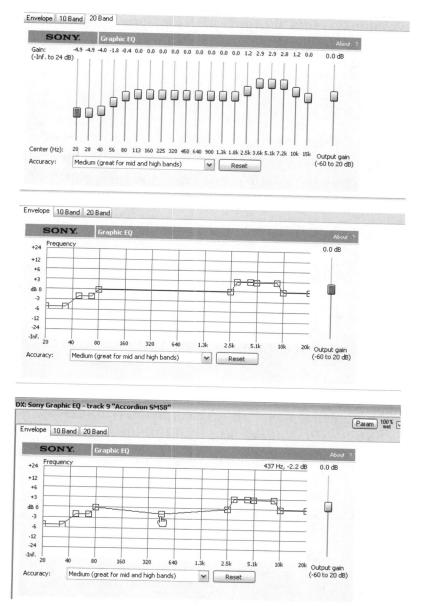

Figure 4.2   Sony's Graphic EQ includes a graphical interface that adds extra functionality.

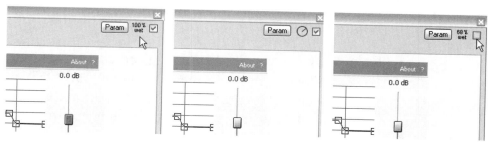

Figure 4.3   REAPER's plug-in interface adds a wet/dry mix control and a bypass toggle to every plug-in. Here it is shown with the Sony Graphic Equalizer.

A parametric equalizer employs four main types of controls for shaping the sound of the item to which it is being applied. These are:

- **Frequency.** This determines the frequency or frequencies that are being modified. This is essentially the same concept that you encountered earlier in the examples that used a graphic equalizer.

- **Gain.** This determines the extent to which the audio signal is modified (increased or reduced) at the selected frequency or frequencies. Again, this is essentially the same concept that you experienced earlier in the examples that used a graphic equalizer.

- **Band type.** This is one of two additional factors that will determine how the equalization is applied. Band type is critical in determining the shape that is used to modify the audio stream.

- **Bandwidth (often known as Q).** Together with band type, this also determines how the audio signal is shaped, particularly with reference to the width or narrowness of the frequency range that will be raised or lowered.

There's actually quite a lot to learn here. Don't worry; we'll soon get to some practical examples.

Band Filter Types

Parametric equalization works by applying filters at selected frequencies across the frequency spectrum. Depending on the particular task and your specific objectives, you might wish to use any number of bands, from just one up to perhaps five or six or even more. Some parameter equalization plug-ins allow you to use as many bands as you wish; others impose a limit. In the example shown in Figure 4.4, the Melda Productions plug-in MEqualizer allows you to use up to six bands.

Also shown in Figure 4.4 is a drop-down list of seven filter types. These can be summarized as follows.

Bell filter. Also known variously as peak/dip, peak, band, or bandwidth filters. This gets its name from its shape. It applies a gain or reduction centered on a particular frequency and across a specified range of frequencies. Typically, these are used to emphasize or de-emphasize certain frequencies of the instrument or voice. In Figure 4.5, Bands 2 and 3 are both bell filters with some gain around 300 Hz and reduction around 1,500 Hz, respectively.

Low-pass filter. This type of filter allows frequencies below a specified frequency to pass through but tapers down to eventually eliminate frequencies above that specified frequency. Typically, this is used to prevent high-end hiss or sizzle. An example of a high-pass filter in use is Band 4 in Figure 4.5. Because this kind of filter cuts out frequencies above that specified, it is also known as a *high-cut filter*.

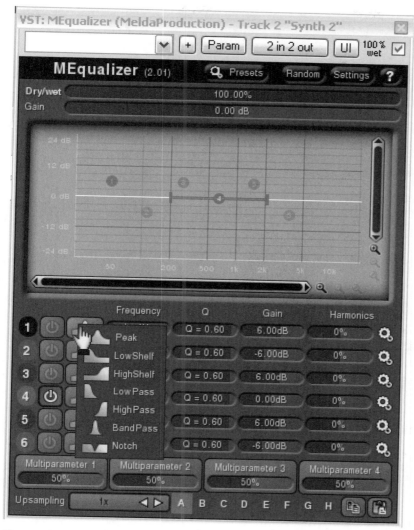

Figure 4.4 This shows the Melda Productions plug-in MEqualizer about to be used as a parametric equalizer. Currently, its settings are all at their default positions, but notice the drop-down list (near the hand that represents the mouse pointer) of seven different band types.

High-pass filter. This type of filter allows frequencies above a specified frequency to pass through but tapers down to eventually eliminate frequencies below that specified frequency. Typically, this is used to prevent low-end hum or rumble. An example of a high-pass filter in use is Band 1 in Figure 4.5. Because this kind of filter cuts out frequencies below that specified, it is also known as a *low-cut filter*.

High-shelf filter. This type of filter can be easily confused with a low-pass filter, as either of these filter types, when used, is likely to be found at the higher end of the frequency spectrum. Whereas a low-pass filter only allows through frequencies *below* that specified, a high-shelf filter's settings apply gain or reduction (attenuation) only to

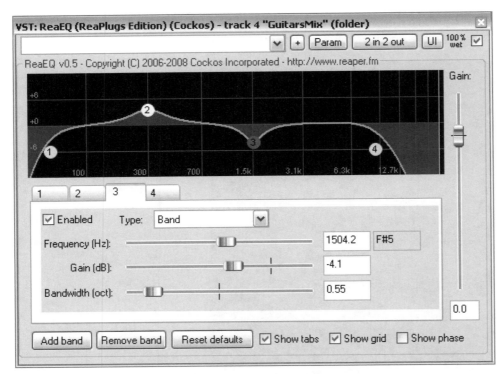

Figure 4.5 This shows the ReaEQ plug-in (supplied on the DVD) in use on an actual track. Four bands are in use—a high-pass filter (Band 1), two peak filters (Bands 2 and 3), and a low-pass filter (Band 4). This example has been set up solely to illustrate these different band types and is not intended to serve in any way as a model.

frequencies *above* that specified. The term *shelf* is used because the curve resembles the shape of a shelf. An example of a high-shelf filter is shown in Figure 4.9.

Low-shelf filter. This type of filter can be easily confused with a high-pass filter, as either of these filter types, when used, is likely to be found at the lower end of the frequency spectrum. Whereas a high-pass filter only allows through frequencies *above* that specified, a low-shelf filter's settings apply gain or reduction (attenuation) only to frequencies *below* that specified.

Band-pass filter. This filter type allows through only those frequencies within the specified band range. It can be invaluable in identifying key frequencies for any recorded item. These can be frequencies where the instrument sounds particularly strong and interesting, or problem frequencies, or some combination of both. As this book progresses, you will see that band-pass filters have quite an amazing range of applications. Figure 4.6 shows an example of a band-pass filter in use.

Notch filter. In a sense, this filter type is the opposite of the band-pass filter. It allows through everything except those frequencies within the specified band range. It is sometimes used where a specific sound (such as sibilance or popping) needs to be removed from a track. Figure 4.7 shows an example of a notch filter in use.

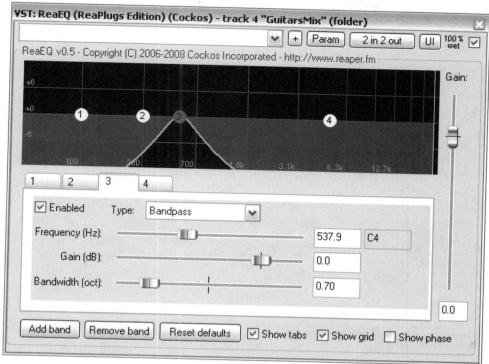

Figure 4.6 This shows a band-pass filter (in use with ReaEQ). Only those frequencies in the selected range will be heard.

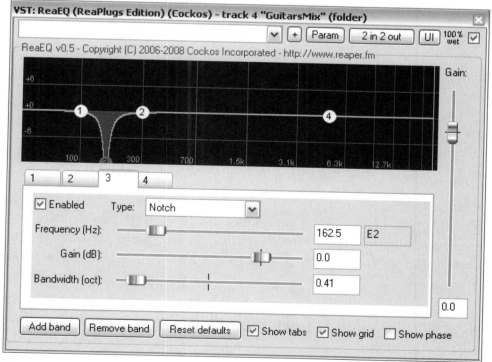

Figure 4.7 This shows a notch filter (in use with ReaEQ). Sounds in the narrow range of selected frequencies are filtered out.

Corrective Equalizing   One technique commonly used to resolve problems that may occur with the sound of an instrument or vocal is corrective equalizing. This can happen, for example, if a guitar sounds too muddy or a vocal sounds too shrill.

The process consists of identifying the offending frequencies (perhaps with the aid of a band-pass filter) and then introducing some attenuation to the problem frequency range. In Figure 4.5, this has been done around the 1,000-Hz frequency.

High-Pass and Low-Pass Filters   High-pass filters and low-pass filters are not only important when you are working with equalization. As you'll see in later chapters (in particular in Chapters 6, 7, and 8), these filters can also play an important role when you are using other effects, including noise gates, compressors, delay, and reverb.

Bandwidth

Take another look at Figure 4.5. You can see that it includes two peak (band) filters—one (Band 2) centered around 300 Hz and the other (Band 3) around 1,500 Hz. Look carefully, and you can observe that Band 2 covers a greater width than Band 3. In each case, the width of the frequency range affected by the gain or attenuation is determined by the bandwidth setting. In the example shown, the bandwidth for Band 3 has been set at 0.55 octave and that for Band 2 has been set at 0.9 octave. This particular equalizer allows the bandwidth to be set at any value between 0.01 and 4 octaves.

This observation leads us to have to consider a rather unfortunate fact. There is no one single universally employed scale for measuring bandwidth. ReaEQ, for example, uses octaves. The higher the octave setting, then the wider the bandwidth. Many other parametric equalizers, however, use a scale of measurement called *quality,* often referred to as simply *Q*. By this standard of measurement, the more finely targeted (or narrow) the bandwidth, the greater the value of Q. This makes comparisons between bandwidth settings on different software something of a problem.

You might find Table 4.3 to be useful whenever you need to make such comparisons.

In this section so far, you have seen two examples of parametric equalizers, the MEqualizer and ReaEQ. Just these two items together are enough to demonstrate that although in some respects all parametric equalizers are similar, many will bring with them their own special qualities and features that might lead you to prefer one over another in a given situation.

For example, ReaEQ lets you use as many or as few bands as you want. If you need seven, you can have seven. If you only need one band, you can delete all the other bands from that instance to avoid screen clutter and help you to maintain focus. You cannot do that with MEqualizer. On the other hand, it does have three other very nifty features. Take another look at Figure 4.4. Near the bottom you'll see eight buttons, labeled A to H.

Table 4.3 Approximate Equivalent Bandwidths Expressed in Octaves or Q Values

Octaves	Q Value	Octaves	Q Value
0.01	144.3	0.70	2.04
0.02	72.1	0.80	1.78
0.03	48.1	0.90	1.58
0.04	36.1	1.00	1.41
0.05	28.9	1.10	1.28
0.06	24.0	1.20	1.17
0.07	20.6	1.30	1.07
0.08	18.0	1.40	0.991
0.09	16.0	1.50	0.920
0.10	14.4	1.60	0.857
0.12	12.0	1.70	0.802
0.14	10.3	1.80	0.752
0.16	9.01	1.90	0.707
0.18	8.01	2.00	0.667
0.20	7.21	2.20	0.596
0.22	6.55	2.40	0.537
0.26	5.54	2.60	0.486
0.30	4.80	2.80	0.443
0.35	4.11	3.00	0.404
0.40	3.60	3.20	0.370
0.45	3.19	3.40	0.340
0.50	2.87	3.60	0.313
0.55	2.61	3.80	0.289
0.60	2.39	4.00	0.267

These enable you in each instance of the plug-in to save up to eight different sets of settings and to switch between them each time with a single click. To the left of these is an upsampling option. This has the potential to improve sound quality by sampling at a higher rate, thereby avoiding aliasing. (Aliasing is a form of distortion that can occur when data is sampled at too low a rate.) As if that wasn't impressive enough, at the top you'll see that the plug-in has its own wet/dry mixer, thus enabling you to easily tweak the overall amount of EQ applied within any host DAW.

Again, the moral of the story is that you should make yourself thoroughly familiar with whatever parametric equalizer is supplied with your DAW. In particular, get to know and understand any special features or characteristics that it might have.

Tutorial 4.1: Understanding Bandwidth

The best way to understand how changing the bandwidth of any filter affects the overall sound of the voice or instrument is to conduct a simple experiment or two. The technique in this example uses a process known as *sweeping*. This consists of setting up a band-pass filter at the lower end (left) of the frequency spectrum and then slowly dragging it along the frequency spectrum (to the right), stopping from time to time in order to isolate and identify how the material sounds at various different frequencies.

1. Insert a parametric equalizer in the track's FX bin.

2. Add a band-pass filter and sweep the frequency range until you identify approximately the frequency on which you wish to work.

3. Adjust the bandwidth until you get the sound just right.

4. Change the bandwidth filter to a peak filter. Increase or attenuate the gain value as appropriate.

5. If necessary, fine-tune the bandwidth.

In this tutorial we'll be doing just that, using for practice the vocal harmony track in the song *Foggy Desperation*.

1. Open the file Foggy40 and save it as Foggy41.

2. Solo the VoxHarmony track and (for convenience) create a loop from 2 min 28 sec to 2 min 56 sec.

3. As is often the case with a backing vocal track, we might wish to remove some of the presence from this track to make it easier for it to sit more behind the lead vocal in the mix. One way to do this is to alter the balance between the bottom end and the presence of the voice.

4. Add a parametric equalizer of your choice. For the examples in this section, this must be one that includes band-pass filters.

5. Create a band-pass filter with a bandwidth of approximately 1 octave (or Q 1.4). As you play the song, sweep the frequencies from about 80 Hz to about 300 Hz until you find the spot where the voice sounds warmest and deepest. In the example in Figure 4.8, this is shown close to 170 Hz, but you should use your own judgment. When you have selected a frequency, adjust the bandwidth to see whether you can improve on the quality of the sound. Figure 4.8 suggests this might be 1.12 octaves (Q 1.28), but again, you should decide this for yourself.

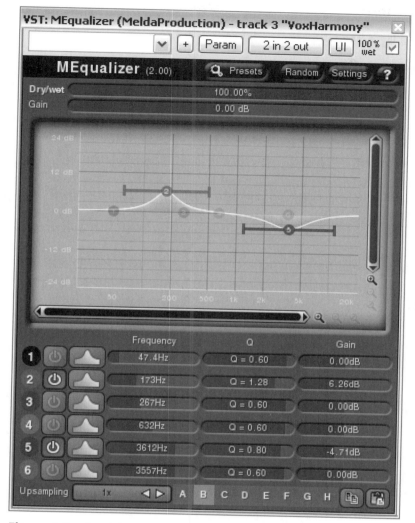

Figure 4.8   Applying two band filters to a vocal track. The two horizontal bars on the graph (labeled 2 and 5) indicate the bandwidth applied in both cases.

6.   Change the filter type to peak and add about 6 dB of gain.

7.   Add another band-pass filter with the same bandwidth as before. Repeat the procedure explained in Step 5, but this time within the range of 2,000 Hz to 5,000 Hz. This time, you are looking for a strong, clear presence. Figure 4.8 puts this at about 3,600 Hz, with a bandwidth of about 1.76 octaves (Q 0.8).

8.   Change the filter type to peak and reduce the gain by about 4.6 dB.

9.   Save the file.

10.   Compare how the vocal harmony sounds with the EQ alternately engaged and bypassed.

11. Unsolo the track and again compare how the song sounds with this effect alternately engaged and bypassed.

12. Remove the loop and save the file.

Using Vocals as an Aid to Learning   It's in the nature of the human ear and the human brain to be more discriminating and sensitive when dealing with the sounds of human voices than with any other sound. Even on the telephone, for example, most of us can instantly identify any individual voice out of the scores or even hundreds with which we are familiar. By way of contrast, how many of us can with equal ease distinguish the sound of one acoustic guitar from another, even in perfect listening conditions?

For this reason, it is often a good practice to experiment with vocal tracks when you are trying to understand what exactly various audio effects do to sound and how their various parameters do this. Changes quite subtle and difficult for the untrained ear to identify on the sound of, say, a guitar or a harmonica can often be easier to identify on a vocal. Of course, this doesn't mean that when you come to mix your vocals down you should saturate them with every conceivable effect known to humankind!

Tutorial 4.2: Learning to Use Parametric Equalizers

The purpose of this tutorial is to give you more practical examples of using equalization and with that develop your abilities to use it. We're not aiming for what is necessarily the perfect mix here; what is important is that you increase your understanding of how changes you make to EQ parameters will shape sound.

In part, the aim is to add more zest and life to the mix, keeping in mind that an arrangement that includes two male vocals (but no female vocals), a bass guitar, a kick drum, and two acoustic guitars runs the risk of being somewhat bottom-end heavy. Table 4.4 includes some suggested possible solutions for these examples, *but you should not just blindly use those settings!* Try out your own ideas. There is no reason why these shouldn't produce results as good as or better than those suggested in the table.

1. Open the file Foggy41 and save it as Foggy42.

2. Apply a parametric equalizer to the lead vocal track, designed to make it a little fuller in sound and more present.

3. Apply a parametric equalizer to the bass guitar track, designed to make it a little fuller in sound with a little more attack and more present.

4. Apply a parametric equalizer to the electric guitar track, designed to make it a little fuller in sound with a fair amount of added crispness and sparkle, even to the extent of bordering on tinny.

Table 4.4   Possible EQ Changes for Various Tracks in Tutorial 4.2

Track	Possible EQ Settings
Lead Vocal	Peak filter at about 160 Hz, 2.2 octave (0.6 Q), +3.5 dB gain Peak filter at about 2,200 Hz, 0.85 octave (1.6 Q), +3.5 dB gain Peak filter at about 5,500 Hz, 1.4 octave (1.0 Q), −1.4 dB gain Overall: +1.7 dB gain
Bass Guitar	Peak filter at about 60 Hz, 0.9 octave (1.6 Q), +5.5 dB gain Peak filter at about 700 Hz, 0.45 octave (3.2 Q), +5.5 dB gain Peak filter at about 1,500 Hz, 1.0 octave (1.4 Q), +4 dB gain Overall: −4.5 dB gain
Electric Guitar	Peak filter at about 120 Hz, 0.9 octave (1.6 Q), +3.5 dB gain Peak filter at about 2,500 Hz, 0.55 octave (2.6 Q), +9 dB gain Peak filter at about 8,000 Hz, 2.0 octave (0.6 Q), +8 dB gain Overall: −1.5 dB gain
Mandolin	Peak filter around 3,500 Hz, 2.0 octave (0.6 Q), +1.8 dB gain
Kick	Peak filter around 80 Hz, 1.8 octave (0.75 Q), +6 dB gain Peak filter at about 400 Hz, 0.8 octave (1.8 Q), −6 dB gain Peak filter at about 4,250 Hz, 1.8 octave (0.86 Q), +5 dB gain Overall: −2.0 dB gain
Snare	Peak filter around 200 Hz, 1.4 octave (1.0 Q), +5 dB gain Peak filter at about 900 Hz, 0.45 octave (3.2 Q), +4.3 dB gain Peak filter at about 3,300 Hz, 1.7 octave (0.8 Q), +7 dB gain
Percussion Mix	High-shelf filter at about 6,000 Hz, 1.15 octave (1.2 Q), +3.0 dB gain

5.   Apply a parametric equalizer to the mandolin track, designed to make it stand out a little more clearly in the mix.

6.   By now the acoustic guitars might be starting to get a bit overwhelmed. In this case, simply raise the sound on these two tracks to about −2.5 dB each.

7.   Apply a parametric equalizer to the kick, designed to give it some more punch and attack.

8.   Apply a parametric equalizer to the snare, designed to make it a little fuller and with more attack.

9.   Add a parametric equalizer to your percussion submix. Use a high-shelf filter to add a little shimmer to your overall drum mix (see Figure 4.9).

10.   You may need to make adjustments to the relative volumes for the different tracks in order to keep the balance about right.

11.   Quite likely, the net effect of these changes has been to raise the overall volume of the mix. If so, lower the gain setting on the volume/pan plug-in on the master to about +2.5 dB.

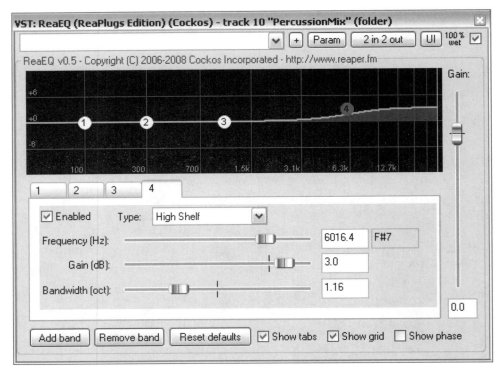

Figure 4.9   Using a high-shelf filter to add a little high-end shimmer, in this case to a drum mix.

12.   Play the file alternately with all effects engaged and all bypassed. You should notice quite a difference!

13.   Save the file.

14.   If you are able to create mixer snapshots, save this project with your EQ settings as one mixer snapshot. Create and save an alternate mixer snapshot using the settings shown in Table 4.4. Save the file and compare how the song sounds with the different mixer snapshots.

We're Not There Yet   In this tutorial you've explored how EQ can help to add qualities to a voice or instrument such as warmth, presence, attack, or punch. So far, so good, but that's only part of the story. In Chapter 6, "Changing Dynamics: Compressors and More," you'll see how other techniques (such as the use of compression) can also play a part in achieving these outcomes.

Table 4.4 shows one possible way in which your EQ settings could be changed in the file Foggy42 as a result of completing Tutorial 4.2. In this example, the changes have been made mostly by boosting certain frequencies. You need to listen carefully when doing this, as there is always the possibility that you may be boosting unwanted sound as well.

Here's an alternative approach you can also try: Rather than boosting those frequencies that you do like, lower the others.

Figure 4.10 illustrates this. The two sets of EQ levels shown will yield broadly similar results, one (left) using additive equalization and the other (right) using only subtractive equalization.

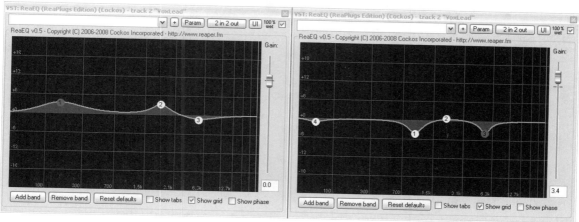

Figure 4.10 Two similar outcomes, but the one on the right uses only subtractive equalization.

There are a couple of points particularly interesting about these suggested possible equalization changes for these tracks when you take them as a whole:

- As far as possible, gain has not been added at the same frequency on more than one instrument.

- There are a number of instances where subtractive equalization has been used to attenuate some of the muddier frequencies.

- You've probably noticed that most of these examples use peak filters. We haven't even looked at notch filters or high- and low-pass filters yet. That's because these filter types, though important, tend to be used less widely.

Figure 4.11 shows an example of a high-pass filter. Its purpose in this instance is simply to eliminate any very low-frequency noise that may have been recorded below the frequency of the instrument itself. You'll learn more about low- and high-pass filters when we deal with noise gates and compressors in Chapters 5 and 6.

Notch filters tend to be used for corrective equalization, sometimes called *surgical equalization*.

Tutorial 4.3: Using a Notch Filter

An example of where you might want to use a notch filter can be found in the recording of the song *Lying Back*. This project was recorded in far from ideal circumstances and

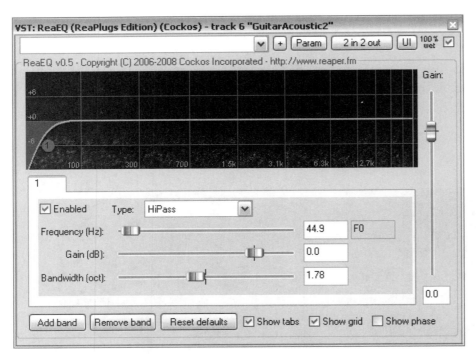

Figure 4.11 An example of the use of a high-pass filter. Only those frequencies higher than that specified are allowed through. In this case, a high-pass filter has been applied to an acoustic guitar, primarily to eliminate any extraneous bottom-end noise.

will be used from time to time to showcase various problems and how audio effects can be used to correct (or at least ameliorate) them.

1. Open the file Lying23 and save it as Lying43.

2. Because several tracks were recorded together, you will find that there is a lot of bleed on some tracks, including the double bass. However, the double bass track has, for whatever reason, also picked up some unwanted background noise. Figure 4.12 shows the spectral analysis of the first few seconds of this track, before the performance even starts.

3. Solo this track and play the first few seconds (before the performance starts). You should notice an unpleasant high-pitched sound. This will be more apparent if you use headphones. We can use a notch filter to remove this.

4. Apply a parametric equalizer to the double bass track and create a notch filter around 4,750 Hz, as shown in Figure 4.13. This is beyond the normal frequency range of the instrument and should not affect its sound adversely.

5. Play the track again. You should notice that the unpleasant high-pitched sound is no longer there. The spectral analysis of this track at this point now resembles that shown in Figure 4.14.

6. Save the file.

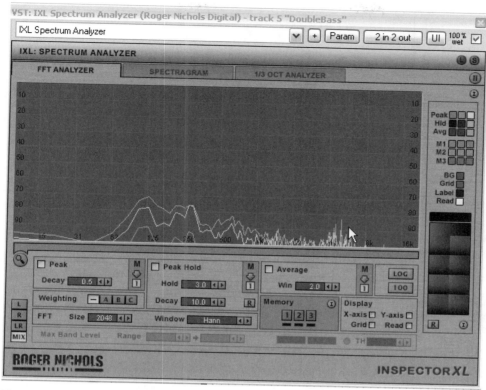

Figure 4.12 The background noise on this track includes an unwanted and unpleasant high-pitched sound just below 5,000 Hz (where the mouse cursor is pointing).

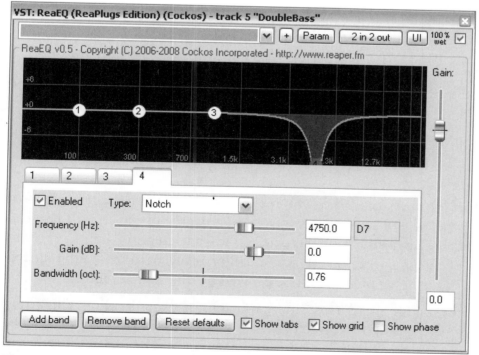

Figure 4.13 Using a notch filter to cut out unwanted frequencies.

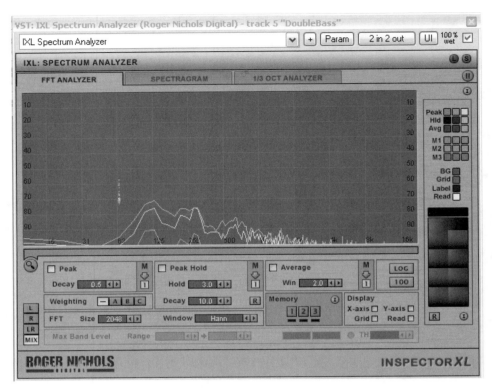

Figure 4.14   The spectral analysis of the same track as in Figure 4.12, after adding the notch filter.

Checkpoint 1

If you'd like some more practice, open the file Mud40 and save it as Mud41. Now explore at your leisure how you could use EQ to improve the sound of this project.

As you make progress, you should notice something quite interesting. Because this project is purely instrumental, there are no vocals that you might be tempted to hide any of your instruments behind. This gives you much more opportunity to really bring out the best in each instrument.

One last point before we move on. When you make changes to the frequency response of an instrument or vocal, you will always introduce a degree of phase shifting. This isn't simply an incidental byproduct of the process; it's an integral part of it. That's because it is inherent in the nature of the type of filter being used that different frequencies within the range being filtered will be delayed by different amounts.

Figure 4.15 illustrates this, showing two different instances using ReaEQ. This particular plug-in includes an option for you to display a phase-shift curve. The steeper the EQ change, the greater the degree of phase shifting that occurs. The bad news is that in theory this can lead to problems when mixing. The good news is that when equalization

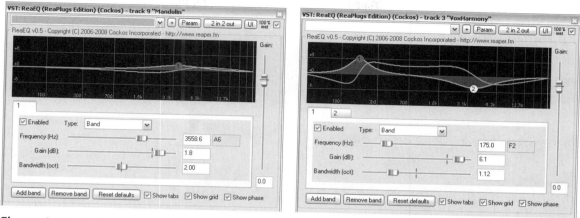

Figure 4.15   Using a parametric equalizer to increase or reduce gain at selected frequencies will always result in some phase shifting.

is used in the ways explored in this section, this is not likely to be a problem. Nevertheless, this is another reason why it makes good sense to check how your mixes sound in mono as well as in stereo.

Using an ordinary parametric equalizer creates phase shifting. The more vigorous the use of equalization, the greater the amount of phase shifting that will occur. In the two examples shown in Figure 4.15, the line passing through the numbers is the frequency response after EQ adjustments have been made. The other line in each case shows how this causes phase shifts.

This is because the human ear isn't really designed to pick up the differences between two intricate audio signals that have the same spectral content but different phase relationships. In this respect, you shouldn't confuse phase shift with phase modulation. On the contrary, you will find that your ears are very well tuned to respond to *modulated* changes in phase, such as happens with some audio effects like flange and chorus. We'll get to these in Chapters 7 and 9.

That said, there may be occasions when you wish to avoid this phase shift, most commonly when you are adding touches of EQ to your mixes. In this event, you can consider using linear phase EQ. We'll come to this topic shortly.

What Is Transparency?   You may from time to time come across people using the word *transparency* when talking about EQ. That's because you might put identical versions of the same signal through two different equalizers with identical settings and find that the sound that comes out from both is not identical. These differences may often be barely discernible to the human ear, if at all. The process of equalization requires the use of algorithms that may to some extent color the sound. The more natural the sound, the more it is said to be transparent.

Semi-Parametric EQ

The term *semi-parametric* is a fairly loose one and, as such, embraces a type of equalizer sometimes called *paragraphic*. These terms usually describe equalizers that combine some of the characteristics of graphic equalizers with some of the characteristics of parametric equalizers. An example of this is Sony's Paragraphic EQ (see Figure 4.16).

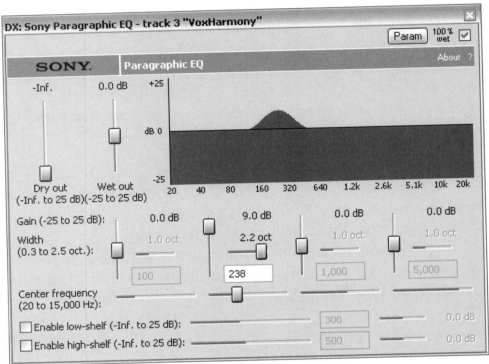

Figure 4.16   Sony's Paragraphic EQ combines some of the characteristics of a parametric equalizer with some of those of a graphic equalizer.

Generally speaking, paragraphic equalizers are less powerful and less flexible than parametric equalizers. Once you know how to use both graphic equalizers and parametric equalizers, then you should have no problem coming to terms with semi-parametric equalizers.

Sweeping the Waves   By now you should know how you can use a frequency analyzer to identify the frequency response of a voice or instrument, and an EQ with a band-pass filter to sweep the frequency spectrum to identify problem frequencies.

One handy plug-in that lets you do both at the same time is Voxengo Span. Inserted into a track's FX bin, it will display the frequency response of the material being played back. Hold the Control key while you click at any point to hear a restricted frequency range (see Figure 4.17).

For download details, see Table 1.2 in Chapter 1.

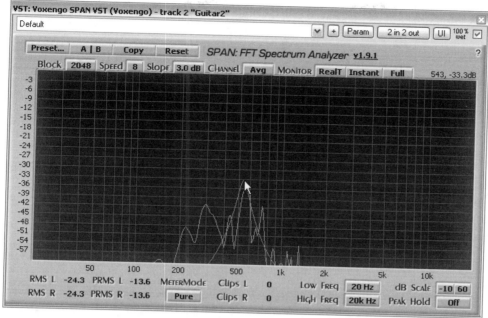

Figure 4.17 Voxengo Span: Control-click on any frequency to hear a band-pass filter imposed at this frequency.

Linear Phase EQ

You have already seen how the use of a standard parametric (or graphic) equalizer introduces some elements of phase shifting to an audio signal. Linear phase equalizers produce a different kind of phase shift, where the shift in phase remains proportional to the frequency of the sound. As the frequency increases, so does the degree of phase shift. This might sound strange at first, but you need to keep in mind the fact that as a waveform's *frequency* increases, its *period* (the time required for one iteration) decreases. These two factors effectively balance each other, resulting in a constant amount of delay on all frequencies. This maintains the integrity of the signal's original waveform.

If you find the theory difficult to get your head around, don't worry. The important points to understand are summarized below. For the technically minded, there are any number of articles available on the web that explore these points in greater depth. However, you do not need that much technical understanding to be able to use linear phase EQ.

- Debates about which type of EQ is inherently "best" are futile. The answer is that it depends on what you want to do.

- As a general rule, you would expect an ordinary parametric EQ (sometimes called a *program EQ*) to be better for use on individual tracks, especially if you are dealing with sounds that have noticeable transients and/or where you are likely to want to make quite substantial boosts or cuts at selected frequencies.

- Linear phase EQ is more CPU-intensive than other forms of EQ.

- Linear phase EQ, because of the way it works, will often be preferred in circumstances where you wish to shape the waveform gently. This is likely to be the case, for example, when you are adding the finishing touches to an overall mix.

- Linear phase EQ should not introduce phase incoherence in the way that program EQ can. Nevertheless, it is still a good practice to check the results in mono as well as in stereo.

- Linear phase EQ is generally preferred in situations where a signal is to be split and multiple filters applied, as happens, for example, when a multiband compressor is used. We'll get to multiband compressors in Chapter 15, "Multiband Compressors, Mastering Limiters, and More."

- Because linear phase EQ needs to look ahead in order to perform its calculations, it can create a degree of delay which can introduce latency. This need not matter, however, if your DAW incorporates and uses latency compensation (in the form of plug-in delay compensation, or PDC). It would be worth your while to check this before you start using linear phase EQ in your projects. Most of the more popular DAW programs do support plug-in delay compensation, a notable exception (at the time of writing) being Pro Tools LE.

- Regardless of whether your host DAW supports PDC, because of the "look ahead" way in which it works, it is inadvisable to use linear phase EQ when you are recording. Think about this for a moment: The plug-in can look ahead to incorporate into its calculations material that has already been recorded, but it cannot look into the future and allow for material that does not yet exist! See also the upcoming "Recording with Effects" note.

Recording with Effects   The question of whether you should use effects at the time that you are actually recording is one on which different people hold different views. Only a small number of DAW hosts offer you the option of doing this with your plug-in effects, although with any DAW you can attach outboard hardware items (such as a reverb effects unit) to your audio chain before the signal enters your computer.

Whether you're using outboard hardware equipment or software plug-ins, I suggest that for the most part, you should avoid this practice. If an audio effect is recorded along with the actual material, then the only way to remove it later may be to record the whole track again. Recording a signal *dry* (that is, without effects) is likely to give you more flexible options for post-production than will recording it *wet* (with effects). However, there are a number of exceptions to this rule. For example, the use of a hardware limiter to prevent clipping on a percussion instrument or when recording a live concert performance can sometimes make good sense.

Tutorial 4.4: Using Linear Phase EQ

I've thought twice and then a third time before introducing this tutorial at this point because it involves adding an effect to the master FX bin. Up until now, the only effects that we have used in the master have been to control the volume of the incoming signal (JS volume/pan) and as a safety measure to prevent clipping (JS limiter). Neither of these has been added in order to modify the shape or color of the mix. This next example will do just that: It will modify the overall sound of the mix. You therefore need to be clear about what you are doing here and why.

What you are *not* doing is mastering. I'll have more to say about this later, when we get to working with effects such as multiband compressors, stereo imagers, and the like. At that time we will also revisit the subject of linear phase EQ. Mastering is a huge topic. It is an art and a science in its own right and involves much, much more than just tossing a few plug-ins into an FX bin. Many volumes have been written on the subject, including *Mastering Music at Home* (Course Technology PTR, 2007) by Mitch Gallagher.

What you *are* doing is gaining a basic understanding of what linear phase EQ is and exploring one example of where it can be applied.

For this example, you can use any linear phase EQ that is supplied with your DAW or a third-party plug-in of your choice. I'll be using the freeware plug-in LinearPhase-GraphicEQ 2.

1. Open the file Foggy42 and save it as Foggy44.

2. Insert the linear phase EQ plug-in of your choice into the master FX bin, after the volume/pan plug-in but before the limiter.

3. As you play the song, experiment with fairly modest EQ adjustments (see Figure 4.18). Try adding a little warmth, a little presence, and a little air. Experiment with cutting back the low mids a little. You'll soon find out how easy it is if you overdo it to make your mix sound *worse* rather than better! You'll probably want to put back the reduction you made to the lower mids.

4. When you are finished, set your linear phase EQ to bypass. We'll come back to it later, but there's a lot more to learn before we do!

5. Save the file.

Quite often, knowing what *not* to do is every bit as important as knowing what you *should* do. This is certainly the case when you are using EQ on a mix. In particular, take note that:

■ This is definitely not the place to correct deficiencies or solve problems with individual tracks. For example, if a kick needs more punch or a vocal needs to be more present, go back to the individual track or tracks and fix it there.

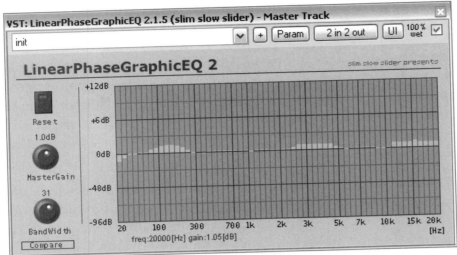

Figure 4.18   Using a linear phase EQ in the master FX bin. The plug-in shown is LinearPhase-GraphicEQ 2. Download information can be found in Table 1.2 in Chapter 1.

- Any changes that you make in the master FX bin will be applied to the entire mix—that's *every* track! If you add, say, more body around 200 Hz to 240 Hz, then that body will be added to each and every vocal and instrument, including some that may actually sound worse as a result.

- Different instruments and voices tend to be dominant at different frequencies. Therefore, any EQ changes that you make in your final mix run the risk of changing the perceived balance between the different tracks.

It's no wonder, therefore, that among those sound engineers most experienced and capable in their field, you will find several who never use EQ on a final mix.

The Pros and Cons of Using Presets   Finally for this chapter, here are a few words about using presets.

Many plug-ins (including EQ plug-ins) come with a range of presets that you can try out if you wish. If you feel compelled to use any of these presets, then do so with caution. I'm saying this for two reasons.

The first is that there is no substitute for knowing and understanding what you are doing. That preset called, say, Electric Guitar was not designed with your musical genre, your particular guitar, your playing style, your recording techniques, your interpretation, your overall arrangement, and your directions and objectives in mind. It was designed to suit some sort of generic electric guitar in some sort of generic context that probably doesn't exist anyway.

Presets can perhaps sometimes be helpful as a starting point, especially when you are in the early stages of learning, but for pity's sake don't become dependent on them and don't trust them more than you trust your own ears. For example, a preset with a name like Bass Attack might be helpful in indicating a range of frequencies where you might want to begin your quest if you wish to add more attack to your bass guitar.

This brings me to the second point. You will never produce a great or really interesting sound if you stick to presets. Doing so will stifle your creativity and condemn you to mediocrity. Aim to develop confidence to trust your ears over and above any other clues that might be available to you.

Bonus EQ and Filter Plug-Ins (Overview)

The DVD supplied with this book includes an extraordinary assortment of more than a dozen EQ and filtering plug-ins. Armed with what you now know about equalization and filtering, you should explore these at your leisure. Don't be put off by their strange names or decidedly bland interface. Their quality ranges from good to excellent. Table 4.5 describes some of these.

Table 4.5 Summary of JS EQ and Filter Plug-Ins

Name	Description
LOSER/3BandEQ	A simple 3-band (low, medium, and high) EQ allowing you to set the frequency range and gain for each band.
LOSER/4BandEQ	A simple 4-band (low, low mid, high mid, and high) EQ allowing you to set the frequency range and gain for each band.
SStillwell/rbj4eq	A 4-band semi-parametric EQ based on the Robert Bristow-Johnson (RBJ) Filter Cookbook.
SStillwell/rbj7eq	A 7-band semi-parametric EQ based on the RBJ Filter Cookbook.
SStillwell/3x3	A 3-band EQ with harmonic excitement.
Teej/rbj4eq	A more sophisticated 4-band semi-parametric EQ based on the RBJ Filter Cookbook.
Teej/rbj12eq	A 12-band EQ with high-pass filter, based on the RBJ Filter Cookbook.
Teej/rbj4notch	A notch filter with 4 bands, based on the RBJ Filter Cookbook.
Filters/autopeakfilter	An FFT peak-detecting filter with controls that include range, gain, and attack time.
Filters/bandpass	A filter that can be used as a band-pass filter or a notch filter, with wet/dry mix control.
Filters/lowpass	A low-pass filter with shape control ranging from sharp to dull.
Filters/parametric EQ	A simple one-band bell filter EQ.
Filters/sweepinglowpass	A sweeping resonant low-pass filter with frequency range, sweep time, and resonance controls.

Project Files Log

If you have completed all of the examples and tutorials in this chapter, you should have created the following files:

Preparation: Mud40, Foggy40

Tutorial 4.1: Foggy41

Tutorial 4.2: Foggy42

Tutorial 4.3: Lying43

Checkpoint 1: Mud41

Tutorial 4.4: Foggy44

Your complete project file log should now be as follows:

Alone00

AudioExperiment21

Foggy00, Foggy41, Foggy42, Foggy43, Foggy44

Lying00, Lying23, Lying43

Mud00, Mud40, Mud41

Whiskey00, Whiskey22, Whiskey30, Whiskey31, Whiskey32, Whiskey33

5 Shutting the Gate: Noise Gates

Stripped to their bare essentials, the concept and purpose of a noise gate are about as easy as it gets when it comes to understanding audio effects, what they do, and why we use them. Getting them to actually do exactly what you want, however, is one of the more challenging of the many tasks involved in audio post-production.

Figure 5.1 illustrates the essential concept of what a noise gate does. In this example, it might be being used to eliminate unwanted background sounds that can sometimes be picked up by a microphone during those passages when the vocal or instrument itself is silent. This can be a useful technique for eliminating bleed when more than one track is recorded together. It can also be used, for example, to eliminate the noise of a singer shuffling some paper or making some minor movements between verses, or simply to eliminate ambient background noise.

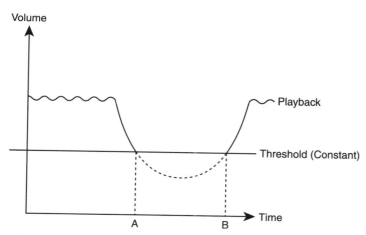

Figure 5.1   The basic concept of a noise gate. When the volume of the material being played back on the particular track falls below the threshold level, no sound is allowed to pass through the gate. Only when its volume rises back up above the threshold level is the material on the track heard again. In this diagrammatic representation, the output of the track shown will be silent during the period from A to B.

Take the example of a vocalist. In Figure 5.1 the threshold would be set below the quietest volume at which she actually sings. In this example, this has the result that during the period between the two moments in time marked A and B, the output from that track would be completely silent.

That, however, is where your understanding of noise gates needs to begin, not end. During this chapter you will learn about the following:

■   Setting up and using a simple noise gate: threshold settings

■   Controlling a noise gate: attack, release, and hold

■   Noise gate filters: high-pass and low-pass

■   Sidechain gating

■   Downward expander gates

■   Applying noise gate controls

■   Noise profiling and noise reduction

■   Bonus noise gate plug-ins (overview)

Preparation

At different times in this chapter, you will be working with two of the sample projects, *Foggy Desperation* and *Lying Back*. It should take you only a few minutes to prepare the sample project files.

Preparation: Preparing the Project Files

The project file Foggy43 that you created in Chapter 4 should be in a state where it is ready to be used for these tutorials. The other project, however, needs just a little work done to it to obtain a rough working mix.

1.   Open the file Foggy43 that you created earlier and immediately save it as Foggy50.

2.   Open the file Lying00 that you created earlier and immediately save it as Lying50.

3.   This file currently has no effects in it (for example, no EQ). This is intentional; we will be using some effects in various later chapters.

4.   Set a pan law of −3.0 dB.

5.   Insert in the FX bin for the master first the JS Utility Volume/Pan plug-in and then the JS Utility Limiter. Leave the volume/pan at its default settings and specify a threshold of −1.0 dB for the limiter.

6.   Adjust the track controls for each of the tracks approximately as follows:

   LeadVox: volume −1.6 dB, pan 7% right

   BVox1: volume −7.2 dB, pan 33% left

   BVox2: volume −7.6 dB, pan 23% left

Bvox3: volume −7 dB. pan, 16% right

DoubleBass: volume −2 dB, pan center

Guitar: volume −3.7 dB, pan 43% left

Mandolin: volume −4.1 dB, pan 45% right

Banjo1: volume −7.1 dB, pan 60% left

Banjo2: volume −7dB, pan 60% right

7.   Save the file.

Let's start by looking at an instance of setting up a very basic noise gate. For this example, I'll be using the plug-in GGate because it is very simple and has only three controls. This is included in the GVST bundle of freeware plug-ins. Download details can be found in Table 1.2 in Chapter 1.

Setting Up a Simple Noise Gate

The GGate noise gate has only three controls—threshold, fade, and attack (see Figure 5.2). For the time being, ignore the fade and attack settings (leave them at their default positions) and just focus on the threshold.

Figure 5.2   The GGate noise gate plug-in.

Tutorial 5.1: Setting Up a Simple Noise Gate

On the basis that it can often be easier to understand how an audio effect works if you start by experimenting on a vocal track, we'll be using vocal tracks in the first couple of examples. Don't think, however, that gating is intended for use purely with vocals. Indeed, most DAW programs come with a range of tools and techniques for editing your audio material, and with some software a noise gate might not necessarily be your best option for dealing with the particular problem posed in this first example. Don't let that worry you, as the main point of this exercise isn't to clean up this particular track but to help you understand how to set up a simple noise gate and how it works.

1. Open the file Lying50 that you created earlier and immediately save it as Lying 51.

2. Solo the track BVox2 and create a loop from about 0 min 16 sec to about 1 min 30 secs.

3. Play the song. Insert a noise gate (for this example, preferably GGate) into the FX bin for the track BVox2.

4. Try to set a threshold high enough to cut out the bleed during passages when the vocalist is not singing, but also low enough to allow through all of the vocals, including the natural decay that occurs at the end of lines and phrases.

5. You should be able to find a threshold level (assuming that your DAW processes the effect pre–track faders) around or close to −22 dB where this happens. However, even when you think you've got it nailed, it is still likely that when you play the whole track, there may be some spots where the voice cuts out unnaturally and others in the otherwise silent passages where the bleed still momentarily breaks through.

6. Save the file. To begin to understand what the problem is here, take a look at Figure 5.3.

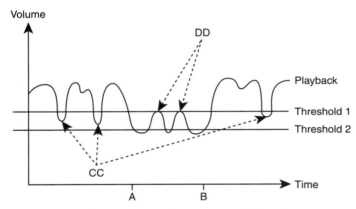

Figure 5.3 A common noise gate problem: Some parts of the sound that you want to allow through the gate (labeled CC) are quieter than some parts of the noise that you want to shut out (labeled DD).

Figure 5.3 is a variation of Figure 5.1. Don't take its exact details literally. The diagram is designed to illustrate and help you understand an important fact about noise gates—nothing more, nothing less. Again, the vocalist is singing up to the point labeled A and after the point labeled B, but not in between. We want to use our noise gate to shut out everything that happens between these two points. However, this time we have a problem.

If you set the threshold at the level indicated by Threshold 1, you will successfully shut out even the highest peaks of the unwanted noise (DD). However, at this level you will also shut out the quieter parts of the vocal (CC). Conversely, if you set the threshold at the level indicated by Threshold 2, you will allow the quieter vocal passages to pass, but you will also allow through the louder parts of the unwanted noise (DD).

That's why you need a few more tools to control not only when but also exactly how the noise gate opens and shuts. GGate has a control that can be used for this—the fade control. If you revisit Tutorial 5.1 and adjust the fade control to the left, this problem will get worse. Move it to the right, and it will get better. In a fairly straightforward application like this, GGate's simple fader can be used to slow down the rate at which the gate is closed, thus ensuring that it won't keep opening and closing for very short periods while the vocalist perhaps pauses briefly between words. It will only close when the volume falls below the specified threshold for enough milliseconds.

The fade control employed here performs a combination of functions that often need to be applied with greater precision by using not one but four separate controls: hold, release, hysteresis, and pre-open. It's time now to take a look at these four functions. Note that on some noise gates the release control is called decay, and that some otherwise excellent noise gates may not include a hysteresis control.

Track Audio Signal Flow   The normal DAW signal flow is that by default your audio effects are processed *before* your track controls (such as pan and volume). If this were not the case, a noise gate would be virtually impossible to use because its settings would need to be adjusted every time you made any change to your track fader levels.

The complete signal flow includes other factors than just your FX and the track faders. For example, you might also have controls and FX on individual media items, send to busses or submixes, and so on. You should definitely take a few moments to check exactly in which order your DAW processes its signal flow and what options it makes available to you.

Controlling a Noise Gate

With the project file Lying52 still open, zoom in on the track BVox1, displaying the region from approximately 1 min 02 sec to 1 min 22 sec (see Figure 5.4). Loop this region and solo the track. Now play it. In addition to the vocal, you will notice an assortment of unwanted noises that happen from time to time.

At Marker 2 there is a strange background noise. At Markers 3, 4, 5, and 6 the vocalist can be heard drawing breath (each instance being different in both length and volume). At Marker 7 there are again some strange background markers. We need to control exactly how the gate will close and open in these various situations. Part of this involves using the hold and release parameters. Figure 5.5 illustrates how these items work.

Figure 5.4   Part of a vocal track to which we can apply a noise gate. Markers 2 to 7 indicate points of special interest.

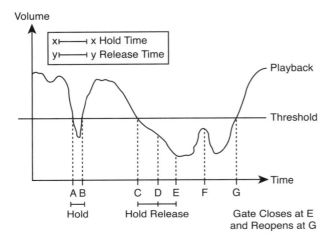

Figure 5.5   This diagram shows how hold and release controls can be used to manage a noise gate.

In Figure 5.5, the hold control has been set to a length of time represented by the line XX and the release control similarly set to a length of time represented by YY. The hold setting ensures that when the volume of the audio signal drops below the specified threshold, it will remain open for that period of time before it starts to close. The release setting will then determine how quickly or slowly it closes.

In the example shown in the diagram, when the playback reaches the point represented by A, its volume falls below the threshold. However, the time it remains below this threshold (until Point B) is shorter than the hold time. This means that in this case the gate never actually closes. It remains open, and the audio signal passes through uninterrupted.

At C the volume again falls below the threshold. The gate remains fully open until D and then (because the volume is still below the threshold) it begins to close. How long it takes to close is determined by the release setting. In this example, by the time it closes (at E) the vocal decay has been allowed through. At F you can see a lift in the volume caused by some unwanted noise (perhaps a singer drawing breath). This is not heard; the noise gate remains closed because the volume of the unwanted noise remains below the gate's threshold setting. This is made possible because using the hold and release controls allows us to set a threshold setting higher than would otherwise be the case. At G the vocalist resumes singing, and the sound is again allowed to pass through the gate.

There are actually three additional controls that can be involved in this process that are not shown in Figure 5.5.

Tutorial 5.2: Managing a Noise Gate's Controls

In this tutorial you will be taken on a journey of experimentation and discovery. As part of the learning process, you will first be shown various combinations of settings that are not quite right for this case, in order to help you understand how the different controls work. By the end of the tutorial, you should have a solution.

1. Make sure the file Lying51 is open. Save it as Lying52.

2. Make sure the track BVox1 is soloed and looped from about 1 min 02 sec to 1 min 22 sec. This is the unaccompanied female backing vocal track. Play the song.

3. Insert an instance of the plug-in ReaGate into the FX bin.

4. Set a threshold level high enough to gate out all the unwanted sounds, especially the louder breathing sounds. You will probably find that this will be at about −24 dB or −25 dB.

5. Unfortunately, this will cause other problems on playback. The fade and decay at the end of phrases will noticeably be cut off (for example, *arms* becomes *arm* in a couple of places), and there will be other instances where the singing is stilted or stuttering.

6. By increasing the hold and release times, we are able to fix this problem. In particular, pay attention to the first *arms,* at around 1 min 07 sec, because it lasts longer than the others.

7. There are a number of permutations you can use—for example, a hold time of 175 ms and a release of 468 ms. However, as soon as we increase the hold and release times, we start to allow the other breath sounds through the gate—for example, at approximately 1 min 11 sec and 1 minute 15 secs. Clearly, we have a dilemma on our hands. The answer is to set the gate for the most common (and in this case the trickiest) situations and then to resolve any individual anomalies afterwards.

8. Try raising the threshold to about −19.2 dB. The relative balance between the hold and release settings is something you can experiment with, depending on how quickly or slowly you want the tail of this backing vocal to fade. You should

find in this case that a hold time of about 60 ms and a release time of about 80 ms will allow most of the vocals through while cutting out most of the unwanted sounds. Notable exceptions are the long slow breath at about 1 min 07 sec (that still passes through the gate), the final *arms* at about 1 min 19 sec, and a couple of places where the voice is late coming back in after a breath (most noticeably at about 1 min 15 secs).

9. As far as the late vocals are concerned, the pre-open control can come to our rescue. The problem is caused by two factors: In a couple of places the soft voice is below the threshold when it starts, and it is also very close to the breathing sound. (In fact, the two sounds virtually run into each other.) By specifying a pre-open value, we can ensure that the gate is actually opened a few milliseconds before the voice reaches the threshold level. Gradually move this fader to the right until it sounds about right. This will probably be at about 14 ms. Figure 5.6 shows a summary of all these suggested settings.

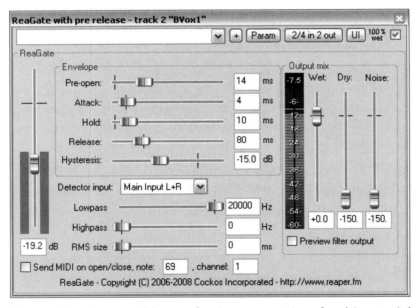

Figure 5.6   One possible set of noise gate settings for this tutorial. The plug-in shown is ReaGate. With some configurations, sudden changes in noise gate parameters brought about by automation can ironically result in an unpleasant crackling sound. To avoid this, try to use only one envelope per track, use linear curves, and avoid sudden, steep changes.

10. We've still got one trick up our sleeve to help us deal with those vocals that cut out too early, and that is hysteresis. You can think of hysteresis as being rather like a thermostat on a heater. By setting a hysteresis level, we are telling the gate to stay open if necessary beyond the specified hold period until the audio signal has fallen the specified number of decibels below the threshold level. This can help prevent a stammering effect that can otherwise occur when a gate opens and closes too frequently.

11. Experiment with moving the hysteresis setting slowly to the left as you play the file. Before long, you should find that the fade on the very last *arms* in the selected loop will once more be heard. However, as you move it left, you will find some of the unwanted noise will find its way back through again. You'll probably want to settle on a level about −15 dB and 10 ms for the hold.

12. Save the file.

13. There are a number of options at your disposal for dealing with any places where your noise gate settings still aren't quite right for the job. One possibility is to manually edit the waveform in those places. Another is to use an automation envelope to vary the threshold levels where necessary. Harnessing the power of automation will be the subject of Chapter 11, but in the meantime you can try adding a threshold envelope to this track, as shown in Figure 5.7.

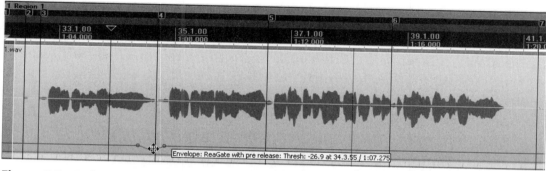

Figure 5.7   Using an automation envelope (in this case, threshold) to fine-tune noise gate settings within a song.

You've probably already noticed that our noise gate includes several other parameters that we haven't yet used. We'll get to these later, but right now there are three more worth mentioning. These are:

■ **Attack.** Think of this as being the opposite of release. The attack setting controls the speed with which a closed gate reopens. The lower the attack value, the faster it reopens when the threshold is next reached. For vocals, a very low setting is usually used; in this case, the default value of 4 ms is quite suitable.

■ **Wet and Dry.** These two very interesting controls work together and are too often overlooked. Strange though it might seem at first, you might actually want to put back into your track some of the noise that you have taken out. In this example, we have been dealing with an especially loud-breathing vocalist. (Compare the breathing on this track, for example, to BVox3.) However, removing the breathing sounds altogether might remove too much life from the vocal. Try setting the wet fader to about −1.7 dB and the dry fader to about −14.0 dB and see what you think.

Unfortunately, not all noise gates include wet and dry fader controls. Don't forget, though, that some DAW programs include a wet/dry mixing control in their standard plug-in interface.

Checkpoint 1

Vocal tracks are always likely to present a challenge when it comes to cleaning out unwanted sounds and noise. The example used in Tutorial 5.2 is about as challenging as it gets. Put what you've learned into practice by gating the VoxLead track in the file Foggy50 to cut out the occasional (and much less challenging) breathing and other sounds that have made their way onto this track. Save the file as Foggy52 when you're finished.

Noise Gate Filters: High-Pass and Low-Pass

In this next section you'll discover a further reason why understanding EQ filters (Chapter 4) is so important. Using such filters with noise gates opens up a whole range of further applications.

Here is an example. When you record a kick and a snare together, you will usually expect to get the bleed from each of these two instruments onto each other's tracks. Take a look at Figure 5.8.

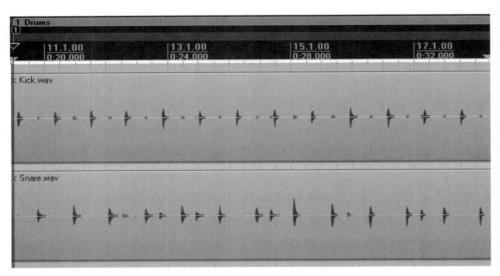

Figure 5.8   A close-up view of part of a kick track and a snare track. In each case the strong parts of the waveform represent the instrument being recorded on that track, and the weaker parts represent the bleed from the other instrument. Of course, the strong parts on the kick track correspond to the weak parts on the snare and vice versa.

You might want to put a noise gate on each of these tracks, in both cases to eliminate the bleed. Let's start by looking at the kick. You would need to set a threshold high enough to cut out the bleed from the snare. With a little bit of patience, it shouldn't prove too difficult to get the hold, release, and hysteresis levels set at values at which they will allow the decay from the kick to pass through each time. However, even after doing this you might notice that there will be times when mixed in with the sound of kick you can hear some of the late (high) harmonics from the snare. A low-pass filter can be used to resolve this.

Tutorial 5.3: Using High-Pass and Low-Pass Filters

In this tutorial, you will use filters to further refine the way in which a noise gate can be used to prevent bleed. The use of filters is possible because the two instruments concerned operate primarily in different areas of the frequency spectrum.

1. Open file Foggy52 (or, if you did not complete the Checkpoint 1 exercise, Foggy50) and save it as Foggy53.

2. Solo the Kick track. Select a fairly representative region of about 30 seconds and loop it. Play the song.

3. Insert an instance of ReaGate in the kick track's FX bin. This should be placed before the EQ that you added in Chapter 4.

4. Set pre-open and attack both to 0 ms. We don't want to open the gate before the kick is struck, and then when the gate does open, we don't want to miss the immediate impact.

5. Adjust the hold, release, and hysteresis level until the snare is effectively gated out, but the kick (including its decay) can still be clearly heard. Figure 5.9 shows one possible set of values that might achieve this.

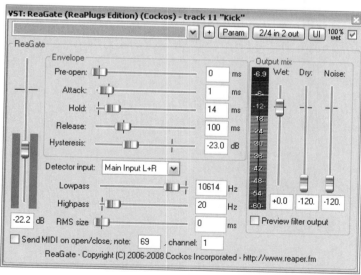

Figure 5.9   A noise gate set to eliminate snare bleed from a kick track.

6. Out of interest, gradually increase the attack value up to about 16 ms. Notice how the sound loses its punch. Return it to 0 ms or 1 ms when you have finished.

7.   Now set the low-pass filter at about 12,000 Hz. This will filter out the very high harmonics from the snare. Because you are operating on very high frequencies, the difference will be subtle.

8.   Out of interest, move the low-pass filter all the way back to about 1,500 Hz. Notice that this makes the kick sound considerably less present. Move it back to the right to what your ears detect as an optimal position.

9.   Save the file.

Checkpoint 2

Now add a noise gate to the snare track to cut out the bleed on this track from the kick. It's unlikely that you will hear any bottom-end bleed from the decay of the kick each time the gate reopens and the snare comes back in, but as a precaution (and for the sake of practice), include in your settings a high-pass filter.

Figure 5.10 shows one possible solution to this tutorial. It is important, however, that you work out a solution for yourself, rather than just reproducing these settings. Don't forget to save your work when finished.

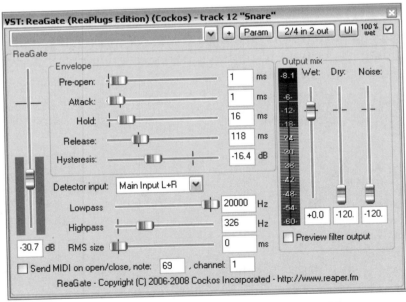

Figure 5.10   A noise gate set to eliminate kick bleed from a snare track.

Sidechain Gating

Up until now, every one of the noise gate examples that we have looked at uses a track's own audio signal to control its own noise gate. Sidechain gating is different. It is what happens when a noise gate placed on one track is controlled directly by the audio signal of another track. One example of this might be if your recorded arrangement includes a bass guitar and a kick drum. Suppose there are a number of occasions when the bass guitar comes in just a few milliseconds ahead of the kick (see Figure 5.11).

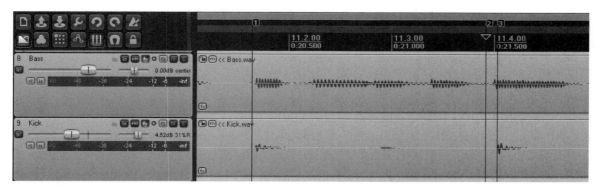

Figure 5.11 There might be a number of occasions (for example, at Marker 3) where the bass comes in just a fraction of a second ahead of the kick. Sidechain gating can often be used to resolve this.

You'd expect to have a number of options for fixing this. Cutting and pasting (or nudging) each offending note individually might be one. For some DAWs, using some sort of beat-snapping facility might be another. Using a sidechain gate to hold back the sound of the bass until the kick comes in is often likely to be the quickest and most effective.

Most major DAW programs support sidechaining, some more flexibly, easily, and powerfully than others. Unfortunately, the methods and techniques used to implement sidechaining vary radically between different programs. For this reason, it isn't possible to include a step-by-step tutorial here. You will need to dip into your DAW's documentation to see exactly how to do this. However, what I can give you is a reasonably comprehensive overview. The main steps and issues involved in sidechain gating are as follows:

■ Sidechain gating requires the use of two distinct audio sources. Most commonly, these are two separate tracks. Some DAWs also allow the use of busses and sub-mixes when sidechaining.

■ The noise gate plug-in is inserted in the FX bin of the track that is to be gated—just as you have been doing up to now. This track is sometimes also referred to as the *main track.* You then need to define which track contains the signal whose volume will control the opening and closing of the noise gate. This is often known as the *sidechain track,* but the terms *auxiliary* and *controlling* track or source are also sometimes used.

■ The threshold setting applies to the volume on the sidechain (auxiliary) track. (In the example used in Figure 5.11, this would be the kick.) The closing and opening of the gate on the gated track is triggered by the volume on the sidechain track falling below and rising above the threshold level.

- The gate itself operates on the gated (main) track. The values that you set for hold, release, and hysteresis (for example) will between them determine how long the gate on the main track will stay open after the volume on the auxiliary track falls below the threshold.

Understanding this is crucial to making sidechain gating work successfully. Refer again to Figure 5.11.

As the playback approaches Marker 1, the gate should be in the closed position. The bass track will be effectively silenced. A threshold level needs to be set to ensure that when it reaches Marker 1, the volume on the kick (auxiliary) track will be sufficient to open the gate on the bass (main) track and allow this instrument to be heard. This gate then needs to be kept open until the position indicated by Marker 2—otherwise, the decay on the bass will be lost. However, at Marker 3 it will again be reopened by the next note of the kick. This will ensure that the small fraction of the second where the bass comes in before the kick will not be heard.

In a situation like this, you are left with very little margin for error. You will need to take into account the following:

- The parameters that are crucial to how long the gate stays open are likely to be hold and release. By all means set a hysteresis level as a fallback, but it is unlikely ever to be applied. This is because a percussive instrument, such as a kick, has a very short decay. In the example shown in Figure 5.11, any meaningful hysteresis level that you set would be reached on the kick long before you want the gate to shut.

- For this reason, the key is to work with the tempo and beat of the particular song. This should enable you to establish workable hold and release times. Most likely, in this case you would be inclined to use a long hold time and a shorter release time.

- The attack should be initially set to 0 ms or 1 ms. You want the bass to come back in with the kick, not behind it. However, be prepared to increase this attack time if you find that these lower settings introduce any distortion. (See the upcoming "Applying Noise Gate Controls" section.)

- When sidechaining, it is especially important to understand your DAW's signal flow—in particular, whether the auxiliary signal being used to control the noise gate is dry (pre-FX, pre-faders), post-FX but pre-faders (after processing any effects in its own FX bin), or post-FX and post-faders. Most likely it will be pre-FX and pre-faders. This means that the signal being used for sidechaining may not be exactly the same as that which you hear during playback.

Take the example used in Figure 5.11. If the sidechaining signal coming from the kick is dry, then any effects in the kick's FX bin will not be used in the sidechaining signal. These would be likely to include the kick's own noise gate and EQ. However, on playback you would be hearing the kick track with these effects applied. This leads neatly to the next point.

■ Pay attention to whether you will need to use a filter. This may be necessary, for example, to prevent your gate from being opened by bleed from perhaps a hi-hat or a cymbal recorded on the auxiliary track.

Downward Expander Gates

Some noise gates include a ratio control. This adds a further level of refinement, allowing some noise through even when the gate is technically closed. It can be used to produce a result not dissimilar from that which can be produced using the wet/dry faders that were discussed earlier in this chapter. The further the signal falls below the threshold, the greater the degree of attenuation.

The concept is quite similar to that which governs the ratio setting on a compressor. The ratio is expressed as 1:2, 1:4, 1:6, and so on. Thus, at a ratio of 1:4, a signal falling 1 dB below the threshold will be reduced by 4 dB. A signal 2 dB below will be reduced by 8 dB, and so on.

This kind of noise gate is known as a *downward expander*.

Applying Noise Gate Controls

In the examples used in this chapter, you have gained some valuable practice at using a noise gate. Unfortunately, it takes more than a few tutorials to become really proficient. You should find the following tips and techniques useful when it comes to using noise gates in your own projects.

Threshold

How you should go about setting your initial threshold level will depend largely on what is being gated.

As you have seen, with vocals a good starting point is to set a threshold just a little above the level of the quietest passages (such as decay) and then use hold, release, and hysteresis settings to allow the quieter vocals through. This will help to stop the gate from being opened by background noise during the silent passages.

On the other hand, the recording of a drum kit is likely to have used close miking to minimize bleed. That being the case, you might wish to use a significantly higher threshold level.

Attack Time

As a general rule, you should aim to set an attack time as short as possible without causing any clicks or distortion. Very fast attack times may have the unwanted effect of generating distortion as a result of modifying the waveform. At 100 Hz, for example, a waveform has a cycle of 10 ms. This is long enough to allow an attack such as 1 ms time to alter and distort the waveform. You will need to let your ears be the judge.

Much will depend on the nature of the sound to which the gate is being applied. With vocals, for example, an attack of about 1 ms to 2 ms is often ideal. This is short enough to allow through the attack of percussive consonants (such as b, p, or t). Electric guitars, on the other hand, vary so much in their characteristics that it is impossible to suggest any generally sensible level.

Hold and Release Times

Generally speaking, the more percussive the sound being gated, the shorter the hold time (and release time) will be. This does not necessarily apply, of course, when side-chain gating is being used.

As with attack times, the optimum release time for an instrument such as an electric guitar will vary enormously. A crisp, clean guitar might sound best with a release time as low as 30 to 50 ms, whereas an instrument with a lot of sustain could benefit from a release setting of 500 ms or more.

Hysteresis

Of course, all of the various controls on a noise gate are important, and to be able to gate sound effectively, you need to understand them all. That said, if there's one control that is likely to save your life more than any other, that is hysteresis. As you have seen, it won't be useful in every situation, but where it is appropriate, it will add a dimension of intelligence to your gating that at times may seem almost spooky.

Using Hold and Hysteresis Together When you stipulate both a hold time and a hysteresis level below 0.0 dB, then every time the gate closes, whichever of the two in that instance lasts longer will be applied.

For example, suppose you have specified a hold time of 10 ms and a hysteresis setting of −25 dB. If after falling below the threshold it takes 15 seconds for the sound level to decay to −25 dB, then the gate will stay open for 15 seconds and then begin to close. If, on the other hand, it takes only 5 seconds for the sound level to decay to −25 dB, then the gate will stay open for 10 ms before it begins to close.

RMS Size

There's one significant control on the ReaGate noise gate that we haven't yet mentioned, and that is the RMS size. RMS means *root mean squared*. RMS is a different way of measuring the level of a track's output. Without getting too technical, rather than taking peak levels, it is calculated according to a formula that uses the square root of the mean of the squares of values. If that explanation just leaves you blinking, don't worry. What it means in practice is that it calculates sound levels closer to the way in which our ears actually hear sound.

As you slide the RMS fader farther to the right (starting at 0), the balance of peak and RMS levels used to calculate the level of the audio signal shifts more and more in favor of RMS. The more you increase this RMS element, the more you will need to lower the threshold level to compensate for it. I haven't gone into too much detail here because very few noise gates include this feature.

The topic of RMS will be revisited in more detail when we look at compression in Chapter 6, "Changing Dynamics: Compressors and More."

Noise Profiling and Noise Reduction

You have already seen how using features such as EQ filters and hysteresis seems to endow a noise gate almost with its own intelligence, to enable it to respond accurately to changes in a track's dynamics. Noise profiling takes this concept to the next level. Noise reduction software works by capturing a profile of some unwanted sound that has found its way onto your track (perhaps some hiss, hum, or rumble) and removes it from the entire track.

Strictly speaking, this isn't really noise gating. With gating, sounds are only removed from playback during periods of intended silence. With noise profiling, the offending sounds are removed for the entire duration of the track, including when the instrument is playing or the vocalist is singing. It's really an example of what we might call a *hybrid application,* since it combines various characteristics of different types of effect (for example, EQ and noise gating) in order to create a new and different one.

Tutorial 5.4: Creating and Using Noise Reduction Filters

In this example, we will use the project file Lying52. We'll go back to the noisy Double Bass track that we attacked earlier (Chapter 4) with a notch EQ filter. This time, we are instead going to capture a profile of the noise and remove it.

1.   Open the file Lying52 and save it as Lying54.

2.   Solo the Double Bass track. If it is still there from an earlier tutorial, disable (bypass) the EQ plug-in with the notch filter.

3.   Select the first second of the song and loop it. Play the song. Especially if you are using headphones, you should clearly be able to hear the unpleasant background noise.

4.   Stop playback. Insert an instance of ReaFir in the kick track's FX bin.

5.   ReaFir is a multipurpose tool that can function as an EQ, a compressor, a noise gate, and more. In this case, we wish to use it to subtract (remove) unwanted noise.

6.   Select Subtract from the Mode drop-down list (see Figure 5.12) and select the option to Automatically Build Noise Profile. Commence playback.

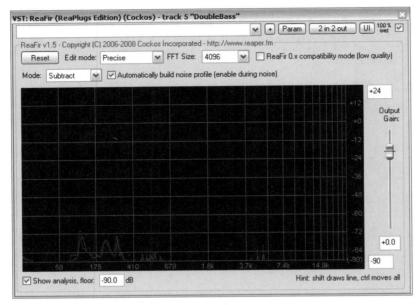

Figure 5.12   Using a noise reduction program to capture a noise profile to remove background noise from an entire track.

7.   As the playback loops over the one-second sample (which consists entirely of unwanted noise), ReaFir will display a frequency profile of this noise.

8.   Stop playback. Uncheck the Automatically Build Noise Profile option.

9.   Remove the loop and commence playback from the beginning of the song. The unwanted noise will not be heard.

10.   Save the file.

Noise reduction effects such as ReaFir are quite powerful, but they cannot work miracles. There will be times when the level and/or nature of the background noise is just too great and too intrusive to enable it to be removed without seriously disturbing the dynamics of the recorded material. If you want an example of this, try using ReaFir on the Bvox2 track to remove the background bleed from the other voice and instruments.

ReaFir and Impulse Response Filters   Despite its name, ReaFir does not use Finite Impulse Response (FIR) algorithms for filtering frequencies.

Instead, ReaFir uses a type of algorithm known as *Fast Fourier Transform (FFT)*. This works by dynamically analyzing the incoming signal and using that data to create its filters. If you like, think of this as being rather like a graphic equalizer with not tens but thousands of tiny bands. Happily, you don't need to understand the mathematical theory behind it in order to use and benefit from it. All you really need to know is that its method of computation is generally fast, efficient, and accurate. The plug-in includes an option for you to specify the FFT size: the larger the size, the more of your computer's CPU it will use. If in doubt, leave this at its default setting of 4096.

If you want to dig deep into the theory behind FFT, go to www.dspguide.com/ch12/2.htm.

Bonus Noise Gate Plug-In (Overview)

The DVD supplied with this book includes a simple noise gate called JS: Misc/noisegate. It lacks the sophistication of ReaGate and the other software used or mentioned in this chapter, but it is ideally suited for simple applications that require just the threshold, silence length for fadeout, fade-in response, and fade-out response controls.

Project Files Log

If you have completed all of the examples and tutorials in this chapter, you should have created the following files:

Preparation: Foggy50, Lying50

Tutorial 5.1: Lying51

Tutorial 5.2: Lying52

Checkpoint 1: Foggy52

Tutorial 5.3: Foggy53

Tutorial 5.4: Lying54

Your complete project file log should now be as follows:

Alone00

AudioExperiment21

Foggy00, Foggy41, Foggy42, Foggy43, Foggy44, Foggy50, Foggy52, Foggy53

Lying00, Lying23, Lying43, Lying50, Lying51, Lying52, Lying54

Mud00, Mud40, Mud41

Whiskey00, Whiskey22, Whiskey30, Whiskey31, Whiskey32, Whiskey33

6 Changing Dynamics: Compressors and More

Arguably, no audio effect is harder to master than the compressor. That's largely because when you are using a compressor, you are changing the dynamics of the original sound. Your recordings may have captured a vibrant and exciting performance by the musician or singer, but therein often lies the problem. The delivery and capture of the sound may have been too dynamic, with too great a difference between the loudest and quietest parts. If that's the case, then some action is needed if you are to obtain a mix that will be pleasing to the listener's ear.

The problem is that compression is a complex area and one that has many facets. It can be applied in any number of different ways and in any number of different given situations. The answer is never as simple as "Just add some compression." The keys to getting successful outcomes with compression are largely about being clear as to your objectives and getting the application right.

It's a big topic. That's why this chapter is the longest in this book. Be prepared to take your time with it, and you will learn about the following:

- Dynamic compression: what it is and why we use it

- How dynamic compression works

- Compressor controls and how to use them

- Matching compressor settings to wave patterns

- Compression zones for different voices and instruments

- Using compression with equalization

- Using auto make-up

- Sidechain compression

- Serial compression

- Parallel compression

- Limiters

- Multiband compression on instruments and vocals

■ Upward expanders

■ Bonus compressor plug-ins (overview)

Dynamic Range Compression versus File Compression Don't confuse dynamic range compression—the subject of this chapter—with audio file compression. The two topics are entirely different; the only thing they have in common is that both use the word *compression*.

Audio file compression is the process of taking a recorded media file (such as a WAV or AIF file) and reducing its file size (in megabytes) by converting it to a different format (such as MP3). That most certainly is not what we're talking about here!

Preparation

At different times in this chapter, you will be working with the sample projects *Foggy Desperation*, *Lying Back*, *Mud Sliding*, and *Whiskey*. It should take you only a few minutes to prepare the necessary sample files.

Preparation: Preparing the Project Files

In each case, the only preparation required will be to open the latest version of each project and save it to the new name required for these tutorials.

1. Open the file Foggy53 that you created earlier and immediately save it as Foggy60.

2. Open the file Lying54 that you created earlier and immediately save it as Lying60.

3. Open the file Mud41 that you created earlier and immediately save it as Mud60.

4. Open the file Whiskey33 that you created earlier and immediately save it as Whiskey60.

Compression Myths and Realities There seems to be a belief in some audio circles that compression always means squeezing the life and natural dynamics out of otherwise pure and pristine music. This is simply not the case.

Compression can be used in a variety of circumstances and for a variety of reasons. It is true that with some applications the effect can be dramatic, even overpowering. However, it is also true (depending on how it is used) that compression can help to create subtle and almost subliminal effects. Using headphones in conjunction with your monitor speakers can often aid you when you are working on some of the more subtle applications of compression.

Dynamic Compression: What It Is and Why We Use It

Before you can really come to grips with the role that compression has to play in sound engineering, you need to dig a little more deeply into what actually is going on when your recorded material is played back. Take a look at Figure 6.1. Like the other sketches used throughout this book, this is an illustrative diagram only and has not been drawn to any particular scale.

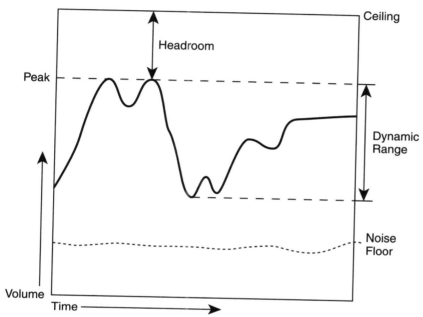

Figure 6.1   Concepts and terms that you will need to understand if you are to appreciate how to use compression include noise floor (or just floor), ceiling, dynamic range, and headroom.

The main wavy line that goes from left to right represents the changing volume of a piece of audio material as it is played back through time. The difference between its loudest (peak) point and its quietest is its dynamic range (also sometimes known as its *dynamic window*). The ceiling of the graph represents the maximum volume that can be allowed before clipping will occur. The distance between the loudest peak and this ceiling is known as the *headroom*. You can think of this as being rather like a safety buffer.

The horizontal line at the bottom of the graph represents the lowest limits of human hearing. Unfortunately, between this line and the quietest passages of our audio material, you can see a wavering dotted line that also weaves its way from left to right. This represents the unwanted noise that also finds its way onto your recordings. This noise can consist of elements such as hum, hiss, and buzz or perhaps some background room noise.

In trying to make our audio material (perhaps a guitar or a vocal) sound its best, there are always any number of issues that need to be addressed, and one of these issues is often the dynamic range. What if the difference between the loudest and quietest passages is so great that the quieter parts get all but lost in the mix? We could of course raise the overall volume, but then the louder parts would be too loud and might even cross the ceiling to produce digital clipping.

One possible approach might be to use a volume envelope to add a few decibels of gain to the quieter passages. This may well be (and often is) your preferred solution. However, it is also possible that making a large number of adjustments to a volume envelope might not be the best answer. For example:

- Simply lifting the volume of the quieter passages might by itself produce short fluctuations in volume that seem to the listener to be too sudden or unnatural.

- It may be that the amount of time it would take to make perhaps a very large number of these extremely fine adjustments is just too great.

- Even after taking the time and trouble to make the many changes required, some other decision made later in the mixing process might well mean having to go back and adjust each of these settings all over again.

In any of these cases, dynamic compression can often be worth considering as an alternative approach and one that might offer a better solution. Take a look at Figure 6.2. This series of three graphs serves to illustrate several things, but for now just focus on the first and the last. I'll explain what happens in between in the section immediately following this one. These two graphs represent what could be the shape of an audio wave before (left) and after (right) dynamic compression has been applied.

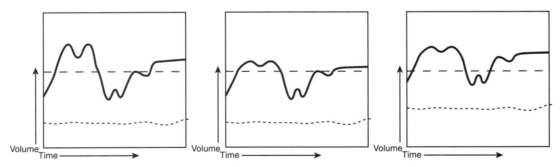

Figure 6.2 Compression can be used to lower the loudest parts of a vocal or instrument, thereby reducing the dynamic range of the recording. If you then lift the volume of the output back up toward the original peak level, the average or overall perceived level of the track will be increased without reducing the amount of original headroom.

You can see that in the third graph, the volume of the quietest parts of our material has been raised with the peaks remaining at their original levels. In doing this, we have modified the shape of our audio wave at its loudest parts, so that the peaks do not stand out as much as they did before. During the quieter passages, the shape is unaltered. This is the opposite of what happens if you resolve the problem using a volume envelope. In that case, the shape of the wave would be unaltered at the top but significantly modified at the bottom.

How Dynamic Compression Works

In Chapter 3 you were introduced to some very basic examples of using dynamic compression using just two of its parameter controls, threshold and ratio. You learned that by setting a particular sound threshold level, you are able to ensure that every time the sound passes above that threshold, its output will be reduced by an amount determined by the ratio setting. Figure 3.8 illustrates the concept of these two controls and how they work together.

Before examining the other compressor controls in detail, there's one more that needs to be mentioned, and that is output gain. Figure 6.2 shows an example of what can happen when output gain is added. The first of the three graphs shows the audio signal as it would be if not compressed. The second shows it after compression has been applied, using simply a combination of the threshold and ratio settings. In the third illustration, output gain has been added in order to lift the overall volume of the track so that the loudest passages will be returned to the same volume as they were before compression. Notice that the entire compressed signal is lifted. Because of this, the level of quieter passages will be louder than before, and the dynamic range will have been reduced. Tutorial 6.1 will demonstrate this.

The term *output gain* is used because the gain is added to the signal as the very last change that is made to it before it leaves the compressor.

Output Gain by Any Other Name . . .   Unfortunately, output gain is another area where terms and terminology used are not universal. Sometimes it is called *makeup gain*. Where a compressor has two separate gain controls (as is the case, for example, with MCompressor), one will be for input gain (lifting the signal before it is compressed), the other for output gain.

Where a compressor has an output gain control but no input gain control, then the output gain is sometimes called just *output* (as is the case with Kjaerhus Classic Compressor) or (somewhat ambiguously) just *gain* (as is the case, for example, with the Sonitus compressor). Other compressors may use other terms. (ReaComp's equivalent fader, for example, is labeled Wet.) You'll just have to get to know your software.

Tutorial 6.1: Simple Compression: Threshold, Ratio, and Gain

In this example you'll be given the opportunity to apply simple compression to a vocal harmony track. This should help you understand how different permutations of threshold, ratio, and output gain settings will produce different outcomes. This example uses ReaComp, but you can substitute a different compressor if you prefer.

1. Open the sample project file Foggy60 and save it as Foggy61.

2. Loop the region that runs from approximately 2 min 28 sec to 2 min 56 sec.

3. The VoxLead track should already contain a noise gate and EQ from earlier tutorials. The VoxHarmony should include EQ. Solo these two tracks.

4. Play the song. Adjust the volumes so that the harmony appears to sit not far behind the vocal. This could be with the lead set at 0.00 dB and the harmony at −1.00 dB.

5. Insert a compressor into the FX bin of the harmony track (after the EQ). Make sure that auto make-up is *not* selected.

6. Set the ratio to about 1.5:1.

7. Adjust the threshold until the compressor becomes engaged gently. This will probably be at about −29.0 dB. You can get visual confirmation from the vertical red meter.

8. Alternately engage and disengage (bypass) the compressor. Even at these conservative settings, you should notice that with the compressor engaged, the harmony is pushed farther back behind the lead.

9. Now increase the ratio slowly up to 40:1. Solo just the vocal harmony. Notice how it loses clarity and energy at this high compression ratio.

10. Unsolo the harmony so that you are playing the whole mix. The vocal harmony will be barely discernible. To make it audible at this level of compression, you will need to increase its overall volume. Slowly raise the wet control on ReaComp to about +4.5 dB or +5.0 dB. By doing this, you are adding up to 5.0 dB to the output.

11. If your DAW supports mixer snapshots, save this as a mixer snapshot.

12. Slowly lower the ratio back to 1.5:1. As you do so, the harmony will come up more in the mix. Fade the wet control down to about +0.3 dB. If your DAW allows this, save this as a mixer snapshot.

13. Play back the song, comparing the two different groups of settings. Try this also with both vocal tracks soloed.

14.   Select the mixer snapshot with the settings that you created in Steps 7, 9, and 10. Adjust the threshold down a little to −30 dB.

15.   Lower the threshold to about −38 dB and change the ratio to 60:1. The harmony will be barely audible when the full mix is played.

16.   Increase the wet (output gain) level to about +11 dB. This will bring the harmony back into the mix. By now we have compressed it so much that it plays at an almost constant level. In the overall mix, it sounds like little more than a drone. You should also find that because this has been so compressed, you have little margin for error in adjusting the output gain between the backing vocal being too low to be heard and being so high as to dominate the vocal mix. Of course, it is perfectly possible that this effect might be the one you want. If you are able, save this as another mixer snapshot.

17.   Which group of settings is best? It depends entirely on which sound you are aiming for. Do you want the backing vocal to be very prominent? If so, how dynamic should it be? Or do you prefer it subdued, perhaps even subliminal? There is no "one size fits all" answer to these questions.

18.   Restore the settings closer to those you made earlier at Step 14, with threshold now at −31 dB, ratio at about 30:1, and output gain at about +5 dB. Compression this aggressive would (for most styles of music) be unthinkable on a lead vocal, but in some circumstances it might be just what you want for a backing vocal. In any event, for learning and comparison purposes, you should in this case leave the harmony vocal compressed at these settings.

19.   Save the file.

Figure 6.2 also illustrates another of the important issues that you may need to address when you are using a compressor. Whenever you add output gain, you are raising the level of everything that is on the track *including the unwanted noise*. You can see in the third graph how the noise floor is raised along with the music or vocal that is being compressed.

Serious problems can occur if this noise is allowed to break through and intrude into the mix. Keep this thought in the back of your mind as we go on to start exploring and experimenting with the compressor's other controls. You will see how with a little more knowledge you should be able to set your compressor's controls to prevent this from happening.

Main Compressor Controls

Compressing the backing vocal in Tutorial 6.1 was a relatively straightforward process. This is largely because by squeezing the track's dynamics so hard, we managed to avoid some of the problems that can arise when you want to apply compression to a track selectively while at the same time preserving as much as possible of its dynamic range. Before working through some practical examples of this, you'll need to be introduced to some of the controls that you will be using.

For convenience I've divided these into two groups—dynamic controls and frequency filter controls. Don't make the mistake of thinking that the parameters included in the second group are in some way unimportant. The reasoning behind how these items are grouped in no way implies this. It is simply that the very nature of how these controls work means that the two groups perform different types of functions. As a rule, you should pay attention to getting your settings broadly right in the first group before paying attention to the second group.

Dynamic Controls

This group of controls includes the threshold, ratio, and output gain faders, as well as the attack, release, knee size, and RMS faders and the auto-release, limit output, and auto make-up options. As you have already seen, the threshold control determines when compression will be applied to an audio signal. The other controls together determine exactly *how* that compression will be applied.

Threshold

Finding and setting a suitable threshold setting is essential if you are to achieve the sound you want. Start with a ratio of about 2:1 while you make the necessary adjustments. Figure 6.3 illustrates three of the many possible threshold settings that could be used on a track.

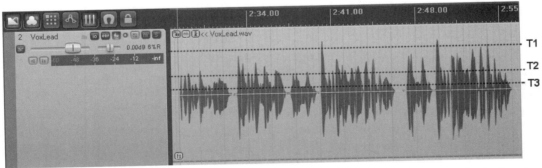

Figure 6.3   Because the threshold setting determines the volume below which the signal will be compressed, it also determines for how long or short a period of time the signal will be compressed.

A threshold level such as represented by the line labeled T1 could be used, for example, if your objective is to tame the peaks on a vocal recording, essentially to pull back the odd syllable or word that jumps out above the mix. In this example, the threshold used would only apply to two of the peaks, and then only briefly. When a threshold level such as this is used with a plug-in such as ReaComp, the vertical bar that shows the amount of attenuation would flash red only very occasionally and then only for very brief moments.

A setting similar to that shown at T3 (or lower) would be used when you want to compress practically the entire track. This is similar to what happened in Tutorial 6.1 when you set (in that example) a level of about −30 dB. The attenuation bar stays in the red to a greater or lesser extent practically all the time. As a result, the dynamics of the sound will be seriously subdued; the higher the compression ratio, the more this will be the case.

Arguably, however, it is the area in between these two levels that is the most interesting. The line labeled T2 represents an example of this. In this instance, the objective is to apply some compression to all or most of the louder phrases while at the same time allowing the dynamics of the more moderate and quieter passages to remain unaffected. The reason this area is so interesting is because of its implications. Consider this . . . .

The situations represented by the lines T1 and T3 could hardly be more different, and yet they share one important characteristic. The issues involved in determining *how* the compression is applied and withdrawn are in both cases not usually too difficult to determine. In the first scenario, the compressor is hardly ever used. When it is engaged, you want the compression to be immediately applied and to finish quickly. Quite often you could probably get by just using your compressor's default attack and release settings, though as you will see shortly, there will often be benefits in fine-tuning these.

In the scenario represented by T3, the opposite is the case. The compressor is applied to almost the entire vocal track. The only times it is released are during the pauses between lines and phrases. These are generally long enough to ensure that a smooth transition should not be too difficult.

It is the remaining scenario, represented by the line T2, that is by far the most interesting and challenging. In this instance, if you follow the line with your eye, you will see that the compressor is repeatedly being applied for often quite brief periods and then released. By way of analogy, think of this as repeatedly, frequently, and quickly turning a light switch on and off, and in circumstances where the timing has to be exactly right. This is the kind of situation in which getting your controls right (including attack, release, and knee size) can require more understanding, skill, and patience and is also more critical.

It is true that as you adjust your compressor settings, including the threshold, the most important information that you need will be relayed to you via your ears; after all, what really matters ultimately is how the track *sounds*. However, in order to get there you should be prepared to also take in, understand, and use the important and useful clues that are also being fed into your brain via your eyes!

Ratio

There's not really much more to say about the ratio control that hasn't already been said. Just to recap, the ratio decides the amount by which the uncompressed signal will be reduced after the volume crosses above the threshold. For example, if the ratio is set at 4:1 and the dry signal passes 8 dB above the threshold, then the processed signal will be not 8 dB above the threshold level, but only one quarter of that—in other words, 2 dB above that level.

Figure 6.4 shows an example of this in action. The Sonitus compressor uses a graph to give you some visual representation of the compression as it is being applied.

Figure 6.4   A picture paints a thousand words. Cakewalk's native Sonitus compressor includes a graph that visually displays how the ratio and threshold settings combine to compress the audio signal.

Most compressors allow you to push the ratio all the way up to infinity:1 if you wish. A ratio of infinity to one can be used to prevent any sound that passes above the threshold from being delivered to the mix. This process is known as *limiting*. It will be considered in a separate section later in this chapter.

Attack

The attack setting works to determine how quickly the compression is applied after it reaches the threshold. It is the period of time that is taken after the threshold is crossed for the audio gain to be squashed down according to the specified ratio. Figure 6.5 is a diagrammatic representation of this. The wave pattern shown is, to say the least, an extremely unlikely one. It has been chosen to help illustrate the point and should not be interpreted too literally.

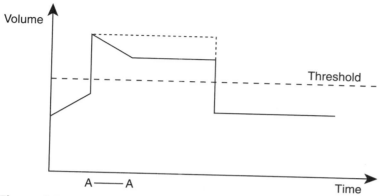

Figure 6.5   This shows how the attack control works to determine how compression is initially applied. For illustrative purposes, the waveform shown here follows a simplified straight and angular pattern. The diagram is adapted from an original that appears on Wikipedia at en.wikipedia.org/wiki/Dynamic_range_compression.

In Figure 6.5, a ratio setting of 2:1 is assumed. The attack time is represented by the distance AA (shown on the horizontal axis). At the point where the waveform jumps sharply above the threshold, instead of being immediately compressed, the signal is initially allowed through and the compression applied gradually over the attack period. This technique can be effective in allowing through a sharp and perhaps dramatic burst on (for example) percussive instruments before the compression is applied. The solid line shows the path taken in this case by the audio signal. The dotted line shows what would have happened had the compressor not been engaged.

Release

The release time setting is used to determine how quickly or slowly the compression is taken off the audio stream when a compressed track drops back below the threshold. This is illustrated in Figure 6.6.

This example builds on that used in Figure 6.5. The audio signal that is being compressed drops back below the threshold level when it reaches the moment in time represented by the first R on the horizontal axis. A release time equal to that represented by the line RR has been specified. Were the compressor to be instantly and fully stopped at this point (a release time of 0 ms), the signal would (in this example) continue along the path of the broken line. Instead, the compression is gradually eased, and the signal follows the path of the solid line.

From this simplified diagram, it might not be immediately apparent that using a release control in this way makes the transition from a compressed signal to an uncompressed

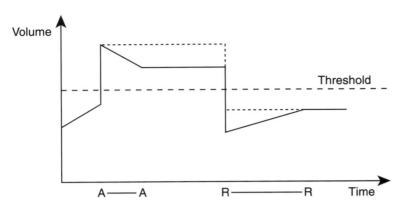

Figure 6.6   The release setting can be used to control how quickly or slowly compression is stopped when a signal drops back down below the threshold level. Because of their role in helping to shape the waveform, attack and release are sometimes known as envelope controls.

signal smoother and less obvious. The greater the degree of compression, the longer the release time required is likely to be if a smooth transition is what you want.

Another key factor relevant to arriving at an appropriate release time is the dynamics of the song itself, including how sharp or smooth the transition into and out of transients is. Too short a release time may create a pumping effect as the signal rises and falls. Of course, this effect might be exactly what you want. Too long a release time runs the risk of the compressor needing to be re-engaged for the next transient before it has been fully removed from the previous one.

I'll have more to say about these issues shortly, including some specific examples, but meanwhile here's something to look out for. Some compressors (including but not limited to ReaComp and Sonitus) include an *auto release* or *transient release control* function (both essentially similar), which, if engaged, will calculate and apply a release time automatically, according to the dynamics of the sound being compressed.

Output Gain

There probably isn't a lot more that needs to be said about the output gain fader. Notice in particular that as long as the compressor plug-in is not set to bypass, the output gain will be applied to the entire track or item as it is played back, not only to those parts that are actually compressed. It therefore follows that if you set the output gain to restore the most heavily compressed notes to their original volume, you will make the audio signal louder than it would have been if not compressed.

Figure 6.7 illustrates this point. It follows from the example used in Figure 6.6. Output gain equivalent to the amount represented by the line marked GG has been applied to this track. The solid line shows the result of this; the dotted line shows the path that would have been taken after compression had the output gain not been applied.

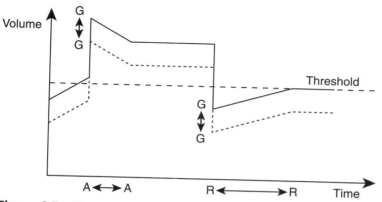

Figure 6.7 Output gain can be applied to a compressed track to raise its entire level.

Note that in this example, the threshold level is shown for reference only. Once the signal has passed through the compressor, it has no more relevance. Obviously, raising the output level back up above the threshold will not cause the signal to be compressed again! Indeed, if too much output gain is added, you may introduce the risk of clipping the output signal. To prevent this, it is advisable to engage the limit output option where this is present.

RMS

You can think of the RMS (root mean square) value as being a sort of moving average of the output level. I say "sort of" because it is calculated according to a formula rather more complex than a straightforward arithmetical average, although the concept is broadly similar. It uses as the basis of its computations not the different levels of output themselves, but the square root of the mean of the squares of the values. If you're not mathematically inclined, don't worry. All you need to understand is that this method of calculation tends to smooth out the more extreme peaks and troughs in an audio stream and produces a continuous series of values with less fluctuation.

Figure 6.8 illustrates a perfectly smooth and regular sine wave. Because it follows such a regular pattern, the peaks and troughs cancel each other out when RMS is calculated, so that the RMS would actually be computed at a perfectly flat level with no variation.

Of course, with real music you would not expect to get a sound pattern anything like that regular. Figure 6.9 is closer to the mark. It shows the VU of a single instrument (an acoustic guitar) as a chord first peaks and then starts to trail away. The two thick bars in the center show the peak signal; the two thinner outer bars show the RMS values. Notice in particular:

- The RMS meters offer a better reflection of how we hear and interpret sound than do the peak meters. This is because our brains tend to focus less on short and sudden fluctuations than they do on sustained levels.

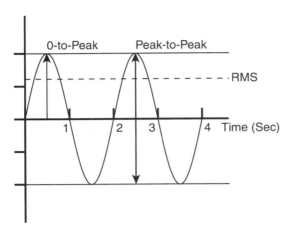

Figure 6.8   A perfectly even sine wave such as shown here would produce a constant root mean square value.

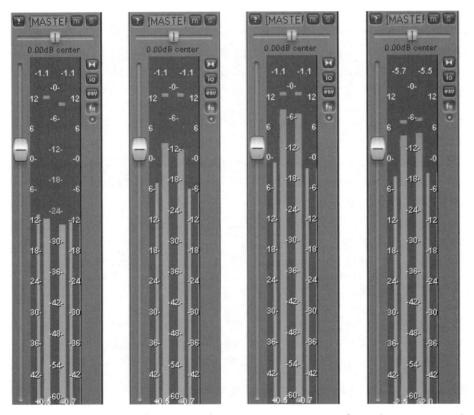

Figure 6.9   Because the RMS value represents a sort of moving average, it will generally be subject to less dramatic fluctuation as the audio signal rises and falls.

■   Not all compressors include an RMS fader. For those that do, it allows you to specify whether the threshold at which compression is applied should be determined according to the peak value or the RMS value. The RMS parameter is specified as a number of microseconds. The lower the RMS setting, the shorter the time period used for calculating the RMS values will be, with the result that these values will closely resemble the peak values.

■ As with all things, optimum RMS settings will depend on the audio signal and the effect that you are trying to achieve. Quite often, however, a modest RMS setting of around 10 ms or so may have the effect of smoothing off rogue fluctuations in signal strength, thereby preventing the compression from being applied in too finicky a manner. Depending on the dynamics of the song, too high an RMS value may result in the compressor's response becoming too sluggish and unresponsive. In any event, the greater the difference between a signal's peak and RMS levels, the greater the difference in compression caused by increasing the RMS setting will be.

In any event, as you increase the value of the RMS setting, you would normally want to lower your threshold value to compensate.

Knee Size

The knee size is another factor that plays an important part in shaping exactly how compression is applied.

All of the examples of compression that we have used up to now (in Chapter 3 and in this chapter) have employed *hard knee* compression. The signal remains unchanged until it reaches the threshold, at which point the compression is suddenly applied according to the ratio setting. Especially at higher ratio settings, this can result in an unnatural and somewhat harsh-sounding transition. For this reason, most compressors provide you with other options.

These usually come in the form of a knee control rotary or fader, which is adjustable within a continuous range. At its lowest limit (0.0 dB), its application is known as *hard knee* because it causes the compression to be applied very abruptly. At its uppermost limit (typically 25 dB or 30 dB), it causes the compression to be applied very gradually and is therefore said to be at its softest. Some compressors use other names for this control, such as *softness, hard/soft,* or something similar.

Figure 6.10 illustrates the shifting change in how compression is applied as you move from hard knee to medium knee to soft knee. The first of the three examples shown uses hard knee, so that the compression is applied suddenly and in its entire 8:1 ratio as soon as the threshold (in this case, −25.1 dB) is reached. The third example shows the same setup but with a very soft knee setting. The compression begins to be gently applied at a ratio barely above 1:1 as soon as the volume reaches a level (in this example) 29 dB below the threshold level and does not reach the full 8:1 ratio until some considerable time after it. The second example shows a compromise halfway between these extremes, with a medium knee setting of −15 dB being used.

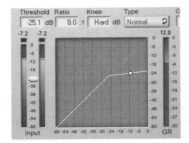 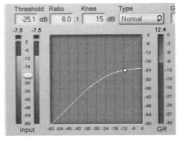 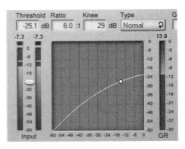

Figure 6.10   This group of three pictures illustrates how the knee size setting affects the way compression is applied.

Don't make the mistake of thinking "hard knee bad, soft knee good." As you will see for yourself in the tutorials that soon follow, it really does depend upon circumstances, including the nature and volume of the sound being compressed. In the example illustrated in Figure 6.10, with a threshold of about −25 dB and soft knee setting of 29 dB, compression would begin to be applied to the audio signal at levels as low as −54 dB. While it is possible that this might be what you want, there aren't too many practical applications that come to mind.

The various controls discussed earlier (such as attack and release) work in the same manner regardless of which knee size setting is chosen, but of course the exact implementation and details of how they modify the compression will vary. The attack and release settings work with the knee size setting, not against it. For instance, a softer knee setting is often used when compression is added to mixes and submixes, whereas a harder setting can be used to create interesting effects, especially on vocals and percussive instruments. We'll explore some examples of this shortly.

Look Ahead (Pre Comp)

Look ahead (or pre comp) is another control that is found on some but not all compressors. It allows you to specify that as the volume of the audio signal increases, the compression will begin a given number of milliseconds before the threshold is reached.

This function can help when you are faced with a potential dilemma between using a slower attack to produce smooth changes or using a faster attack in order to trap transients. What actually happens is that the input signal is split: One side is then delayed by the specified period. The non-delayed signal then controls the compression of the delayed signal, thereby allowing a slower attack rate to trap transients.

Confused? Too Much to Learn?   Take a moment and pause for breath before you continue.

By now you might be starting to get somewhat bewildered, if not demoralized, by the sheer number of different controls that you might find on a compressor. Don't be.

You don't need to become expert in every one of these items to be able to use compression effectively in many if not most situations. Here's a comforting fact: The Kjaerhus Classic Compressor, as an example, has only six controls—threshold, ratio, knee size, attack, release, and output gain. Start by getting on top of the basics, and then as you develop confidence, you can familiarize yourself with the others.

Other Controls

We're at last nearly ready to move on to the next tutorial, but there are just a few more compressor controls that really should be mentioned first. These are all on/off options, so happily you don't need to learn too much about how to set them! Some have already been mentioned in passing, but it's worth collecting them all together.

Normal Mode versus Vintage (Classsic) Mode. Normal compression is compression applied pretty much as you would expect it to be. All gain above the threshold is attenuated according to whatever ratio has been specified. This can be seen in the first of the two examples shown in Figure 6.11.

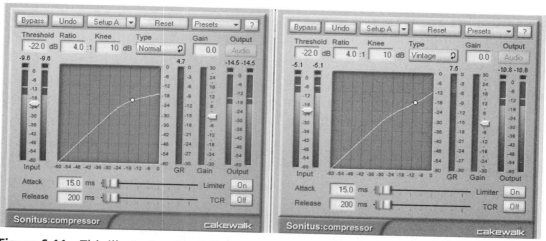

Figure 6.11 This illustrates the different ways in which normal mode (left) and vintage mode (right) will compress the same audio signal.

Vintage mode, on the other hand, emulates an approach taken by some analog compressors, so that at a certain level above the threshold, the compression ratio is gradually reduced back to 1:1. This results in rather less compression, in particular with the loudest peaks passing through uncompressed. Especially with percussive instruments, this can produce a warmer, punchier sound.

Auto Release Control. The auto release function enables the compressor to calculate and apply release values intelligently according to the changing dynamics of the audio signals. Unless you are using compression to create a particular effect, enabling auto release may often prove to be the easiest and most reliable way to obtain the optimal release periods.

Auto Make-Up. This option may also be called by a variety of other names, including *maximize signal.* If enabled, it will raise the output level (before any output gain controls are applied) so that the audio stream will be lifted as close to 0.0 dB as is possible. In some circumstances, such as those we are discussing in this section, it is unlikely that you would want to enable this option. We will look at auto make-up later, in a separate section.

Limit Output. Enabling this option will prevent the output of the compressed signal from clipping, even after output gain is applied.

Other ReaComp controls that we haven't yet mentioned include the dry output fader and the low-pass, high-pass, and preview filter controls. The dry output can be used for parallel compression, which is the subject of a separate section later in this chapter. The other three are used as frequency filter controls and will be explained in the section immediately following the next tutorial.

Tutorial 6.2: Getting Serious about Compression

In this example you will most definitely learn by doing! One useful technique to help you understand what the different controls do and what sorts of settings are appropriate to different circumstances is to see (or rather, hear) what happens when you get these settings wrong! To that end, in this tutorial you will on occasion be deliberately guided into making some bad settings before being steered toward more appropriate ones.

Before you begin, remember again that the content of this tutorial is not intended to imply that you should or should not use compression on any or all of the various tracks in this song. Rather, its aim is to help you to understand how to apply compression if you do wish to use it.

1. Open the sample project file Foggy61 and save it as Foggy62.

2. Loop the region that runs from approximately 2 min 28 sec to 2 min 56 sec.

3. Solo the VoxLead track and insert your preferred compressor plug-in in the track's FX bin. If you inserted a noise gate into this track at Checkpoint 1 in Chapter 5, the compressor should be placed after the noise gate. For this example, I shall be using ReaComp, but you may use a different compressor if you wish. Make sure that any auto make-up (or equivalent) control is turned off.

4. Suppose that you wish to use a compressor here primarily to tame any extra-loud peaks that might otherwise jump out of the mix. Start with a ratio of about 3:1 and adjust the threshold until the compressor seems to be catching those peaks. This will probably be at about −24 dB.

5. The vocal waveform includes reasonably sharp transients, and you do not want to miss the loudest parts. This means you should not set too long an attack time. As an experiment, slowly increase the attack setting. As you gradually increase this setting, the degree of attenuation applied to the compressed signal becomes less and less. By the time you get to 500 ms, the length of time taken to build up to the required ratio means that almost no compression is applied at all. Fade the attack level back to about 2 ms.

6. For learning purposes, make sure that any auto release control is turned off. Now slowly fade the release setting up toward 2000 ms (two whole seconds!). With such a long release time, the compressor each time becomes re-engaged at the next peak before it has recovered from the previous peak. Add about 3.5 dB to the output gain (wet) signal. As a precaution, engage the limit output control.

7. Unsolo the track. Play the looped part of the song with the compressor alternately engaged and bypassed. It should be noticeable how the dynamics have been squeezed out of the vocal.

8. Restore the release setting to about 90 ms and the output gain to about +1.0. A longer period would give you a smoother sound (as you might want, for example, for a ballad or slow smoochy love song). Fine-tune the attack, release, ratio, and threshold settings so that the vocal sits nicely (but not too much) above the mix and is delivered with both clarity and warmth. You are likely to find in this case that a threshold around −22.0 dB, a ratio around 2.5:1, an attack around 50 ms, and a release around 60 ms will give you this—*but use other settings if you prefer them!*

9. Once again, solo the VoxLead track. Gradually change the knee shape from hard to fairly medium. (Try a setting about 14.0 dB or 15.0 dB.) Add an extra 1 dB to the output gain to compensate.

10. Unsolo this track and play the whole mix (still looped). Adjust the output gain to get the overall vocal level about right. Probably you will need to bring it back down a little.

11. Experiment with the pre comp (look ahead) setting. You probably don't really need it. A high setting will likely cause enough delay to make the compressed vocal sound a little muffled. Leaving pre comp at about 2 ms might make the vocal a touch more polished in the more heavily compressed areas.

12. Now experiment with the RMS setting. A high RMS setting (above about 500 ms) will average out the signal too much and cause a little compression to be applied all the time rather than the required amount of compression to be applied to the louder parts only. Set at about 5 ms, you should find that some of the sharper jumps in signal attenuation will be evened out a little.

13.   Save the file. For something different, let's now turn to the bass track. If you completed Tutorial 4.2, this track's FX bin will already include an EQ plug-in.

14.   Place your preferred compressor in the bass track's FX bin after the EQ. The example that follows uses ReaComp.

15.   Still using the loop from about 2 min 28 sec to 2 min 56, solo the bass track and play it. In this case, we might wish to not simply tame the peaks, but also to add some punch to the sound of this instrument as it drives the song along. This means that at the same time as applying compression, we also want to accentuate rather than smooth out the dynamics of the instrument.

16.   At about −23.0 dB, the threshold should be about right for capturing the louder notes. Try a ratio of about 6:1 or 8:1. For more punch, choose a hard knee setting.

17.   Set the attack to 0 ms and then slowly increase it to the point where it seems to allow some punch through before the compression kicks in. This will probably be at about 6.0 ms.

18.   Starting at 0 ms, slowly increase the release setting up to the point where the sustain seems to hold up well before dropping more steadily away. In this case, this will probably be at about 200 ms. For illustration purposes, if you extend this release period out to, say, 1,000 ms, you will find that you take almost all the punch out of the instrument. You will be effectively compressing it all or most of the time.

19.   Select classic (vintage) mode. You should notice a definite increase in punch.

20.   Set RMS to a very low value, no more than 2.0 ms. Set pre comp (look ahead) to 0 ms.

21.   Unsolo the track and adjust the output gain so that the instrument sits nicely in the mix. This will probably be at about +1.0 dB to +1.5 dB.

22.   Play the loop over and over with the bass compressor alternately engaged and set to bypass. Make any adjustments that you think will improve the sound.

23.   Save the file. In a later tutorial, you will return to this project and apply some compression to your percussion and other instruments.

24.   For comparison purposes, play this file with global effects bypass alternately on and off. You should notice quite a difference. When you have finished, set global bypass to off and save the file.

Frequency Filter Controls

Three of the compressor controls that we have not explained yet are the low-pass filter, the high-pass filter, and the preview filter option. The good news is that given what you already know about frequency ranges and EQ, these are quite straightforward and easy to use.

We have already seen (with frequency analyzers and their like) that most of the dynamic energy and volume of most music tends to be concentrated around the lower frequencies. As the frequencies get higher, the volume tends to decline. A quick look back at Figures 2.10 and 2.11 will remind you of this. There is a case to be made, therefore, that quite often you may wish to leave these higher frequencies uncompressed, so that their natural sparkle can still shine through. That's when you might wish to use a low-pass filter.

Conversely, you might find that an instrument begins to sound rather boomy when compressed even quite gently. A high-pass filter might help to prevent this.

The preview filter option allows you to check and assess your filter settings by restricting output (as long as it is engaged) to that range of frequencies between the high- and low-pass filters that is actually being compressed. Of course, you would not leave this engaged during normal playback.

Tutorial 6.3: Using Frequency Filters with Compression

In this next tutorial, you will explore using compression on your snare and kick and experiment with the use of frequency filter controls.

1.   Open the sample project fileMud60 and save it as Mud63.

2.   Loop the region that runs from approximately 1 min 28 sec to 2 min 08 sec.

3.   We are going to apply enough gentle compression to the two guitar (dobro) tracks to just lift them above the mix a little. By using a high-pass filter, we will also preserve the clarity and sparkle of the high harmonics of the instrument.

4.   A fair starting point when compressing a guitar in this way is to take a similar approach as you might with a vocal. Solo the track Guitar1 and insert ReaComp into the track's FX bin. Use a different compressor if you wish. If there are any other plug-ins there as a result of any previous experiments, set them to bypass. Play the song.

5.   Set an initial ratio of 5:1 and lower the threshold until the compressor becomes engaged for the louder notes. This is likely to occur at about −25 dB. Select normal rather than classic or vintage attack.

6.   Set low values at or close to 0 for both pre comp and RMS.

7. Set a low attack time sufficient to let the initial attack through uncompressed; this is likely to be somewhere between 2 ms and 5 ms. Set a release time that will ensure that the compressor is released after each peak before it encounters the next one. Examine the range 100 ms to 200 ms and see where you get the best outcome.

8. Start with a fairly hard knee setting of about 6 dB. Soften it a little if you think this improves the sound.

9. Now enable the preview filter option. Fade the low-pass filter to the left until you hear the sparkle and clarity being noticeably diminished. You are now hearing only those frequencies that are being compressed—in other words, frequencies below this setting. For this first experiment, try setting this at about 4,000 Hz.

10. Disengage the preview filter. Add output gain of about 1.5 to 2.0 dB. Compare how this instrument sounds with the compressor alternately engaged and bypassed.

11. Apply similar compression to the track Guitar2, this time without using a high-pass filter. Play the song alternately with and without the FX bypassed. You should find that by using a high-pass filter on one of the two tracks, you have enhanced the clarity of the instrument.

12. Save the file.

High- and Low-Pass Filter Preview   This next point is a tricky one, so take it slowly and be prepared to maybe read it twice or more!

When you engage the filter preview option, you will hear only those frequencies that are being compressed. A handy trick is to use the other pass filter to check which frequencies are being allowed through uncompressed. For example, in Tutorial 6.3 a low-pass filter is set around 4,000 Hz. If you return the low-pass filter control all the way to the right and instead set a high-pass filter at 4,000 Hz, you will then hear only those higher frequencies that you want to be allowed through uncompressed.

You can use this trick to help determine where exactly you want to set your low-pass filter. Then, by returning the high-pass filter all the way back to the left, setting the low-pass filter at that frequency, and disengaging the filter preview, you will achieve your goal.

Matching Compressor Settings to Wave Patterns

In this section we'll dig a little deeper and aim to understand more about why we need to set different compression ratios and attack and release times (to name but three of the many settings) to get the best results for different voices and instruments. The old adage that when working with sound you should always let your ears be your main judge is good advice. However, it does no harm to also trust your eyes when they are able to give you visual confirmation. If you look carefully at Figure 6.12, you might be able to glean some visual clues.

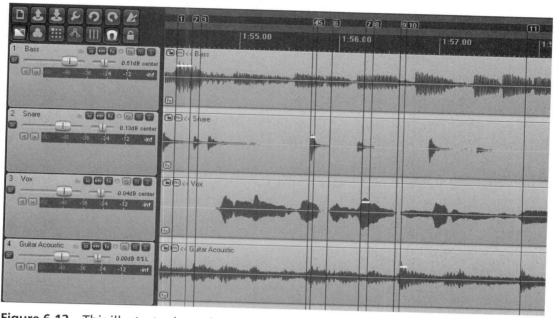

Figure 6.12   This illustrates how the sound waves produced from different sources (in this example, bass guitar, snare, vocal, and acoustic guitar) exhibit different characteristics. These need to be taken into account when compression is applied to these sounds.

Illustrated here are the waveforms of a few seconds of playback from four tracks that are part of a project. We have a bass guitar, a snare, a vocal, and an acoustic guitar. Of course, the project would contain other instruments than just these—these four have been selected to help illustrate a point.

Knowing how to read waveform patterns can be a useful asset. Let's assume that a compressor is to be used on each of these tracks.

Look first at the bass. Suppose that a threshold has been set at the level represented by the horizontal white line shown on Track 1 between Markers 1 and 2. As the song is played, the compressor will become engaged at Marker 1. The short transient length means that a reasonably short attack time will be sufficient to allow the transient through. At Marker 2, the compression will be eased. We actually have a reasonably large window (starting at Marker 3 and ending shortly before the 1:55 mark) within which we can set a release time, depending on how we wish to shape the sound. This is because a bass guitar's notes generally decay fairly slowly and reasonably steadily. We have a window of about half a second (500 ms) before the next mini transient.

Moving on to the snare, you can see that compared to the bass, its transients are much shorter and sharper, and the decay is much faster. With a threshold setting as represented by the horizontal white line shown on Track 2 between Markers 4 and 5, a very short attack is needed if we are not to miss the transient altogether. Similarly, the quick decay means that a short release time should also be preferred.

The next track is a vocal track. The attack may be slower than the snare and even the bass, but the transients are held for shorter periods. If our aim is to use compression simply to bring back into the mix peaks such as those shown above the white threshold line on Track 3 (between Markers 7 and 8), then a short attack setting will be needed. You do not want too long a release period, but too short a setting might result in an awkward and uncomfortable transition.

Finally we come to the acoustic guitar. Using compression to tame the peaks is relatively straightforward. Assuming a threshold setting as indicated by the horizontal white line on Track 4 (at Marker 10), finding suitable relatively short attack and release times should not be too difficult a task. Notice, however, that the nature of this instrument is to decay slowly and sustain quite strongly. Too low a threshold and too long a release time could between them see the compression that kicks in at Marker 10 being continued all the way to Marker 11 and beyond.

This demonstrates the point that especially with less percussive sounds, getting your threshold level right is the first and one of the most important keys to using compression well. Look at Figure 6.13. Here I have zoomed in very closely on one note of a bass guitar track. From what you have learned in this section, you should be able to work out for yourself why a threshold level set at the white line labeled X will require different treatment (particularly different ratio and release settings) from one set at the line labeled Y—and that each would produce different outcomes.

This might lead you to ponder the question of what you should do when a track's transients vary substantially in their strength throughout the song. If your objective is simply to pull the loudest peaks back into the mix, then you clearly do not have a problem. Just set the compressor to catch the loud ones and allow the others through. If, however, your goal is to use compression to shape the sound in some way, then you have a situation that needs addressing. Hold that thought for a moment, and we'll return to it shortly. Right now it's time to apply what you have learned in this section to using compression with drums and percussion.

Tutorial 6.4: Compressing Percussive Instruments

In this next tutorial, you will explore using compression on your snare and kick and experiment with the use of frequency filter controls.

1.   Open the sample project file Foggy62 and save it as Foggy64.

2.   Loop the region that runs from approximately 1 min 28 sec to 2 min 08 sec.

3.   Our aim is to add a little more impact to the snare. Solo this track and play the song. Add your compressor of choice after the effects already in this track's FX bin.

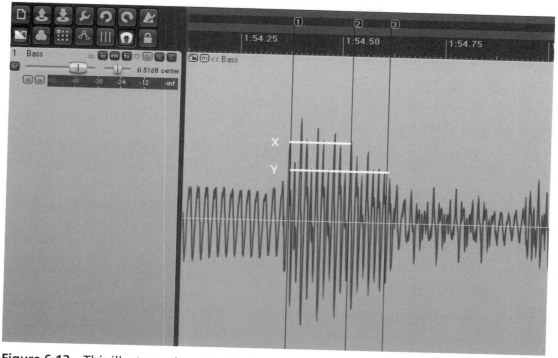

Figure 6.13 This illustrates how the level at which a compressor threshold is set plays an important part in determining how many of your other compressor controls should be set.

4. Make sure that auto make-up and auto release are both disabled. Select the limit output option. Set pre comp to 0 and RMS size at or very close to 0.

5. Start with a ratio of 7:1 and a threshold level that gives about 6-dB attenuation on the peak. Add 6 dB to the output gain to compensate for this.

6. Start with an aggressive attack time of 1.0 to 2.0 ms (no higher) and a tight release time within the range of 150 ms to 200 ms, no more.

7. Start with a hard knee (0 dB) but soften it just a little to 2 or 3 dB if this sounds too harsh.

8. If the option is available to you, try alternately the classic (vintage) attack and normal attack options. Which do you prefer?

9. Compare the sound of the snare with the compressor engaged and disengaged. The compression should make the sound sharper.

10. Now add a compressor to the kick. Like the snare, it is a percussive instrument. The same guiding principles used in arriving at settings for the snare should also apply to the kick.

11. Unsolo the soloed tracks when you have finished. Play the whole song. Compare how it sounds with and without global FX bypass.

12.   Turn global FX bypass off. Make any adjustments that you feel are necessary to the various tracks' volume faders if the balance between the different tracks needs adjusting as a result of the changes made in these tutorials.

13.   Save your work.

Compression Zones

When you understand the general relationship that exists for any instrument between its normal sound pattern and the various compressor controls, you can start thinking in terms of the instrument's natural compression zone. By that I mean the ranges of settings within which it by and large makes sense to work when you are applying compression to that instrument. These are, of course, guidelines, not rules. Depending on the kind of sound or effect that you are trying to achieve, there could be any number of reasons why you might want to operate outside of the normal compression zone of any instrument. However, in many circumstances these settings offer you a fairly sensible starting point.

As a general guideline, aim to be consistent and holistic in your settings. Be mindful of how the different controls work together. Remember, too, that you can always try using the auto release control where it is available.

Table 6.1 Examples of Compression Zones for Different Instruments and Voices

Instrument	Comment
Vocal	Soft knee for smooth, mellow sound; hard knee for hard-edged rock. Starting ratio 4:1. Fast attack. Release generally 200 ms to 500 ms. Normal mode.
Acoustic guitar	Knee size depends on style (like vocals). Starting ratio 4:1 to 6:1. Attack 5 ms to 10 ms. Release between 100 ms and 500 ms. Normal mode.
Bass guitar	Hard knee for more punch; softer knee for more mellow sound. Start at 4:1 ratio and increase if necessary. Fast attack. Release 100 ms to 500 ms depending on tempo, etc. Use classic mode for extra punch.
Electric guitar	So many different circumstances could apply as to make generalization impossible. That said, try hard knee for more urgency. Ratio around 8:1. Fast attack and relatively slow release, 200 to 500 ms, to add sustain. Classic or normal mode depending on which is preferred.
Kick	Hard knee for percussion. Higher ratio, around 5:1 or more. Very fast attack, fairly smart release, 150 ms to 250 ms. Classic mode for more impact.
Snare	Hard knee for percussion. Higher ratio, around 5:1 or more. Very fast attack, fairly smart release, 150 ms to 250 ms. Classic mode for more impact.

Checkpoint 1

You can never have too much practice! Open the file Lying60 and save it as Lying61. Explore the use of compressors on various vocal and instrumental tracks until you feel that you are truly in control of what you are doing.

Feel free to experiment with pushing the boundaries, even to the extent of creating unusual dynamics. All that matters is that you understand what you are doing. This particular version of this project (Lying61) will not be used in any further examples (unless you wish to), so you can really give yourself a free hand.

Compression with Equalization

You may have noticed that in several of the examples used in the tutorials in this chapter, equalization was already added to the track in Chapter 4. The use of EQ and compression together is not unusual. In most cases the equalization is applied first, but this does not necessarily have to be the case. You have (as always) a number of options, and (also as ever) each possibility will yield a different outcome. Consider, for example, these scenarios:

- You have added EQ to a track, perhaps a vocal, to add more presence. You now wish to use compression to prevent rogue peaks from jumping up above the mix. In this case, the compression is applied only occasionally and then very briefly. Placed after the EQ, it is unlikely to affect the frequency response of the track in any discernible way.

- You have used EQ to improve the sound of a track, perhaps to make a guitar sound warmer. You wish to use compression on the whole track in order to reduce its dynamic range and push it back a little in the mix. In this case, placed after the EQ, the compression could squeeze out of the track some of the qualities that you were using EQ to put in.

Tutorial 6.5: Using Compression with EQ

In this example, we will explore what happens when you place a compressor after and before a track's EQ. The EQ settings used might be considered somewhat extreme; this is to help illustrate the point.

1. Open the sample project file Mud63 and save it as Mud65.

2. Loop the region that runs from approximately 1 min 28 sec to 2 min 08 sec.

3. Select and solo the harmonica track. Suppose that we wish to boost certain frequencies (with EQ) to add an increased feel of urgency to this track, while at the same time squeezing the dynamics a little to make it sit back a little more in the mix. Play the song.

4. Add a parametric EQ of your choice, with a single bell (peak/dip) filter with gain of 10 dB around 4,000 Hz and a bandwidth of about 0.5 octave (Q approximately 3.0). This is a rather severe use of EQ; these settings have been chosen for illustrative purposes only.

5. Now add a compressor after the EQ. Set the ratio to 5:1 and the threshold to a level where the compressor is generally engaged (about −30.0 dB).

6. Set a low attack time (about 0.3 ms) and a release time of about 500 ms (to ensure the compression is released slowly). Use a medium knee setting, such as 10.0 dB. Use normal attack and low RMS and pre comp settings. Do not use any high- or low-pass filters.

7. As you play the song, change the effects' order so that the compressor is placed before the EQ. You should notice the difference in the harmonica sound. Interestingly enough, this difference might actually become *more* noticeable when you unsolo the track and listen to the entire mix!

8. Save this file.

Using Auto Make-Up

Where a compressor includes an auto make-up (or maximize signal) control, it can be used to really squeeze the track's dynamics and pump up the sound. Using this control makes the otherwise quieter passages much more pungent. Whether and when you might wish to do this is, of course, a matter for your artistic and creative judgment. The example in this section shows how you could go about using auto make-up, but with it comes no implied value judgment that you *should* be doing it.

Tutorial 6.6: Using Auto Make-Up

By way of demonstration, let's see how you might use auto make-up to really pump up a drum mix.

1. Open the sample project file Foggy64 and save it as Foggy66.

2. Loop the region that runs from approximately 2 min 28 sec to 2 min 56 sec.

3. Set to bypass the compressors that you inserted earlier in the kick and snare tracks. These brought up the punch of the percussion a little; this time, we're going to really go to town.

4. Solo the Percussion Mix bus and play the song.

5. Insert ReaComp (or any other compressor whose feature set includes auto make-up) in the FX bin for this bus. You may have an instance of an equalizer here from an earlier example. If so, place the compressor before the equalizer. If not, don't worry about it!

6. Set a threshold that engages the compressor for the loud transients, probably at about −25.0 dB. Set ratio at 4:1, knee size at hard (0.0 dB) attack very short (3.0 ms), release fairly tight (100 ms), and RMS size and pre comp both to 0.0 ms.

7. Engage first the limit output option and then auto make-up. The difference should be dramatic as the percussion mix is really pumped up.

8. Unsolo the bus, then fade the wet (output gain) control down until you are happy with the level of the percussion within the overall mix.

9. Save the file.

Serial Compression

At times you may be faced with a dilemma when trying to work out suitable compressor settings. This can arise when you have two objectives—for example, you might wish to squash down the occasional peak that is trying to jump out of the mix, but you might also want to use a compressor to restrict the instrument or vocal's dynamic range. In that case, the answer might be as simple as placing two compressors into the FX bin, one after the other. They can, of course, be two separate instances of the same plug-in. This practice is known as *serial compression*.

When using serial compression, most commonly you would use a high threshold, high ratio, hard knee, and very fast attack on the first one so as to trap and tame the peaks. You would then use the second compressor to shape the sound according to whatever you are trying to achieve.

Checkpoint 2

If you like, try this example, which will demonstrate an example of serial compression in action. It does not require you to learn any new skills; rather, you have the opportunity to apply what you have learned in a slightly different way.

Open the file Whiskey60 and save it as Whiskey65.

Add a compressor to each of the two vocal tracks purely to tame their peaks. This will be applied in each case before the output is passed to the vocal submix, where it will be passed through a second compressor that was inserted during Tutorial 3.4, which you completed in Chapter 3.

Make any changes you think appropriate to perhaps make this second compressor a little less severe and more mellow. Save the file when finished.

Having multiple instances of the same plug-in can become confusing, especially when you are returning to work on a project after a long break. Check your DAW's feature set to see whether it allows you to rename individual plug-in instances within individual track FX bins. As Figure 6.14 shows (follow the mouse pointer) this can be a very helpful trick.

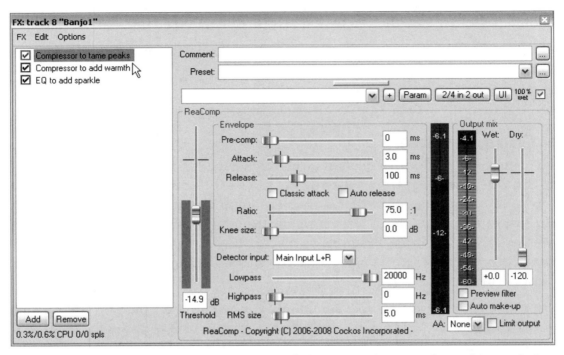

Figure 6.14   Renaming individual instances of plug-ins within a track's FX bin can help provide you with a useful record of your actions.

Serial compression may sometimes offer a solution to a problem we touched on earlier. This is the question of what can be done when different parts of the same track need to be treated differently. However, often this will not be the case. Consider the example illustrated in Figure 6.15. This happens to be a recording of a choir, but it could equally well be a musical instrument. Look at the top image first.

If we wish to compress this track for almost any reason other than to prevent possible clipping, then it is likely that the various settings required between Markers 1 and 2 would be different from those required after Marker 2. You have several different ways of resolving this, each slightly different. You need to be aware of the implications of each. Your most feasible options (in no special order) are as follows:

■ Split the media item at Marker 2 and place a separate instance of your compressor directly into each item rather than into the track's FX bin. This is illustrated in the lower image. (See the mouse pointer.) This might appear to be a simple solution, but you need to take into account your DAW's signal flow (refer back to Figure 3.15). This would cause you problems if you wanted to place any effects (such as perhaps a noise gate) in the *track* FX bin that you want applied before the compression.

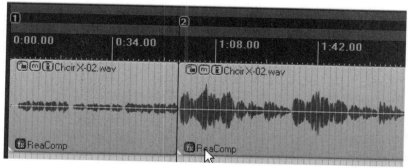

Figure 6.15   Dealing with a situation where the dynamic range varies markedly in different parts of a track.

- Use a single compressor, with automation envelopes to change the settings as the song progresses from its first part to its second. This could be a good solution if, say, the threshold is the only setting that needs changing, but it could become unnecessarily complicated and clumsy if it means creating half a dozen envelopes and perhaps having to readjust them every time you make some other change to your mix.

- Use two different compressor instances—one for the first part of the song and one for the second. Create a bypass envelope for each instance to ensure that it is engaged only when required. This solution can often prove to be the simplest and most elegant.

Parallel Compression

Parallel compression is a term that describes the process of splitting an audio signal in two, compressing both streams simultaneously but differently, and then joining the two streams together. Figure 6.16 illustrates a relatively simple example of parallel compression. In the example shown, the signal is passed through an equalizer before being compressed, but of course this does not have to be the case. The compressor used is one like ReaComp, which has its own built-in parallel compression capabilities.

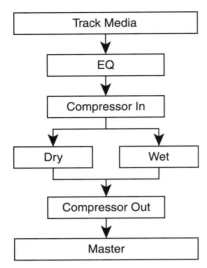

Figure 6.16   In this example of parallel compression, after passing through an equalizer the signal is passed to a compressor, where it is split into two streams. The stream labeled dry bypasses the compressor settings, while the wet stream carries the compressed signal. The two streams are then joined back together and passed either to the next effect in the chain or, as in this example, directly to the mixer.

The advantage of using parallel compression is that it enables you to create a blend of the original audio with its full dynamic range intact and the compressed audio with perhaps the extra punch, sustain, or whatever quality the compression is adding. Its more popular applications are with vocal and percussion submixes.

Tutorial 6.7: Using Parallel Compression

By way of demonstration, let's see how you might use parallel compression on a vocal submix.

1.   Open the sample project file Whiskey60 and save it as Whiskey67. We are going to use parallel compression with the vocal submix that was created earlier in Tutorial 3.4.

2.   Remove the compressor that you added to the vocal submix in Tutorial 3.4. Add a volume envelope to this submix and adjust its level so that the vocals sound about right in the mix. You will find that you will need to lower the volume when both people are singing.

3.   Add an instance of ReaComp to the FX bin. Use another compressor if you prefer, but be sure to choose one that allows you to specify a wet/dry mix for the compressor's output. Not all compressors permit this.

4.   Loop the section from about 3 min 20 sec to 4 min 16 sec. Solo the vocal submix.

5.   Start with the wet fader at +0.0 and the dry fader at −infinity.

6. We are going to use the compressor to create a very smooth and mellow vocal effect. Set a ratio of 6:1 and a threshold around −30 dB, so that the compressor will be engaged during the entire length of the vocal passages. To make the sound smoother, keep a short attack, set the release at about 500 ms, add 10 ms pre comp, a soft knee of about 20 dB, and fade the RMS period up to about 200 ms.

7. Now fade the wet output gain down to about −1.8 dB and bring the dry output fader up to about −5.4 dB. Compare the sound with the compressor alternately engaged and bypassed. Decide for yourself if in this case you have a preference for normal mode or classic mode. If you are able to save mixer snapshots, save a mixer snapshot.

8. Unsolo the submix, remove the loop, and continue to make the comparison. You should find, as in Tutorials 6.5 and 6.6, that the difference is more noticeable when you listen to the whole mix than when the item being compressed is soloed. This is because with the full mix playing, you are able to hear the change in its context.

9. Now swap the wet and dry gain settings, so that dry is around −1.6 dB and wet is around −5.3 dB. The compressed signal now sits behind the uncompressed signal. The difference may be subtle at first, but it is likely that you will prefer this mix.

10. Save the file.

More sophisticated forms of parallel compression are available using two compressors with different compression settings, rather than one compressor with a wet/dry mix. However, this technique usually requires you to create the two separate audio streams yourself. Some programs (notably REAPER) can handle this with channel splitting, but with most host programs, if you want to use this technique, you will need to either create extra tracks or use extra auxiliary busses.

We'll come back to this topic in Chapter 13, "The Chain Gang: Serial FX Processing," when we look at parallel effects chains.

Sidechain Compression

The principles governing sidechain compression are similar to those governing sidechain gating, which we encountered in Chapter 5. With sidechain compression, the level of the volume of the audio signal on one track or bus is used to control a compressor on another track or bus. This process is also known as *ducking*. A typical example of ducking would be to use the volume of a vocal track or vocal mix to push back any tendency in an instrument mix to jump out and distract from the vocals. In that particular example, the instrument mix would be the compressed track, and the vocal would be the auxiliary or sidechain track. The process can be summarized like this:

■ Sidechain compression requires the use of two distinct audio sources. Most commonly, these are two separate tracks. Some DAWs also allow the use of busses and submixes when sidechaining.

■ The compressor plug-in is inserted in the FX bin of the track (or bus) that is to be compressed—just as you have been doing up to now. This track is sometimes also referred to as the *main track*. You then need to define which track (or bus) contains the signal whose volume will control the compressor's behavior. This is often known as the *sidechain track*, but the terms *auxiliary* and *controlling* track or source are also sometimes used.

■ The threshold setting applies to the volume on the sidechain (auxiliary) track (in the example quoted a moment ago, this would be the vocal submix). The application of compression to the compressed track is triggered by the volume of the sidechain track rising above and falling below the threshold level.

■ The compression itself operates on the compressed (main) track. The values that you set for attack, release, and knee (for example) will between them determine how the compression is applied.

Not all DAWs (or all compressor software) support sidechain compression. Those that do each have their own method of implementation. For these reasons, it is not possible to include a step-by-step tutorial with this section. However, if your DAW supports sidechaining, you should be able to work through an example for yourself, aided no doubt by its documentation. For this example, you can use the file Whiskey67. Try using the vocal submix as an auxiliary (controlling) track to apply sidechain compression to the guitar submix. If you wish, save the file to the same name.

More often than not, when using sidechain compression you will want to be gentle. For example, if you find that you have to use compression settings that squash down the compressed signal all the time the controlling signal is present, then you probably have your basic levels wrong. Adjust your track volume faders or use volume envelopes to ensure that the relative levels are such that the compressor is engaged only as much and as little as is necessary.

Limiters

You've already encountered limiters—several times, in fact—earlier in this book, when you inserted the ReaJS utility limiter into the master track of your various projects as a precaution against clipping. At its simplest, you can think of a limiter as being like a compressor, but one with a very restricted range of controls and functions. In the case of the ReaJS limiter, it behaves as a hard knee compressor with a ratio set at 100% and just one control—threshold. Every time the audio signal tries to rise above the threshold level, it is ruthlessly squashed down.

Limiters vary in their degree of sophistication: As they become more sophisticated, they start displaying more of the controls that you should recognize from what you now know about compression and compressors.

Figure 6.17 shows one such an example. The attack, release, and knee controls can be used to soften the result of limiting. A limiter such as this might be placed last in the FX bin of a track or bus to tame any excessive peaks, perhaps produced as the result of applying other effects.

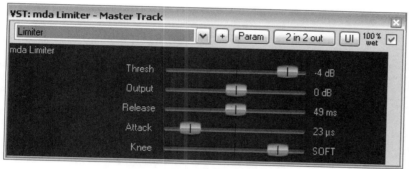

Figure 6.17   The MDA Limiter includes controls such as attack, release, and knee. These can be used to prevent limiting from producing too harsh or brittle an effect. For download information, see Table 1.2 in Chapter 1.

The other main use for limiters is in the track master. For now, we'll be content just to use the simple ReaJS Limiter, but when we examine mixing and master track effects in more detail (in Chapter 15, "Multiband Compressors, Mastering Limiters, and More"), we'll take a look at a slightly different application for limiting.

Multiband Compression

A multiband compressor combines many of the characteristics of an equalizer with many of the characteristics of a normal compressor. It can be used to compress different frequencies by different amounts, thus giving you more control over how you can shape the sound. It is more often used on a mix than on individual tracks, and for that reason we won't look at this item in detail until we get to Chapter 15. Nevertheless, you may find there are times when a multiband compressor can usefully be added to an individual track (such as perhaps a vocal or percussion track) to enable you to compress and boost one particular range of frequencies.

Tutorial 6.8: Using Multiband Compression

In this example, a multiband compressor is going to be used to shape the sound of a female vocal to make it sound more haunting and wispy. The plug-in used is GMulti from the GVST bundle (download details in Table 1.2 in Chapter 1). You can, however, use any multiband compressor of your choice.

1. Open the sample project file Whiskey67 and save it as Whiskey68. Loop the section from about 3 min 20 sec to about 4 min 16 sec. If you are able, save its current settings as a mixer snapshot. Play the song.

2. In the female vocal track, set the existing EQ and compressor plug-ins to bypass.

3. Insert a multiband compressor at the end of the FX bin for this track.

4. Make all bands except Band 2 inactive. If the bands do not have a toggle control for this (as is the case with GMulti, shown in Figure 6.18), the same result can be achieved by raising their threshold to 0.0 dB so that they are never engaged.

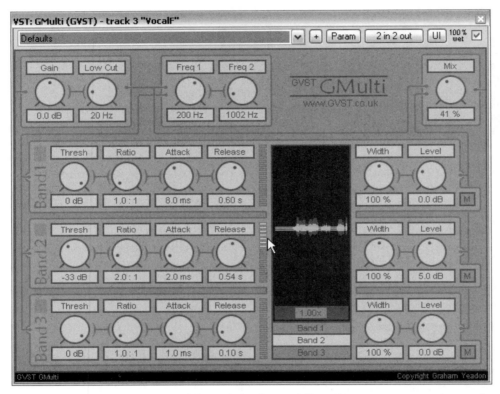

Figure 6.18 Using one band (Band 2) of a multiband compressor to shape the sound of a track.

5. If there is an input gain control (in Figure 6.18, this is top left), set it to 0.0 dB. Set the lower limit for Band 2 at 200 Hz and the upper limit at about 1,000 Hz. This is the vocal range that we are going to work on. If you are using GMulti, these controls are labeled Freq 1 and Freq 2.

6. Set the Band 2 threshold at a level where the compressor becomes steadily engaged. (See the mouse pointer in Figure 6.18.) This will probably be at about −33 dB. Use a ratio of about 2:1, a short attack, and a release of about half a second (500 ms). Add about 5 dB of gain to this band. (In Figure 6.18, this control is labeled Level.)

7.   Adjust the mix setting to about 40%, so that the dry and wet signals are processed in parallel.

8.   If this track is now too loud, lower the track volume fader, probably by about 3 dB. If your DAW allows, create another mixer snapshot.

9.   Save the file. Play the song. Compare the two mixer snapshots.

Checkpoint 3

The key to using a multiband compressor on an individual track is to get your targeted frequency range right. One technique that can help is to mute all bands other than the one that you are working with while you adjust the upper and lower frequency limits of that band until you get it right. You can then unmute the other bands while you make your other adjustments.

If you like, experiment with doing this with one or more of the vocal tracks in the file Lying60. Save the file to a new name, such as Lying62, before you start experimenting. This new file will not be needed for any of the remaining tutorials.

Upward Expanders

As its name implies, an expander does the opposite of a compressor: It raises rather than restricts the dynamic range of the audio source to which it is applied. Its most popular use is to help restore dynamics to material that has been previously over-compressed. In many cases the same plug-in can act as either a compressor or an expander. The secret is in the ratio. You have already seen how as you fade the ratio up above 1:1, you will increase the rate at which the dynamics are compressed. It therefore follows logically that if you fade the ratio *down* below 1:1, you will gradually increase the rate at which the dynamics are *expanded*.

Figure 6.19 illustrates this concept, using Cakewalk's Sonitus compressor. In the example shown on the left, the incoming signal is compressed at a ratio of 4:1, and to more or less compensate for this, 3.0 dB has been added to the output gain. In the example on the right, using a ratio of 0.5:1 results in upward expansion. For every decibel by which the incoming signal exceeds the threshold, the outgoing signal is raised by two. As a consequence, if we wish to compensate for the extra volume, the output gain fader will need to be lowered accordingly. In this case, after the expansion has been applied and the gain lowered, the loudest parts will be approximately as loud as they were before, but those parts that fall below the threshold will be quieter. Thus, the dynamic range has actually been expanded.

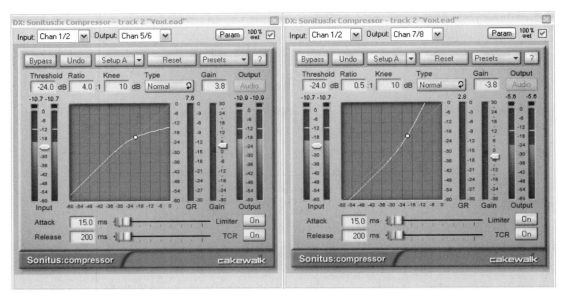

Figure 6.19 Cakewalk's Sonitus compressor gives a good visual representation of the contrast between downward compression and upward expansion.

Tutorial 6.9: Using an Upward Expander

In the example that follows, we can simulate the situation of working with material that was over-compressed when it was recorded. We will simply add a compressor in a track's FX bin to over-compress it and then follow it with an expander to compensate for this.

The example uses the MjCompressor from the Magnus range of plug-ins. Download details can be found in Table 1.2 in Chapter 1. You can, of course, use any compressor you wish, provided it allows you to set ratios lower than 1:1.

1.   Open the sample project file Foggy60 and save it as Foggy69. Loop the section from about 1 min 10 sec to about 2 min 9 sec. Solo the VoxLead track. Play the song.

2.   If there are any effects in this track's FX bin other than a noise gate, remove them.

3.   Insert a compressor plug-in after the noise gate.

4.   Set ratio at 2:1 with a threshold around −23 dB. Use a low attack (about 2 ms), a moderate release (about 300 ms), and ensure that auto make-up (if available) is not engaged. Add about 6 dB to output gain to restore the perceived volume of this track to around its former level. Unsolo the track. Compare the mix with this compressor alternately engaged and bypassed, and you should notice how the dynamics on the vocal have been squeezed. Now suppose that what you are hearing now is exactly how the track was recorded.

5. Add another instance of the same compressor after the first one. This time, set threshold again to −23 dB, but specify a ratio of about 0.65:1 so that it will function as an expander (see Figure 6.20). Use the same attack and release settings as before. Lower the output gain by about 7.5 dB. You may need to tweak the ratio and threshold settings a little, but you should soon find that by adding this second plug-in, you have pretty well restored to the track its original dynamics.

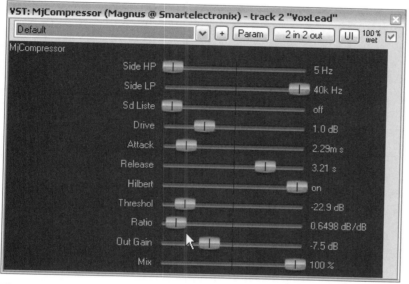

Figure 6.20 Using a compressor (MjCompressor) as an upward expander. Notice (near the position of the mouse cursor) a ratio below 1:1 is used, together with a reduction in output gain.

Bonus Compressor Plug-Ins (Overview)

The DVD supplied with this book includes an assortment of interesting, varied, and sometimes unusual compressor and expander plug-ins. They tend to be targeted at specific types of applications. Armed with what you now know about dynamics, you should explore these at your leisure. Don't be put off by their strange names or decidedly bland interface. Their quality ranges from good to excellent. Table 6.2 describes some of these.

Table 6.2 Summary of a Selection of JS Compressor Plug-Ins

Name	Description
LOSER/DDC	A digital drum compressor with a sidechaining capability.
LOSER/DVC2JS	A versatile digital compressor/limiter that includes the option for auto make-up.

(Continued)

Name	Description
LOSER/DVCJS	Another versatile digital compressor.
LOSER/SP1LimiterJS	A simple peak limiter.
LOSER/TransientKiller	A simple attack/release compressor with auto make-up gain.
LOSER/Transient Controller	A simple compressor designed to add sustain to transients.
LOSER/Transhape	Another simple compressor designed to add sustain to drums.
LOSER/UpwardExpander	A compressor/expander with sidechain capabilities.
SStillwell/1175	A fast attack compressor with program-dependent release.
SStillwell/autoexpand	A program-dependent expander whose controls include threshold, ratio, gain, and knee, as well as peak/RMS detection modes.
SStillwell/eventhorizon	A peak limiter with hard/soft clip knee control.
SStillwell/fairlychildish	A compressor limiter modeled on the Fairchild F670, especially suited to drums.
SStillwell/hugebooty	A compressor/bass enhancer.
SStillwell/louderizer	A compressor with only two controls—mix and drive. Makes an audio source louder.
SStillwell/majortom	An unusual and remarkable program-dependent compressor. This has no attack or release controls, but it calculates and sets these automatically in similar fashion to the legendary classic stealth DBX160. Incredibly versatile: Apply it gently to vocals, aggressively to drums, or to just about anything else in between.
SStillwell/mastertom	A variation of majortom more suited for use on the master track.
SStillwell/realoud	Even easier to use (with just one control) than the louderizer. Makes an audio source louder.

Project Files Log

If you have completed all of the examples and tutorials in this chapter, you should have created the following files:

Preparation: Foggy60, Lying60, Mud60, Whiskey60

Tutorial 6.1: Foggy61

Tutorial 6.2: Foggy62

Tutorial 6.3: Mud63

Tutorial 6.4: Foggy64

Checkpoint 1: Lying61

Tutorial 6.5: Mud65

Checkpoint 2: Whiskey65

Tutorial 6.6: Foggy66

Tutorial 6.7: Whiskey67

Tutorial 6.8: Whiskey68

Checkpoint 3: Lying62

Tutorial 6.9: Foggy69

Your complete project file log should now be as follows:

Alone00

AudioExperiment21

Foggy00, Foggy41, Foggy42, Foggy43, Foggy44, Foggy50, Foggy52, Foggy53, Foggy60, Foggy61, Foggy62, Foggy64, Foggy66, Foggy69

Lying00, Lying23, Lying43, Lying50, Lying51, Lying52, Lying54, Lying60, Lying61, Lying62

Mud00, Mud40, Mud41, Mud60, Mud63, Mud65

Whiskey00, Whiskey22, Whiskey30, Whiskey31, Whiskey32, Whiskey33, Whiskey60, Whiskey65, Whiskey67, Whiskey68

7 Playing with Time: Delay and Chorus

In Chapter 3 you were introduced to some very simple examples that used delay to fatten or add atmosphere to a sound. This chapter will teach you more about delay, what it is, and how to use it before going on to introduce a further time-based effect—chorus. Understanding delay and chorus will provide you with a solid foundation for understanding other related effects, such as flanging, phasing, and reverb.

Introduction

One question often asked by newcomers to audio processing is, "What is the difference between delay and reverb?" It's actually a very good question. Typically, it is answered with a technical explanation of the different ways in which these two types of effect are created. Although there's nothing wrong with this response, I suspect that quite often such an answer misses the point of the question. For that reason, I'm going to approach the subject from a different angle and say that by and large, whereas you can use delay to create an *effect*, with reverb you can go a step further and simulate an *environment*. When you appreciate this distinction, you will be less inclined to try to use the sledgehammer of reverb to achieve a reasonably simple effect that could more easily and more appropriately be created by using delay.

For example, reverb might be used to give the listener the impression that she is hearing a performance that was recorded live in perhaps a church, a basement nightclub, or a concert hall. Delay, on the other hand can be used to change certain qualities of a sound, perhaps to make it appear fuller, more haunting, or wider. Later, you may come to see that there can be gray areas that reflect both these concepts, but we'll save that discussion until Chapter 8, "The Fourth Dimension: Reverb," when we look at reverb.

This chapter has been divided into the following sections:

- Basic delay concepts

- Delay parameters and controls

- Simple delay: single-tap

- Spatial delay: multi-tap

- Slapback delay

- Delay effects chains

- Chorus

Preparation

At different times in this chapter, you will be working with the sample projects *Alone Again, Foggy Desperation, Mud Sliding,* and *Now Is the Time for Whiskey*. It should take you only a few minutes to prepare the necessary sample files.

Preparation: Preparing the Project Files

In each case, the only preparation required will be to open the specified version of each project and save it to the new name required for these tutorials.

1. Open the file Alone00 that you created earlier and immediately save it as Alone70.

2. Open the file Foggy64 that you created earlier and immediately save it as Foggy70.

3. Open the file Mud65 that you created earlier and immediately save it as Mud70.

4. Open the file Whiskey67 that you created earlier and immediately save it as Whiskey70.

Basic Delay Concepts

In Chapter 3 you saw that as its name implies, delay works by repeating a sound somewhat later in time than the original. It is most often, but not exclusively, applied to vocals and guitar tracks. It usually takes one of three forms:

- Simple echo delay, either single- or multi-tap: The delay effect merges in with the original sound.

- Ping-pong delay: As the name implies, the delay effect appears to bounce around from side to side.

- Slapback delay: The delay is heard as a distinctly separate series of notes.

We'll come to examples of each of these shortly, but first it pays to understand something about how the delay is produced.

Before the digital era, delay effects were achieved using analog magnetic tape. The technique involved the use of tape loops mounted on reel-to-reel recorders. The echo-like effect was shaped by a combination of adjusting the length of the loop and the position of the read and write heads on the tape deck. The process was rather imprecise, but paradoxically these imperfections brought with them one distinct strength: They helped ensure a smooth and natural-sounding echo.

The digital delay software that you use with your DAW offers you much greater precision and control over the decay time and the repeat spacing (tap) but is in some ways too perfect. For example, unlike tape delay, digital delay will produce a perfect frequency response. This means you do need to be careful how you use it to prevent your delay from falling out of time with the tune. This is especially the case with musical instruments such as a guitar or a mandolin.

You have a number of weapons in your armory to help resolve this. For example:

- Some delay software provides you with an option of using tape mode or digital mode. Selecting the former causes a series of subtle variations (or imperfections) in the delay, which may help produce a more natural-sounding effect. You may also have the option of analog mode. This attempts to simulate the way in which analog delay machines, such as the Boss DM-2, generated delay. This is one of those topics that can be debated forever, but in short, the conventional wisdom is that analog delay may be less flexible than digital delay, but it is likely to produce a warmer sound.

- Many of the best DAW plug-ins provide you with some method of telling them that when you import material, you want them to work out a song's time signature and tempo automatically for you, usually based on a time selection. Often they will then allow you to specify delay periods as fractions of a note rather than as a set number of milliseconds if you wish. This should help prevent the problem of the delayed signal getting out of sync with the tune.

- The sound of natural echoes loses its clarity with each repetition. Look for and use controls in the delay program that will let you use high-cut or low-pass filters, which can help simulate this and make the delay sound more natural.

Delay Parameters and Controls

With so many products to choose from, you will find considerable variation in the parameters that you are likely to find in delay software. The following are generalized summaries; do not expect every plug-in to have exactly the same or all of these features. Of course, core features, such as length and feedback, will always be there—you'd be hard-pressed to produce delay without them. Which of the other controls matters likely depends on what you are trying to do at the time.

Single-tap delay allows you to create one stream of regular delay at the period specified. For example, if you specify a delay of 50 ms, a copy of the exact same audio stream will be repeated, which will be played exactly 50 ms behind the original. Multi-tap delays let you create multiple streams of delayed audio. Look for the controls listed in Table 7.1. For a multi-tap system, separate length, feedback, filter, volume, stereo width, pan, volume, and possibly wet/dry mix controls should be available for each tap (delay instance).

Table 7.1 Summary of Commonly Used Delay Parameters

Name	Description
Input gain	When present, this allows the strength of the dry signal to be adjusted *before* the delay is added.
Mode	Where present, this allows you to choose between tape, digital, and perhaps analog.
Length (time)	Specifies the delay length, usually in milliseconds.
Length (notes)	Specifies the delay length as a fraction of each note.
Feedback	Usually expressed as a percentage; specifies the amount of the delayed signal that will be fed back into itself. See the upcoming "Feedback: Handle with Care" note.
Low-pass filter	This allows only frequencies below that specified to be delayed.
High-cut filter	As an alternative to a low-pass filter, this determines that delay is cut from frequencies above that specified.
High-pass filter	This allows only frequencies above that specified to be delayed.
Low-cut filter	As an alternative to a high-pass filter, this determines that delay is cut from frequencies below that specified.
Stereo width	When applied to a stereo track, bus, or submix, this determines the width of spread of the delayed signal.
Volume	This determines the strength of the delayed signal.
Pan	This enables the delayed signal to be panned to the left or right of the original.
Wet/dry mix	This determines the relative amounts of the dry (original) and wet (delayed) signal that are mixed together.
Level or output	This determines the level of the output signal.
Unlink/link	This allows/prevents the various controls to be set differently for left and right channels.

Because delay can be and is used for so many creative purposes, you are also likely to find that individual items of delay software may well include additional controls not listed in Table 7.1. For examples of this, you only need to browse through some of the items listed in the "Bonus Delay and Chorus Plug-Ins (Overview)" section near the end of this chapter.

Feedback: Handle with Care   Feedback controls need to be handled with extreme care. Too high a level of feedback will create that dreadful high-pitched whistling tone that can damage your equipment, not least of which are your ears.

If your DAW has an option to automatically mute output when output exceeds a specified level (such as +10 dB), you are strongly advised to engage this option when working with feedback.

Single-Tap Delay

The first few examples of using delay will be relatively modest in their scope and simple in their implementation. Don't underestimate their value because of this. For many styles of music, these represent examples of the kind of situation in which you are most likely to want to use delay. One common application is to use delay to fatten or thicken a sound. This is sometimes known as *doubling delay* or *doubling echo*.

Tutorial 7.1: Simple Echo Delay

This first tutorial will work through two examples of how delay can be added to a vocal, each time to create a different effect. It will use Kjaerhus Classic Delay (see Figure 7.1) for the first example and ReaDelay (see Figure 7.2) for the second example. You can, of course, use any other delay plug-ins that you prefer, provided they include all of the necessary controls.

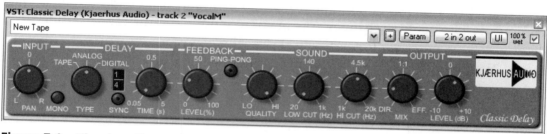

Figure 7.1   Kjaerhus Classic Delay is single-tap only, but it has some impressive features, including tape/analog/digital selection mode.

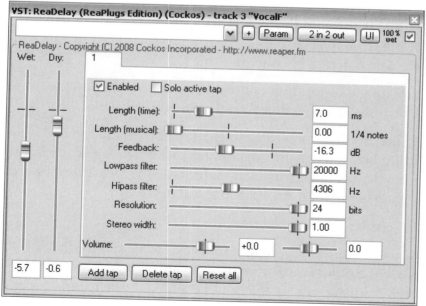

Figure 7.2   ReaDelay is a solid if uninspiring no-nonsense delay plug-in. It can be used as either single-tap or multi-tap.

1. Open the file Whiskey70 that you created earlier and immediately save it as Whiskey71.

2. Loop the section from about 1 min 36 sec to about 2 min 53 sec.

3. Solo the male vocal track (VoxM). This track should already include an EQ plug-in that is still there from Tutorial 3.1.

4. To add more body and depth to this vocal, insert Kjaerhus Classic Delay into this track's FX bin. Place it after the EQ that should still be there from Tutorial 3.1.

5. Leave the first (input pan) at its default setting in the center. Select the mono option. Set the delay mode to digital for now. Make sure the sync option is *not* selected. This would be used to set the delay period as a fraction of a note. Instead, set the time all the way down to 5 ms (.05). At such a low level, the delayed signal, for all practical purposes, will be merged with the dry signal. Set the feedback (30%) and quality (high) controls approximately as shown in Figure 7.1. The quality setting works in conjunction with the mode setting to determine how perfectly (or otherwise) the echo generator emulates the chosen mode. Now adjust the delay time within the range of 5 ms to 10 ms until you are happiest with the sound.

6. Set a high-cut filter at about 4,500 Hz and the mix and output levels as shown in Figure 7.1.

7. Try each of the three delay type settings. Even with such a conservative amount of delay as this, you may notice that the digital setting seems a little harsher than the others. Set it at analog.

8. Now unsolo the male vocal and solo the female vocal. If there is still a delay plug-in left in the FX bin from the tutorials in Chapter 3, set that to bypass. Add an instance of ReaDelay in the FX bin after this.

9. Time to get creative. Fade the wet output control (left) up to 0 dB and the dry control all the way down. Now you will hear only the delayed signal.

10. Adjust the high-pass filter so that you are adding delay only to the top end, probably at about 4,000 Hz. This might run counter to what you already know about the top end normally trailing away from natural delay. However, we are aiming to create an effect here, not necessarily natural delay.

11. Fade the wet and dry settings up to the levels shown in Figure 7.2.

12. Set a delay time period of about 12 ms, length (musical) to 0, and feedback at about −16 dB. Leave the other controls at their default levels. You should now hear only the high-frequency delay that will be added to the female vocal to give it a slightly mystical effect.

13. Unsolo the track. Play the loop with the delay plug-ins alternately engaged and bypassed. You may need to adjust the dry and wet output faders to obtain a mix that sounds right to you. The difference is subtle but definite. The vocals should be just that little bit fuller with the delay engaged.

14. If you like, slightly adjust the settings for the compressor on the vocal mix to restore just a little more of the natural dynamics to the vocals. This will involve some combination of lowering ratio, raising threshold, setting pre comp to 0, lowering RMS size, introducing a low-pass filter at about 4,500 Hz, and possibly lowering the wet and dry output faders a little.

15. Save the file.

Ping-Pong Delay

Ping-pong delay is achieved by taking two inputs (or a single input split into two channels) and using each to drive a separate delay line. Feedback from each is directed not back into itself (as happens with normal delay), but to the other one. By then panning each of these hard left and hard right, respectively, you are able to create a bouncing effect. Figure 7.3 illustrates this concept.

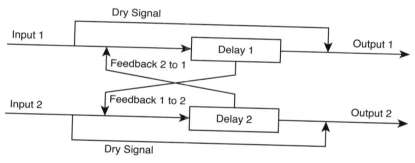

Figure 7.3 Ping-Pong delay is created using two separate channels, sending the feedback of each of these channels to the other, and then panning the two channels opposite each other.

Not all delay software is capable of delivering ping-pong delay. Those that do tend to use their own individual interface and controls. Because of this, there isn't a lot to be said here by way of further explanation, other than to say that you should familiarize yourself with the features of whichever product you are using.

Tutorial 7.2: Ping-Pong Delay

This tutorial demonstrates the use of ping-pong delay, in this case on a shakuhachi. Like the other exercises, it is presented purely for learning purposes, not as a model for how to treat a particular instrument.

1. Open the file Whiskey71 that you created earlier and immediately save it as Whiskey72.

2. Loop the section from about 2 min 52 sec to about 3 min 23 sec.

3. Solo the shakuhachi track. This track may already include a delay plug-in that is still there from Tutorial 3.3. Set this to bypass. Play the song. Add the Kjaerhus Classic Delay (or equivalent) to the track's FX bin. Click on the ping-pong button to engage it. (It will show in red.)

4. Pan the input full left and set it to mono (see Figure 7.4). Select tape mode. Engage the sync option. (Like the mono option, this should now show in red.) You should now find that you cannot adjust the time rotary control directly. Instead, you should select the fraction of a note to which you want the delay synchronized.

Figure 7.4 Kjaerhus Classic Delay set to create ping-pong delay. Settings such as feedback, low cut, high cut, and mix will be applied independently to both channels.

5. Observe the two small boxes above the sync button. These contain numbers that represent the song's time signature (expressed in beats and bars). Click and drag the mouse up or down over either button to change its value. Set this to 1 over 4.

6. Because the signal is not being fed back to itself, you can be a little more aggressive with the feedback setting. Try about 60%.

7. Set the quality, low cut, and high cut levels as shown in Figure 7.4. Set the mix a little higher than before, at about 1:1. Adjust the output level if necessary.

8. Add a mix automation envelope for the delay plug-in, so that it is completely dry during all of the song except for this break, for which the mix level should be 1:1.

9. Save the file.

10. Now experiment with different pan settings to see how differently the sound bounces around. You can also create some interesting effects by choosing different sync settings.

Multi-Tap Spatial Delay

One great feature of multi-tap delay is that it really allows you to play tricks with time and space. By creating two separate delay streams and panning them differently, you can really add strength to a vocal or instrument and body to an otherwise possibly thin-sounding mix.

Tutorial 7.3: Using Multi-Tap Delay

In this case, multi-tap delay will be used on two tracks. One will be to make a lead vocal more powerful and give it more authority. The other will be to make a backing vocal more distant and obscured. The tutorial suggests that you use ReaDelay, but you may of course use any other delay plug-in with equivalent features, including a multi-tap capability. In both cases, we will also use a handy little tool called a *goniometer* to help you to understand what's going on.

Figure 7.5 shows a goniometer applied to a track before and after multi-tap delay is added. It shows in both cases the amount of stereo present in the two-channel signal. The picture really speaks for itself. The addition of delay makes the sound more powerful and more prominent.

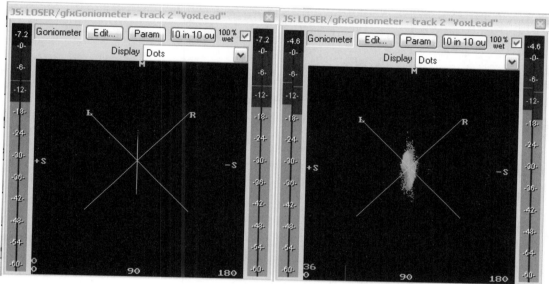

Figure 7.5   A goniometer is used here to show a visual representation of how a sound (in this case, a lead vocal track) is spread across a mix before (left) and after (right) multi-tap delay is added.

1.   Open the file Foggy70 that you created earlier and immediately save it as Foggy73.

2.   Loop the section from about 2 min 28 sec to about 2 min 56 sec.

3.   Solo the VoxLead track. This track may already include a noise gate, EQ, and a compressor as a result of completing various earlier tutorials. Add an instance of ReaDelay at the end of the FX chain.

4.   Purely for reference purposes, insert an instance of ReaJS into this FX bin, immediately after ReaDelay. Load the JS LOSER plug-in gfxGoniometer.

5.   Play the song. Set length (musical) to 0 and length (time) to about 7 ms. Fade the feedback up to about −17 dB, and you may notice that at this level it adds a certain edginess to the vocal. Fade it down again until the feedback blends nicely

with the original signal (probably about −40 dB). Use a low-pass filter of about 4,500 Hz to take the delay off the higher frequencies. Leave the volume at 0.0.

6.   Adjust the wet and dry output faders. Try a dry setting of about −0.5 dB and a wet setting of about −7.5 dB. When you are happy with the wet/dry balance, set delay pan to −0.7 (70% left). The pan fader is the unlabeled item to the immediate right of the volume fader. With some DAWs, you may need to change the track's interleave setting for the panning to be made effective.

7.   Click on the add tap button. This will create a second delay tap with its own page of settings. ReaDelay allows you to create as many of these extra taps (pages) as you wish. By default, all parameters will inherit the values that you specified when you defined your settings for the previous tap. (In this case, this was the original tap; see Steps 5 and 6.)

8.   Lower the delay time to about 3.5 ms and change the pan setting to +0.7 (70% right). Save the file.

9.   Unsolo the track and continue to play the song. As you alternately engage and bypass the delay plug-in, notice the difference in how the vocal sounds and observe the different patterns displayed in the goniometer (refer to Figure 7.5).

10.   There's one other matter you may need to address here. Spreading our lead vocal farther across the breadth of the mix may result in the listener's brain interpreting it as coming from farther away in the distance. I'll have more to say about this when we look at chorus effects. Meanwhile, if you perceive this as a problem, you can add some EQ to the lead vocal immediately after the delay and use this to make the vocal appear more present. You will probably find that a modest gain of about 1.0 dB to 1.5 dB at around 4,000 Hz with a fairly wide bandwidth (about 2 octaves) will be all it takes to fix this.

11.   Try moving the compressor on this track to immediately *after* the delay plug-in. By applying the delay before the signal is compressed, you will help prevent the delay effect from sounding too prominent. If you have completed all of the tutorials that use this project up to this point, the contents of your FX bin for this track should now be similar to that shown in Figure 7.6.

12.   Now select and solo the VoxHarmony track. The song is called *Foggy Desperation*, so let's experiment with making the harmony vocal sound foggy! Insert ReaDelay and the JS gfxGoniometer into this track's FX bin. This time, however, place them before the compressor. Compressing the delayed sound will help to obscure it, which in this case is what we want to do.

13.   For the sake of this example, be more aggressive with your use of delay on this track. In particular, specify a longer period (about 120 ms on one tap, 100 ms on the other) and push the feedback up as high as −20 dB or so. Pull the low-pass

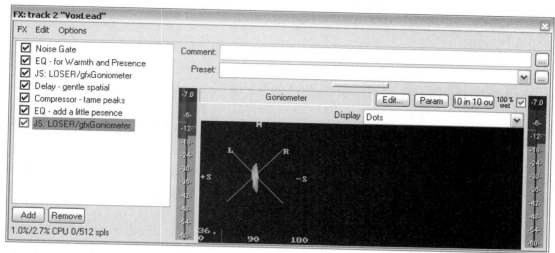

Figure 7.6   By now you should have an effects chain on your lead vocal similar to this. The interface shown is REAPER, but of course you could use any other DAW of your choice. This is also a good example of when renaming individual FX instances can be useful.

filter back below 4,000 Hz. Pan the two taps 90% left and right, respectively. Figure 7.7 shows possible settings for one of the two delay taps.

14.   Unsolo the track, unloop, and play the song. If the delay on the harmony vocal seems rather overdone to you, lower its wet output fader to about −11.0 dB. If it sounds right, also lower the track volume fader a little and increase the track volume fader on the lead vocal. The aim here is to get a balance where the delay helps to make the vocal harmony sound distant and muffled.

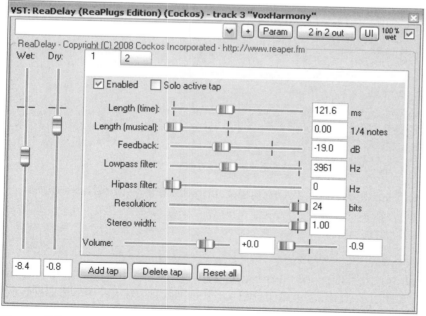

Figure 7.7   An example of delay settings for one of the delay taps used to help make a track sound more obscured in a mix.

15.   Save the file. Compare how it now sounds with global effects bypass engaged and disengaged.

One of the main reasons for setting up this tutorial in the way that we have is to demonstrate two contrasting examples of how effects can be used, in this case on vocals. A number of effects have been added to the lead vocal, all of them quite subtle. The effects added to the backing vocal, on the other hand, have been applied in a manner that is anything but subtle.

Be prepared to experiment and be adventurous when you are learning about delay, but be cautious when applying it. The settings in Figure 7.8, for example, use Cakewalk's Sonitus Delay plug-in to show an interesting delay effect that can be applied to an acoustic guitar to create a doubling sound. The delay is synced to the beat, with one tap added every fourth quarter (whole note) and the other every eighth quarter (second note).

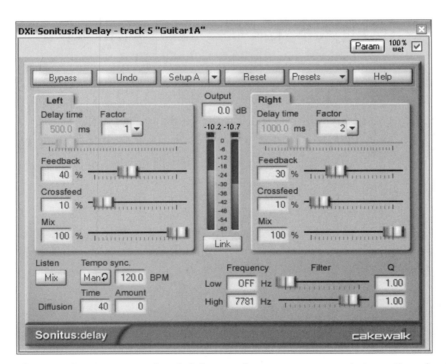

Figure 7.8   An example of delay settings to create an interesting doubling sound on a guitar.

Slapback Delay

The most distinguishing characteristics of slapback delay are its longer delay time (preferably synchronized to the beat), its low level of feedback (to keep the delayed sound distinct), and the relative prominence given to the delayed signal in the mix. Figure 7.9 shows an example.

Figure 7.9 An example of delay settings suitable for creating slapback delay.

Playing tricks with sound also has the potential to play tricks, sometimes quite power-fully, on human emotions. In this case we can use it in our *Mud Sliding* tune to create in the background a feeling of almost anxiety that might seem to suit the tune.

Tutorial 7.4: Using Slapback Delay

In this example, Kjaerhus Classic Delay is used, but any other equivalent delay plug-in would be equally suitable.

1. Open the file Mud70 that you created earlier and immediately save it as Mud74.

2. Add an instance of Kjaerhus Classic Delay at the start of the harmonica track's FX bin. Play the song.

3. Make sure you turn on the sync option in the delay plug-in. Experiment with applying slap delay alternately at 1/8 note, 1/4 note, and 1/2 note. Refer to Figure 7.9 for guidance on other suitable settings.

4. When you're finished, save the file.

Using a Delay Effects Chain

As you become more experienced in the use of delay, you might well wish to experiment with creating and using your own delay effects chains. The idea is that you might wish to apply other effects (for example, compression and/or EQ) only to the delayed signal, but not to the undelayed signal. Alternately, you might wish to create your delayed signal independently of any other effects that you have placed on the track. Either of these scenarios might enable you to create some interesting psycho-acoustic effects. This can be achieved using a technique known as *parallel effects processing*.

Depending on your DAW's feature set, there are a number of ways that you can achieve this. Probably the smartest is to split the track's audio signal into two or more stereo pairs, apply the effects to one pair but not the other, and then mix the different pairs back together again. Unfortunately, very few DAWs support this feature directly. (REAPER is one that does.) With most, however, you can achieve a similar if less ele-gant outcome using sends and busses.

Almost any DAW will also let you use another method. Simply duplicate the track. Add the delay and other effects to one of these two tracks but not the other and then adjust the relative volume of the two tracks until you get the balance you want. It might not be a very elegant solution, and it doesn't make the most efficient use of your computer's resources, but it works. You'll find an example of this outlined in the parallel FX Checkpoint near the end of this chapter.

I've introduced the idea of parallel effects chains here primarily to plant the seed in your mind. Don't worry about it too much right now. This is a topic that we will return to in Chapter 14, "Chaining the Chain Gangs: Parallel FX Processing"—but we've got a fair bit more ground to cover before we do!

Chorus

Chorus is an effect that really belongs in the same group as the modulating effects that are the subject of Chapter 9, "Time Modulation, Pitch Shifting, and More"—flangers, phasers, and so on. The main reason for bringing it forward into this chapter is to help you understand the differences between chorus and the subject of the next chapter, which is reverb.

The concept behind the chorus effect is actually quite simple. Think about what happens when two instruments (for example, two acoustic guitars) are played together in harmony. No matter how proficient the musicians, some variations in pitch, timing, and synchronization will inevitably occur. This is the effect that, at its simplest, chorus aims to imitate. Beyond this, the parameters that control the chorus effect can, if you wish, also be set to produce sounds and effects that would never occur naturally.

Chorus works primarily by creating an audio stream with variable amounts of delay and then mixing that back with the original stream to produce variable changes in pitch. Reducing the delay time will raise the pitch, and increasing the delay time will lower it. Additional factors (such as changing the shape of the waveform) can also be used to offer you more options to help you determine the shape of the delayed waveform; some chorus software offers more such options than others.

Figure 7.10 illustrates these concepts. It will make more sense if you refer to it in the context of the various chorus parameter controls. Some of these controls are more

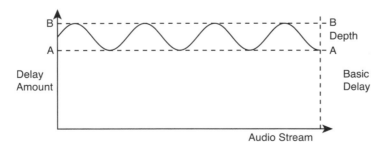

Figure 7.10 This graph illustrates how variable delay is used to create a chorus effect. This example uses an ordinary sine wave.

fundamental than others. For example, without delay and depth controls, it would not be possible to create any chorus effect. A shape control, on the other hand, is not essential but will give you more options.

If you are using a chorus plug-in with features additional to these, you should consult its documentation.

Table 7.2 Summary of Commonly Used Chorus Parameters

Name	Description
Input gain	Adjusts the strength (volume) of the incoming signal.
Delay amount	The basic amount of delay that is fed back into the audio stream. In Figure 7.10, this is represented by the line AA.
Depth or width	This determines how much variation is applied to the delay. In Figure 7.10, this is represented by the difference between the two lines AA and BB. Thus, as the audio stream is played back, the amount of delay applied will vary continuously between that shown between the horizontal axis and AA and that shown between the horizontal axis and BB.
Rate or speed	This determines how quickly (or slowly) the waveform is repeated and hence the speed at which the modulation occurs. This is one of the factors that helps create the pitch modulation.
Shape or LFO	This determines how the sound of the delay is shaped. The steeper the changes in the waveform, the more sudden and stepped the pitch changes will be. At the waveform's peak, the pitch will be at its lowest. At the waveform's trough, the pitch will be at its highest. Figure 7.11 shows four commonly used LFO (low-frequency oscillator) shapes.
Feedback	Where present, this works in a similar fashion to the feedback control on delay plug-ins. It allows a portion of the chorused signal to be fed back to itself. Handle with care!
Dry/wet or mix	This control (or pair of controls) is used to determine the relative amounts of the dry (unprocessed) and wet (chorused) signals that will be mixed together.
Output gain	This is used to increase or decrease the strength of the outgoing signal.
Number of voices	Some chorus software allows you to create as many voices (separate instances of chorus) as you like, each with its own separate parameter settings. Others permit a finite maximum, such as four or six. Most are single-voice only.

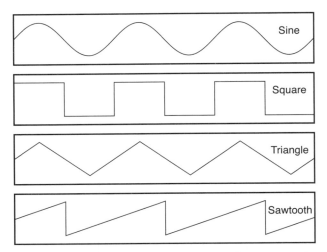

Figure 7.11   Four widely used LFO shapes are the sine, square, triangle, and sawtooth. You might also encounter any of several variations of these four main types.

Stereo Chorus   Some plug-ins can be used to create a stereo chorus effect. This effect is most commonly achieved by creating a second delay stream with the same settings as the first and running this second stream one quarter of a wavelength later than the original. You can then use some form of panning control to determine how far left and right the two streams are panned apart.

Chorus is most commonly used on guitars. If you're experimenting with chorus on a vocal, be very cautious and proceed with care, unless your aim is to create a "munchkin" effect. Remember that as with spatial delay, the wider a sound is spread across the mix (which is what stereo chorus will do), the harder it is for the listener to pinpoint an exact location as its source. This can result in the psycho-acoustic effect of seeming to push the part farther back in the mix.

Don't be intimidated by the term *psycho-acoustics,* by the way. The term simply refers to the fact that the sound messages sent from our ears to our brains will be processed and interpreted according to our previous experiences, established over years.

Tutorial 7.5: Using Chorus

This example will use the Blue Cat Audio Stereo Chorus plug-in (see Figure 7.12). Download details can be found in Table 1.2 in Chapter 1. You can, of course, substitute your own chorus effect if you wish.

1.   Open the file Foggy73 that you created earlier and immediately save it as Foggy75.

2.   Select and solo the first of the two acoustic guitar tracks. Create a loop from about 0 min 45 sec to about 2 min 10 sec.

Figure 7.12   Blue Cat Stereo Chorus—a single chorus plug-in with LFO shape control.

3.   Add the Blue Cat Stereo Chorus plug-in (or equivalent) to this track's FX bin. Fade the delay, depth, rate, and stereo controls all the way down. For now, set both dry and wet output controls to 100%. Select the sine LFO shape. Leave the input gain at +0.0 dB.

4.   Play the song. Fade the delay up to a fairly conservative setting of about 15 ms. Fading depth up to about 35% and rate to about 0.30 should produce a fairly clean chorus effect. The more you raise the depth fader above this, the more the sound will become artificial and twangy (which in some circumstances might be what you want). Increasing the rate too much will cause the original guitar signal to be virtually lost altogether. Bring these two faders back to 35% and 0.30, respectively. Compare how this sounds alternately with the sine and triangle LFO shapes selected. Restore it to sine when you are ready.

5.   Now raise the stereo fader until you are happy with the stereo spread, perhaps around 30%. You will notice this more if you test your settings while wearing headphones.

6.   Lower the dry fader to about 80% and the wet fader to about 40%.

7.   Unsolo the track and adjust this track's volume fader if you feel you need to.

8.   Copy this plug-in to the FX bin on the second acoustic guitar track. This should give you a stereo chorus on this track with identical settings. Increase the stereo setting to 50% and listen!

9.   Save the file. As always, compare how the song sounds with global FX bypass on and off.x

Checkpoint 1

Open the file Alone70 that you created at the beginning of this chapter and save it as Alone76.

Pan the rhythm about 25% left and the lead about 25% right.

Experiment with a little chorus on the rhythm guitar and some delay on the lead. Do not be overly ambitious. Your main goals are to add a little atmosphere and to bind the mix together. Treat this exercise as an opportunity to consolidate the basic skills that you have learned in this chapter.

Adjust the output volume faders of both tracks until you are satisfied with the mix. Save the file.

Bonus Delay and Chorus Plug-Ins (Overview)

The DVD supplied with this book includes about a dozen or so interesting and varied delay and delay-related plug-ins. Given what you now know about delay, you should be able to explore these at your leisure. As before, don't be put off by their strange names or decidedly bland interface. Their quality ranges from good to excellent.

Because delay is an area that offers so much scope for creativity, this is one particular area where it really could prove worth your while to investigate these plug-ins for yourself. They are all easy to use, and once you try out the effects they create, they are easy to understand. Figure 7.13 shows the interface for three of these plug-ins; Table 7.3 describes these as well as several others.

Checkpoint 2

If you really want to push the boundaries and be creative, try using two or even more of these plug-ins in serial (that is, one after the other) or as a chain in parallel with a dry signal. Chapter 14 will cover parallel effects processing in detail, but meanwhile, here's an example you can try if you like.

You can experiment with the project file Whiskey70. Open it, save it as Whiskey77, and select the female vocal track.

Duplicate this track and remove any existing effects from the duplicate. Add your delay plug-ins to the second of these two tracks but not to the original. Adjust the various settings to suit. It can also be worth your while to use an EQ plug-in between the two delay plug-ins to roll off some of the top end.

Finally, adjust the panning and set the relative volumes of the two tracks so that the delay is subtly mixed back in behind the original. Figure 7.14 shows an example of how you might do this.

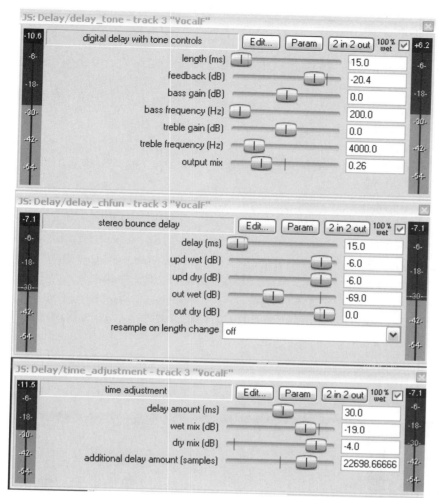

Figure 7.13   Shown here are the interfaces for the JS delay tone, stereo bounce delay, and time adjustment delay plug-ins.

Table 7.3 Summary of JS Delay and Chorus Plug-Ins

Name	Description
LOSER/TimeDelayer	A simple stereo delay plug-in that can be used to add different delays to left and right channels.
Delay/delay	A simple no-frills delay plug-in with limited functionality.
Delay/delay_chfun	A simple stereo bounce delay plug-in.
Delay/delay_chorus	A very easy to use delay plug-in with chorus added.
Delay/delay_lowres	A delay plug-in with resolution loss.
Delay/delay_sustain	A delay plug-in with attack and release controls added to allow sustain.

(Continued)

Name	Description
Delay/delay_tone	A delay plug-in that includes bass and treble frequency and gain controls.
Delay/delay_varlen	A variable-length delay plug-in.
Delay/fft_delay	An FFT delay plug-in with eight bands of delay and feedback controls.
Delay/scratchy	An unusual delay plug-in that can be used to create a scratchy effect.
Delay/time_adjustment	An interesting delay plug-in with additional time manipulation controls—for example, to allow pre-delay.
Guitar/chorus	A chorus plug-in specifically designed for use with guitar.
SStillwell/chorus	A clever but easy to use chorus plug-in that includes all standard chorus controls plus a pitch fudge factor.
SStillwell/chorus_stereo	Similar to the SStillwell/chorus but with channel offset and beat sync controls added for use with stereo tracks, busses, or submixes.

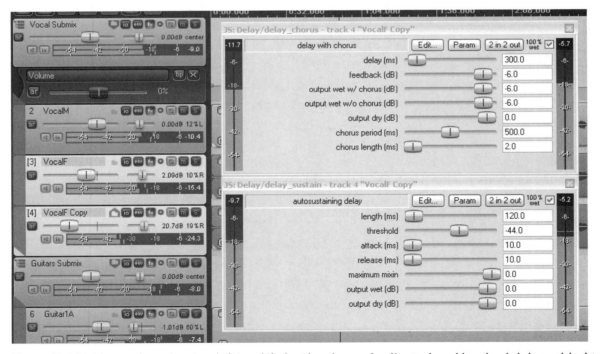

Figure 7.14 Shown here is a track (VocalF) that has been duplicated and has had delay added to the duplicate track. This allows the delay to be processed independently of any effects that might exist on the original track. This example shows the REAPER interface, but using ReaJS you could achieve this outcome with any DAW.

Project Files Log

If you have completed all of the examples and tutorials in this chapter, you should have created the following files:

Preparation: Foggy70, Mud70, Whiskey70

Tutorial 7.1: Whiskey71

Tutorial 7.2: Whiskey72

Tutorial 7.3: Foggy73

Tutorial 7.4: Mud74

Tutorial 7.5: Foggy75

Checkpoint 1: Alone76

Checkpoint 2: Whiskey77

Your complete project file log should now be as follows:

Alone00, Alone 70, Alone76

AudioExperiment21

Foggy00, Foggy41, Foggy42, Foggy43, Foggy44, Foggy50, Foggy52, Foggy53, Foggy60, Foggy61, Foggy62, Foggy64, Foggy66, Foggy69, Foggy70, Foggy73, Foggy75

Lying00, Lying23, Lying43, Lying50, Lying51, Lying52, Lying54, Lying60, Lying61, Lying62

Mud00, Mud40, Mud41, Mud60, Mud63, Mud65, Mud70, Mud74

Whiskey00, Whiskey22, Whiskey30, Whiskey31, Whiskey32, Whiskey33, Whiskey60, Whiskey65, Whiskey67, Whiskey68, Whiskey70, Whiskey71, Whiskey72, Whiskey77

8 The Fourth Dimension: Reverb

In Chapter 7 we examined delay and found that its usefulness comes from the important role that time plays in influencing how the human brain perceives sound. In this chapter we'll go a step further and look at reverb. Before considering what reverb is, however, it's worth taking a moment to understand what it isn't.

Reverb is *not* a magic silver bullet that can take a mundane recording or mix and transform it into magnificence. That doesn't mean it is not one of the most significant tools in your audio kit. It is. But it can't be used to work miracles. Be wary of anyone who asks, "Can't we cover that up with a little reverb?"

Delay is in essence a fairly simple concept. Reverb is a complex one. Reverb is concerned not just with time, but also with the interaction of time and space within any given environment. Its behavior and impact are more intricate than simple delay, largely because it is iterative. This isn't necessarily an easy concept to get your head around, but you will. *Reverb impacts not only the material to which it is being applied, but also itself.*

Introduction

Before you can confidently set about applying reverb, you will need to understand what it is. Even then, this chapter can't take you much further than the first few steps in applying that knowledge and understanding. There is so much about reverb that you can only learn by practice, experimentation, and application. But don't worry—by the time you reach the end of this chapter, you'll be heading in the right direction.

Reverb is a big topic. The approach taken here will be to start with a general overview, which will help you understand the core concepts, then to zoom in on more detailed applications before finally pulling back and dissecting the bigger picture in more detail. This chapter has been divided into the following main sections:

- Key reverb concepts
- Creating a reverb environment
- Core reverb parameters
- Types of synthetic reverb

- Creating reverb effects
- Special reverb effects
- Convolution reverb
- Reverb effects chains

Preparation

At different times in this chapter, you will be working with the sample projects *Foggy Desperation, Lying Back, Mud Sliding,* and *Whiskey.* It should take you only a few minutes to prepare the necessary sample files.

Preparation: Preparing the Project Files

In each case, the only preparation required will be to open the latest version of each project and save it to the new name required for these tutorials.

1. Open the file Alone76 that you created earlier and save it as Alone80.

2. Open the file Foggy75 that you created earlier and immediately save it as Foggy80.

3. Open the file Mud74 that you created earlier and immediately save it as Mud80.

4. Open the file Whiskey72 that you created earlier and immediately save it as Whiskey80.

5. Open the file Lying60 that you created earlier and immediately save it as Lying80.

Key Reverb Concepts

Reverb (reverberation) is something you experience every day of your life—in fact, every time you hear a sound. It is a natural phenomenon, and although you may not consciously be aware of this, it is an area in which you already possess a stunning amount of expertise. This is because over the years your brain has built up a massive data bank that it uses to put the sounds you hear in some sort of context. That is how you can tell the difference between, say, hearing a sound in a small, square dark cellar with little or no furniture and hearing the same sound in a large church, in your living room at home, in a tunnel, or in an open space.

Because of this, you already know that some environments are more suited to listening to music than others are. That's what you are trying to do with your recordings when you add reverb—you're trying to fool listeners into thinking that they are listening to a performance that was recorded in a concert hall, an intimate cellar nightclub, or a church or cathedral, rather than in a cold, clinical, lifeless studio. Your brain already knows what it is looking (or rather, listening) for.

To help understand what the issues involved are, let's take as an example a live acoustic performance, unamplified. The music that you hear doesn't only travel to your ears directly from the various instruments (although, of course, some of it does). The sound waves also bounce around all over the place to an extent that almost defies detailed description and eventually reaches you via an extraordinarily complex series of paths. Key factors that come into play here include:

■ How far from the performer the listener is seated.

■ The size and shape of the venue, including its width, length, and height.

■ Other characteristics of the room (for example, the construction material used, the thickness of the walls, the presence of windows, curtains, and alcoves, and so on).

■ The number of people in the room. The more bodies, the more sound will be absorbed and the less "echoey" the sound will be.

If you try to get your head around every single factor at the same time, it'll probably give you a headache at the very least. Let's start with a relatively simple example.

Figure 8.1 illustrates but also oversimplifies three of the core factors that together help to create reverb. The figure isn't drawn to any accurate scale. It is there for illustration only and as a starting point, not as a comprehensive statement. To help you make sense of it, let's put it in the context of an actual example. To make the example relatively easy to follow, I'll take a few liberties with mathematics, rounding some things up and other things down. If my figures were being used to create actual reverb algorithms, this would matter. Because they are being used for illustrative purposes only, it doesn't.

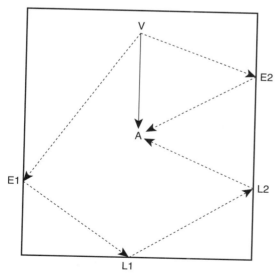

Figure 8.1 This illustrates some important basic principles of reverb. V represents the position of an unaccompanied vocalist; A is a single member of the audience. The various lines illustrate just three of the many paths that will be taken by the sound waves.

First, here are a couple of key facts. The exact speed at which sound waves travel depends on a number of factors, including air pressure and height above sea level. Let's take a fairly representative figure of 1,130 feet (just less than 345 meters) a second. That's just less than 13 inches (about 32 cm) every one thousandth of a second (millisecond). Let's call it about a foot (12 inches, or about 30 centimeters) every one thousandth of a second. You might find that thinking primarily in terms of distance rather than time will help you to understand reverb. Of course, the two concepts (distance and time) are inexorably linked to each other.

Suppose our vocalist (shown at V) sings, unaccompanied, just the three notes *Do Re Mi* and that she does so in about a second. Let's also suppose that you are seated about 30 feet away from her, at the position shown as A. As she begins to sing, you'll hear the clarity of her first attack on the *Do* after about 30 ms. Now follow the line labeled E2 in Figure 8.1. About 30 ms after that, you'll also hear the first reflections of her *Do* as they enter your ears after bouncing straight off the wall. These are often called the *early reflections*. Now follow the line that travels from V to E1 to L1 and to L2 before it finally reaches you. That's taking such a circuitous route that (depending on the size of the room) it could possibly add up to 300 ms or more. This would mean that even as our vocalist begins striking out on her *Re*, the late reflections of her earlier *Do* are only just reaching our ears.

As the performance goes on, the effects of the reverberation will accumulate. For example, depending on the actual environment, you could find that even when the singer is belting out her *Mi*, you in the audience might still be hearing the very last and lingering reflections of *Do* mixed in with some of the late reflections of her *Re*.

You think that's complicated? Well, consider this. Figure 8.1 only shows three of the literally countless number of routes taken by our singer's sound waves. They head off in every direction, more pronounced in some than others, and bounce back off every surface. This doesn't just mean the walls, but *every* surface, including the audience members themselves, and, of course, the floor and the ceiling. What's more, they're doing it continuously, an immeasurable number of never-pausing streams of sound waves. It's a good thing that sound waves aren't visible, because if they were, they'd be so thick that seated at Position A in Figure 8.1, you'd be lucky if you could see through them enough to catch even the occasional glimpse of the performer.

Remember, too, that in the real-world environment, sound is analog. We'll look at some of the technical terms used and how we arrive at their values a little later, but for the time being, focus on just three important facts:

- Every time a sound wave encounters an object (such as a wall), some of it will be absorbed, some of it will pass through, and some of it will be reflected.

- The frequency response of the reflected waves will not be the same as the original. Usually you would expect the higher frequencies to be substantially attenuated.

■ The larger the size of the room or venue, the greater and more noticeable the effect of this reverberation will be.

Creating a Reverb Environment

Let's now take this knowledge about how the real world works and apply it to how you might go about trying to artificially create such a real-world environment for persons listening to your recordings. You simply need to identify and master the tools that you have available to do this job. Those tools are the various parameters and controls that together are used to create artificial reverb. You've now reached the point where you stand to learn more by experimenting than by reading. Before moving on to the first reverb tutorial, however, I'd like to say a word or two about choosing reverb software.

So far, our discussion of reverb has barely scratched the surface, but already you should be getting an idea about what a vast, complex, and multidimensional topic this is compared to, say, EQ or simple delay. For this reason you will find that the quality and capabilities of different reverb software vary enormously. Even this variation isn't simple. A product that might serve you perfectly in one situation might not be as good in another. This topic will be explored in more detail after you've gained a little hands-on experience. Right now, I'd like to introduce what I believe to be four of the better freeware/donation-ware plug-ins available. However, this does not mean that you won't be able to find others at least equally as good.

Shown in Figures 8.2 through 8.5 are the interfaces for four freeware or donation-ware VST reverb plug-ins. You can find download details for all of them in Table 1.2 in Chapter 1.

KR-Reverb (see Figure 8.2) deserves a mention for its graphical design alone. It gives you very informative and helpful visual feedback about your settings. As an example, look at the listener position setting. As you move the fader, the graphic above it shows the listener's position relative to the speakers. My only reservation about using this in a first example is that it measures its parameters as a percentage between 0 and 100, rather than in milliseconds or feet. For the less experienced user, I find this scale of measurement can be difficult to relate to.

OmniVerb (see Figure 8.3) is, in my opinion, very, very impressive. It seems to create a clean sound and give you adequate control over how you create and shape your reverb. Its lack of any visual feedback is the only reason I am not using it in this tutorial. Good reverb doesn't need to give good visual feedback, but I do believe that especially when you are learning, this can be very helpful.

Kjaerhus Classic (see Figure 8.4) is every bit as good as you would expect any plug-in to be that bears the Kjaerhus brand name. Its fairly bleak interface, however, does not make it the ideal choice for the learner, in my view.

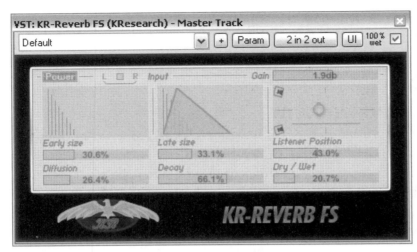

Figure 8.2   KR-Reverb: This reverb plug-in gives you strong visual feedback.

Figure 8.3   OmniVerb: a solid reverb plug-in with a good, clean sound.

Figure 8.4   Kjaerhus Classic: a quality reverb plug-in with a no-nonsense approach.

I have therefore settled on Mo Verb (see Figure 8.5) for this example. It has all the parameter controls you need, and its graphic feedback (including a very cute little goniometer) makes it an ideal choice for this exercise. For this reason, even if you have available to you some other reverb plug-in that you prefer, you should probably use Mo Verb for this first tutorial.

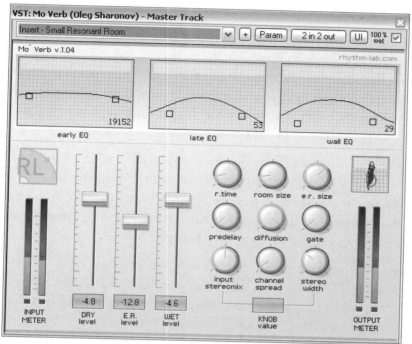

Figure 8.5 Mo Verb: a well-designed reverb, easy to work your way around and with a good visual interface.

Tutorial 8.1: First Steps in Reverb

This tutorial will introduce you to using the core parameters required to create reverb. You'll be doing it by adding a reverb plug-in to a track's master FX bin. We'll discuss later where the best place is and when the best time is to add reverb to a project, and more often than not, the preferred solution will *not* be to use the master track's FX bin. However, purely for this exercise and for learning purposes only, the master track's FX bin is highly suitable in this case.

You'll experiment using different combinations of settings to re-create artificially a variety of possible environments. After you have completed the tutorial, we'll home in more closely on the individual reverb parameter controls and examine each in more detail.

1. Open the file Lying80 that you created earlier and immediately save it as Lying81.

2. This project should include in its master track FX bin an instance of the ReaJS (with the utility volume/pan plug-in) and a simple hard limiter.

3. In between the volume/pan plug-in and the limiter plug-in, insert whichever reverb effect you are going to use for this tutorial. The detailed instructions that follow assume that you are using Mo Verb (refer to Figure 8.5). If you are using a different reverb effect, you may need to modify the instructions accordingly.

4. Notice the dry/E.R./wet faders. When you are sitting in the room or a concert hall listening to a performance, you do not hear the early reflections, the dry sound, and the later reverb separately; your brain absorbs and interprets them all mixed in together. However, when testing parameters to simulate an environment artificially, that is exactly what you may need to do. Different people have different systems that work for them. Try this one.

5. Fade the Wet level all the way down. Set the dry level at 0.0 dB and the E.R. level at about −23.0 dB. We are going to work on this first and then on the later reverb. Play the song, looped from about 0 min 46 sec to about 1 min 32 sec. This gives you a representative sample of the song. Set the gate to the off position (all the way left). We'll come to gated reverb in a later tutorial.

6. Let's try to re-create an environment similar to that shown in Figure 8.1. This looks like a fairly small room; set the room size to about 10 or 12 (close to the 8 o'clock position). Such a small room also implies a small spread. Set both the channel spread and the stereo width to about 20 (about 9 o'clock).

7. Pre-delay is the time it takes for the first early reflections to be produced. In this case, this should be about 30 ms. Experiment with setting the density of your early reflections. In this case (a small room), the density should probably be kept below 30. The higher the density, the more closely the early reflections are pushed together and the "thicker" they sound. Also, be aware that the thicker these early reflections are, the more they will affect the sound of the main reverb (later reflections).

8. Test this (use headphones) with Mo Verb alternately engaged and bypassed. The difference is subtle, but the early reflections should add a little warmth to the mix, as well as binding the different instruments and voices together a little.

9. Now for the reverb itself. Set this close to a full second (perhaps at about 0.9 sec). For a room this size, try setting the diffusion at about 30.

10. Gradually fade the wet level up until it sounds about right in the mix. This will probably be at about −14.0 dB to −17.0 dB. Compare the sound with the reverb engaged and bypassed. The difference should be that between the sound of a collection of individuals playing and a cohesive group playing together. This is because your reverb has given the mix a spatial context that your brain is able to recognize.

11.   Now turn to the EQ graphs. These, as you should by now be able to recognize, can be used to roll off the top and/or bottom end so that reverb is not applied at the very low and very high frequencies. Too much reverb on the bottom end can make a mix sound muddy; too much on the top end can make it sound unnatural. For this example, use EQ filter settings similar to those shown in Figure 8.5.

12.   Be prepared to tweak any of these settings if you think it will improve the sound. One issue that you might encounter is that some parts may seem to have a little too much reverb, others not quite enough. We'll address this in the next tutorial. Save the file. Save this reverb preset. (See the upcoming "Reverb Presets" note.)

13.   Now try moving your band from the smallish room that you have them in now to a reasonably sized concert hall. Set the pre-delay time at about 40 ms, so that our band is now performing some 40 feet away from the first reflective surface. Increase the early reflection size to about 75 so that you are now about 80 feet back from the stage. Restore most of the bottom end to the three EQ filter graphs. Increase reverb time to about 2.5 seconds. Increase the diffusion to 80. Bring up the channel spread to about 50 and the stereo width to 35. Set the E.R. level to about −20.0.

14.   Fade up the wet level to about −5.0 dB. You'll certainly hear the hall effect, probably too much so. Fade this back down until it sounds about right. This will probably be at about −19.0 dB to −20.0 dB. Save this file and save the reverb settings as a preset. This makes it easy for you to compare the two environments.

15.   One last comment before we move on. Even a fairly humble plug-in such as Mo Verb puts a lot of creativity at your fingertips. You can play around with the parameters in such a way as to create environments that simply do not exist in the real world. For example, you can create very small rooms with very long reverb times. You'd be unlikely to want to do this to an entire mix, but as you'll see when you get to the "Special Reverb Effects" section, you can use this technique to create some interesting effects.

Reverb Presets   Many reverb plug-ins include a number of presets, usually with names such as Medium Room, Large Hall, and the like. These can be useful as a starting point, but you should not come to depend on them. Not all so-called medium-sized rooms are the same shape or even the same size, besides which you will not be able to make the most effective use of reverb if you don't really know what you are doing.

More important is the ability to create, save, and recall your own presets. Most DAW hosts allow you to do this using various icons that are displayed within their FX interface. (Ableton Live, shown in Figure 8.6, is an example of this.) Others, such as Samplitude, for example, use menu commands for this.

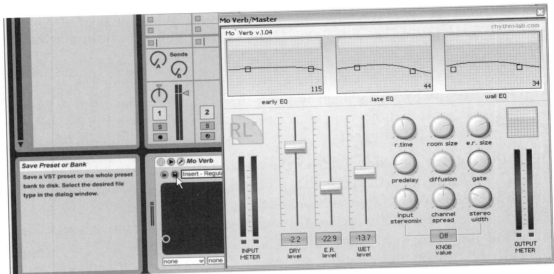

Figure 8.6   Most (if not all) DAW hosts allow you to create, save, and recall your own collection of reverb presets. Shown here is Ableton Live. Notice the two small icons closest to the mouse cursor and the tool tip to the left.

Use this feature to build up your own library of reverb settings that suit your particular needs.

Some plug-ins (such as Mo Verb) include separate presets for *sends* and *inserts*. In most cases this simply reflects the fact that when you are using reverb with sends and a bus, you will want a different wet/dry mix (more wet) than when you are using the same reverb effect inserted directly into a track's FX bin.

If you wish, experiment further with the controls that you have used during Tutorial 8.1. However, if you wish to save any changes, use a file name other than Lying81, as you may wish to use the file Lying81 in a future exercise. As you experiment, keep in mind the following:

- By far the most commonly made mistake with reverb is overdoing it. Try to build in your mind a mental picture of the environment you are trying to create, and remember that more often than not a venue that is praised for its acoustics is one whose natural reverberation is subtle and unobtrusive.

- Where the judicious use of reverb starts and ends is a matter of debate and some controversy. Some producers like to use different reverb effects on different instruments within the same mix. Others believe that this practice can detract from the quality of the mix. In this chapter you'll encounter some examples where this is done. It's your call as to whether or not you like this.

- The more reverb you apply to a mix, the more you will increase the feeling of space and depth, but the less the sense of musical contrast will be.

- The musical genre needs to be taken into account. For example, some new-age styles of music may well be enhanced by long, lingering reverb, but it is unlikely that this will do much for a delta blues band.

- If you are struggling to get just enough reverb to create your environment without the sound being too washy, consider other possible solutions. For example, you could try using reverb with early reflections only or revert to subtle delay, as you did in Chapter 7.

Core Reverb Parameters

In Tutorial 8.1, you were introduced to using the core reverb parameters that you should expect to find in most good reverb software. As with other kinds of effects, however, you may sometimes find that the same control is known under several different names. Table 8.1 summarizes the core controls that you have encountered so far.

Table 8.1 Summary of Commonly Used Core Reverb Parameters

Name	Description
Room size/type	Establishes the basic environment within which your other reverb parameters will operate. In general, the larger the room, the greater the impact of your other parameter settings and the more pronounced the reverb will be. In most circumstances you will want to make your other parameters reasonably consistent with your choice of room size.
Pre-delay (time)	This is a measurement of the delay time between the original sound and the first early reflections. It can fine-tune how the room size is perceived by the listener. The smaller the setting, the smaller the room. A long pre-delay setting can help maintain the clarity of vocals when reverb is added to them.
Early reflection size	Specifies the density of the early reflections.
Reverb time (decay time)	This defines the time it takes for each reverb reflection to trail away. The longer the reverb decay time, the larger the environment it appears to create will be. Remember, though, that the effect of your reverb decay time will itself be partially determined by the early reflection setting.
Diffusion	The diffusion setting will determine the rate at which the reverb reflections will appear to increase in thickness or

(Continued)

Name	Description
	density. This setting can help to create a more interesting environment. For example, a lower diffusion setting will suggest a square or rectangular room with a flat ceiling and few interesting features. An environment that includes perhaps a cathedral-type ceiling, alcoves, pillars, and other such idiosyncratic features will produce a higher diffusion rate. It is no coincidence that you will often find features such as these in theatres and concert halls.
Damping	Damping reflects the way different surfaces will affect the reverberation in different ways. Harder surfaces, such as tiles or concrete, will produce a brighter sound than a softer surface, such as one made of wood or covered with curtains, will.
Low-cut filters	Some reverb plug-ins allow you to specify the frequency above which high-end damping will be applied. Others have this built into their algorithms.
High-cut filters	In most environments, higher frequencies are absorbed at a greater rate than are midrange frequencies. By dampening the reverb at these frequencies, you are able to create a sound closer to that with which the listener may be familiar.
Channel spread and/or pan	This controls how the reverb is spread between the two speakers.
Stereo width	When applied to a stereo track, bus, or submix, this determines how widely across the mix the reverb is spread. The best way to understand the effect of this control and the channel spread control is to experiment with adjusting them while listening to the mix.
Dry level fader	Determines the extent to which the dry signal will be included in the mix.
E.R. level fader	Determines the extent to which the early reflections will be included in the mix.
Wet/dry mix	Determines the extent to which the wet (processed) signal will be included in the mix.

In Tutorial 8.1 you added your reverb to the FX bin of the master track. There may well be occasions when you will wish to do that, such as when you are working with a fairly simple arrangement and you wish to add just a small amount of polish to your overall mix. However, it is much more likely that you will prefer to use a reverb bus. This has the advantage of letting you add as much or as little of the reverb as you want to each track individually, while at the same time using your computer's resources very efficiently.

It is, of course, also possible to use different reverb effects on different tracks and groups of tracks. We'll get to that in Tutorial 8.3.

Tutorial 8.2: Using a Reverb Bus

To use a reverb bus, you will need to create sends from each of the various tracks to which you want the reverb added. These sends can be either pre or post track faders and any track FX. If you are in any way unclear about this concept, you should refer back to Figure 3.15. For this example, you should make all your sends post FX and post track faders.

1.   Open the file Whiskey80 and save it as Whiskey82.

2.   Create a loop from about 1 min 9 sec to about 3 min 20 sec. This will give you a representative sample of the song.

3.   Create a bus called Reverb. Add to this a reverb plug-in of your choice. The instructions that follow will be specifically for the OmniVerb Reverb. If you are using a different plug-in, you may need to modify it accordingly.

4.   Create sends (post FX and post track faders) from each of your two vocal, four guitar, and single shakuhachi tracks to this reverb bus. Solo the bus so that all you hear is its output. Set the level of each send to 0.0 dB. (This will probably be the default.) Play the song.

5.   Ignore the gate controls altogether. There is a strangely unlabeled button to the right of the early reflections rotary fader. This is the gate engage/bypass button. When engaged it is colored green; when bypassed it is colored gray. Make sure it is set to bypass.

6.   Set the room size to about 60% and the early reflections delay (pre-delay) to 35 ms. Specify a level of 30%.

7.   Set T60 (reverb time) to about 1,700 ms or 1,800 ms and density to about 60%. Ignore the modulation settings and make sure that modulation is disengaged. The little button labeled Mod should show as gray and not be illuminated. Modulation will make more sense after you have competed Chapter 9, "Time Modulation, Pitch Shifting, and More."

8.   Set the damping frequency to about 3,250 Hz, the high cut off at about 4,500 Hz, and the low cut off at about 150 Hz.

9.   Unsolo the reverb bus. The song should sound far too "mushy." Fade down the reverb bus output fader until it seems to sit about right in the mix. This will probably be somewhere between −18.0 dB and −25.0 dB. If you are able to, save this mix as a mixer snapshot.

10.   Lower the volume of each of the four guitar sends by about 4.0 dB. Increase the volume of each guitar track by about 0.5 dB to partially compensate for this. If possible, save this as a mixer snapshot.

11.   Play the song and compare both of your two scenarios. Especially during the break, the guitars should sound crisper and clearer with less reverb applied to them. This is not a lesson about guitars particularly, but about reverb. The more reverb, the more distant and the less clear the sound is. The less reverb, the clearer and closer it will appear.

12.   Save this file.

Types of Synthetic Reverb

Reverb comes in two main categories. These are *convolution reverb* and *synthetic reverb*. Convolution reverb will be the subject of a separate section, because its method of working is very different from the synthetic reverb that we have encountered up to now.

Synthetic reverb plug-ins exist in probably greater abundance and variety than just about any other. Many different products will display different characteristics, features, and parameters of their own. This is in part because they are striving to use whatever artificial means they can to create what should be a natural sound and in part because they are trying to carve out a competitive edge—and in some cases, it might be sheer gimmickry.

To begin trying to distinguish which features are important from those that are not, it often pays to go back to basics. When we looked, for example, at equalization, noise gates, or compression, we found that the key to getting good outcomes is matching the available tools, parameters, and controls to the characteristics of the sound to which they are being applied. Reverb can be approached in exactly the same way.

Shortly, we'll look at how you might go about creating the right reverb settings for, say, a vocal track, a snare, or a guitar. First, we need to take a quick look at the history of synthetic reverb. In the days before we had desktop computers with DAW software and VST or RTAS plug-ins, reverb had to be physically created using physical equipment. These different methods are reflected in many of the algorithms used in today's digital reverb plug-ins. Some approaches work better than others in different situations and when reverb is being used for different purposes. When you look through the presets supplied with your various reverb plug-ins, you will often come across words such as *chamber, plate,* or *spring.* Table 8.2 summarizes these. The techniques are listed in the chronological order in which they first appeared.

Table 8.2 Summary of Different Types of Reverb

Name	Description
Chamber reverb	Chamber reverb uses a real environment (often one such as a basement below the recording studio) to generate and capture reverb. Different reverb effects were created by the placement of a microphone and speakers. The dry mix would be fed from the studio to the speakers, so that the reverberation of the room would be captured by the microphone and fed back to the studio.
Plate reverb	Plate reverb is simply ingenious. It is produced by attaching a very thin piece of sheet metal to the front of a speaker and recording the sound that it creates. Various characteristics of the metal piece (such as its thickness) determine the actual texture of the reverb that is produced.
Spring reverb	Spring reverb evolved from plate reverb. It uses a spring with a transducer at one end and a pickup at another. You'll find spring reverb commonly used in guitar amps.
Digital reverb	Enter the digital age, and it's a whole new ball game. Computer technology is not limited to simulating earlier types of reverb. It also opens up any number of new ways of producing and using reverb. We'll look at some of them here.
Hall and room reverb	These reverb types aim to simulate an environment, such as a concert hall or a nightclub. This is what you were doing in Tutorial 8.1.
Gated reverb	This works by applying a noise gate either before the reverb effect or, more commonly, after it so as to cut off the reverb tail sharply. As you're about to find out, gated reverb can be really effective when applied to percussion.
Reverse reverb	A prime example of creating an effect that cannot occur naturally in a real-world environment. The reverb signal is reversed so that it appears to happen before the original sound. Use sparingly and with care.

Creating Reverb Effects

In this next tutorial, the focus will be mostly on using reverb to create an effect rather than an environment. Afterwards, we will be in a position to take an analytical look at the various different parts (instruments and voices) that go into a mix to figure out why some combinations of settings work better with some parts than they do with others.

Tutorial 8.3: Using Reverb Effects

This example uses the *Foggy Desperation* project. We'll start by adding some reverb to the percussion, then to the vocal, then to some of the string instruments. This is a very long tutorial and probably the most difficult in the book. You might wish to break it up into several sessions; there are natural breakpoints after Steps 11, 17, 22, and 24. Also, it will probably be easier for you if you use the same plug-ins as described in the examples as much as possible. However, you may substitute others if you wish. Note, too, that this is another exercise where some of the more subtle of the effects you will be creating may be more easily discernable if you use headphones.

1. Open the file Foggy80 and save it as Foggy83.

2. Create a loop from about 1 min 28 sec to about 2 min 28 sec. This will give you a sample of the song to work with.

3. Solo the snare track and play the song. The snare FX bin should already include (in this order) a noise gate, EQ, and a compressor.

4. Insert an instance of OmniVerb into this FX bin, between the EQ and the compressor. If you use a different reverb plug-in, make sure that its feature set includes gated reverb.

5. Engage the gate (the gate button will show as green) but set the gate sensitivity to 100%. This ensures that at first all of the reverb tail will be allowed to pass through the gate.

6. A snare is usually recorded with the microphone very close and little or no natural reverb. Allow about 30 ms of delay before early reflections with a density of about 20%. For this reason you can start by trying fairly generous settings. Figure 8.7 shows a reverb time of about 1.7 sec, room size 40%, damping about 5,500 Hz, high cut off at 8,000 Hz, and low cut off at 180 Hz. Notice also that modulation is not engaged. Fade the wet output control down so that reverb is not too overpowering; this is likely to be at about −12 dB.

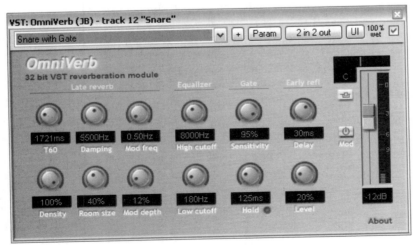

Figure 8.7   An example of possible settings for creating gated reverb on a snare. This example uses OmniVerb.

7. Now fade back the gate sensitivity and adjust the gate hold time until the reverb tail is being cut off just before it starts to lose its impact. These levels will, of course, be in part determined by your earlier track settings and especially the EQ output levels. In the example shown, this happens to be at about 95% and 125 ms. Notice how the gate light flashes as it opens and closes.

8. Compare how this sounds with the reverb before and after the compressor. It should be noticeably crisper and sharper before the compressor.

9. Play the song with the track unsoloed. If necessary, adjust the track volume fader for the gate so that it sits nicely in the mix. If you compare the sound with and without the reverb bypassed, remember that you have not yet added reverb to any other track. Save the file.

10. A bass or kick drum very often will not need reverb. If you do use reverb, be careful not to add mud to the mix. In this example, by being judicious we can use reverb to add a little punch to the mix. Figure 8.8 shows an example of this, with Kjaerhus Classic Reverb inserted in our kick track after the EQ and before the compressor.

Figure 8.8   An example of adding punch to a kick drum. This example uses Kjaerhus Classic Reverb.

11. The key factors here are a fairly spacious room size (about 80 sq m or 880 sq ft), no pre-delay or early reflections, very aggressive high-frequency damping, a conservative low-cut filter at about 40 Hz (to prevent any possible bottom-end rumble), and a wet/dry mix level that makes the impact of the reverb punchy but not dominant. Be willing to experiment with these settings to find the sound you prefer. Save the file.

12. Let's now tackle the tricky issue of adding some reverb to our lead vocal. I say "tricky" because the vocal is the one area where if you get it wrong, your listener will notice most. Both the lead and the harmony vocal had delay added during the tutorials in Chapter 7. So as not to overdo the effects in this case, fade the wet level in the ReaDelay mix on both of these tracks down to about −20.0 dB. Save the file.

13. Create a bus called Vox Reverb and add a pre-FX, pre-fader send from both vocal tracks to the Vox Reverb bus. By making the send pre-FX, you will ensure

that the reverb will be processed independently of the delay, not added to it. This routing brings with it another benefit. We will be able to make any future adjustments to the volume of the vocal tracks completely independently of the reverb send levels. This may not be an easy concept to grasp at first. Figure 8.9 illustrates this.

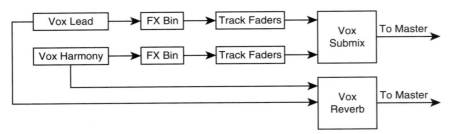

Figure 8.9   An example of a signal flow using pre-FX sends to a reverb bus. This can help prevent the reverb from being made foggy or unnatural-sounding because of unwanted reverb being compounded onto other effects.

14.   Adjust the loop so that it now runs from about 1 min 28 sec to about 2 min 08 sec. Play the song, lowering the volume on the send for the vocal harmony until the balance between the two vocals seems about right. This will probably be at about −6.0 dB. Insert OmniVerb into the reverb bus. Solo the bus.

15.   You should find that with this signal flow, you have a fair range of options as to how you could specify your reverb settings. A fairly safe starting point is with a moderate room size (say, 40%) and (to help preserve clarity) a relatively high early reflections delay setting (say, 30 ms or so). Use a fairly conservative setting (below 30%) for early reflections depth (level). Keep the reverb length (labeled T60) down to about 2 to 2.5 sec with high cut off at about 8,000 Hz to 10,000 Hz. Because this is a bus, keep the vertical wet output fader on the right at 0 dB.

16.   Unsolo the bus and adjust its volume fader to set the amount of reverb that is to be fed to the mix. This is likely to be somewhere in the range of −15 dB to −20 dB—but, as always, above all, trust your ears! If you wish, you can make adjustments to any of the parameter settings and/or to the volume fader on your existing Vox Mix bus.

17.   Save the file. We are now going to turn our attention to the acoustic guitars and the mandolin. The example that follows, like all of the others, has been developed for learning purposes and to teach you a particular technique. Please don't conclude from this that it is necessarily a good practice to use many different reverb effects in the same project.

18.   You are going to learn how reverb can be used to add a big-band feel to instrumental tracks such as these. Create a new bus, call it Guitar Verb, and build post-FX sends from the mandolin track and both acoustic guitar tracks to this bus. It

is important that the sends should be post-FX, because we want the reverb in this case to be applied *after* the chorus.

19.   Insert a reverb plug-in to the FX bin of your Guitar Verb bus. The instructions that follow are for Kjaerhus Classic Reverb, but they can be adapted for a different plug-in if you wish. The aim is to create a reverb that will not be too mushy.

20.   If you're using Kjaerhus Classic Reverb, set pre-delay and early reflection output both to 0. Set damping at 50%, high damp at 50%, and low cut all the way to the left. These are fairly cautious settings. Because this is a bus, set output mix all the way to wet (effect). Experiment with room size between about 20 sq m and 80 sq m (that's about 220 to 880 sq ft) to find the sound that you prefer. Play the song with the bus soloed and the reverb alternately engaged and bypassed. You should find that the reverb enhances the other effects (rather than clashing with them).

21.   Now for the interesting part. Add a stereo imaging plug-in after the reverb plug-in. These instructions are for the SStillwell/seterowidth plug-in, which you can load into ReaJS (see Figure 8.10). We'll revisit this sort of plug-in in Chapter 12, "Making Space: Stereo Enhancement," but this exercise will give you an interesting introduction.

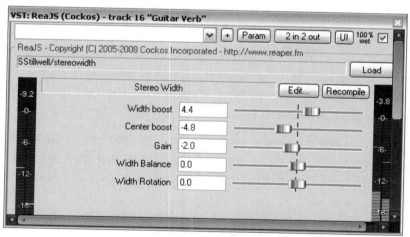

Figure 8.10   An example of adding stereo imaging to reverb. Shown here is the JS plug-in SStillwell/stereowidth.

22.   If you adjust the parameters as shown in Figure 8.10, you will find that the reverb will be pushed out within the stereo field farther away from the signal on the guitar tracks. This will help to deliver a bigger, fuller sound. Unsolo the bus and compare how the song sounds with the guitar reverb FX bin alternately bypassed and engaged. Adjust bus and track volume faders if you need to. Save the file.

23.   Finally, the electric guitar. This has obviously been recorded through a miked guitar amp. Again, the idea is to find a gentle touch of reverb that will enhance this by working with it, not against it. Again, a simple plug-in such as Kjaerhus Classic should be more than adequate for the job. Start with a very modest room size (about 10 sq m or 110 sq ft), modest damping (about 30), and pre-delay (also 30). Push the high damp close to maximum. Set the low-cut filter at about 65 Hz. In the output, add about 2.0 dB to the early reflections (to help preserve clarity) and set the mix level to about 2:1 dry (about 10 o'clock).

24.   You're almost finished! Save the file.

25.   Now play the song over again and review your mix. Don't be surprised if you end up pulling back some of the reverb, either by lowering some of the sends to the busses or by lowering the reverb output itself. It's not unusual (especially for a less experienced person) to be so focused on the reverb when adding it that they overdo it.

26.   After reviewing your work, save your file again.

Hopefully, as a result of completing three reverb tutorials, a light will be opening up in front of you, and a self-evident but often overlooked truth will be dawning. Remember all those questions you've read in magazines and online forums? You know, those "Which reverb plug-in is the best?" questions? Well, maybe those people would have been better off asking, "How do I go about using reverb to get the best results?"

Like the other examples used throughout this book, Figure 8.9 illustrates one example of how you could apply various audio effects. The main purpose of this example is to illustrate how your DAW will apply effects to audio signals that are routed pre-FX rather than post-FX and post–track faders. In no way should you infer that this represents a model of how you should apply reverb to vocal (or any other) tracks.

You will find some general comments in Table 8.3 that are designed to help you when trying out your reverb settings. Keep in mind that they are guidelines and they are only general—any and every one of them could be inappropriate in the wrong circumstances!

Table 8.3 Reverb Tips for Different Instruments

Item	Comment
Kick	Use reverb to add punch rather than a sense of space. Use little or no pre-delay and avoid a long decay time. Try modifying one of the ambient presets if available.
Snare	Use short and/or gated reverb settings with a high wet/dry mix for a live sound. Experiment with modifying one of the plate presets if available.

Item	Comment
Lead vocals	Pre-delay can help preserve clarity; long decay settings will produce muddle. Too much brightness can aggravate sibilance, but insufficient reverb can leave the vocal seeming detached from the rest of the mix. This is arguably the most important one to get right. As a generalization, the faster the pace of the song, the less reverb the vocal needs.
Backing vocals	Use thicker early reflections if you wish to push backing vocals back in the mix. (In Tutorial 8.3 this was not necessary because of the delay already on the track.)
Bass guitar	The bass guitar has such a long natural sustain and decay that it usually should not require reverb.
Electric guitar	Spring reverb presets can be a good starting point. Using compression before the reverb can create a powerful effect.
Acoustic guitar	Because of its long delay, you have a fair amount of scope for experimentation when applying reverb to an acoustic guitar, very much depending on the type of material. Stringed instruments in the guitar family present a number of interesting options. These include using two reverb instances (the first more conservative), or adding reverb after delay or chorus, and/or spreading the reverb away from the original signal to create more of a full band sound.

Special Reverb Effects

No doubt you found that last tutorial hard work. There is a lot to be learned in there. Don't worry if you feel that not all of it has stuck. You can go back to it later and do it over again. But before you do, you're going to have some fun. In this section we'll be looking at some examples of how you can be creative with reverb and use it in ways to create interesting effects, rather than a natural sound. It's not really a question of what is right and what is wrong—rather, it's what you like and what you don't! We'll start by experimenting with the two vocal tracks on *Now Is the Time for Whiskey* in such a way as to use reverb to enhance certain contrasting qualities of the two voices. As with many other tutorials, try to focus on the technique being used here, the bigger picture, rather than the actual example.

Tutorial 8.4: Special Reverb Effects

This tutorial involves splitting each vocal track into two, adding reverb to certain frequencies only, and then joining them up again. Different DAW programs have different tools for doing this. I'll be using the method of creating duplicate copies of the relevant tracks, not because it is an especially elegant or efficient way of working, but because it can be used with any DAW, and it works. Creating a separate track for your reverb will ensure that the reverb audio stream will be kept completely separate from the original track. This might not always be possible by using a send (even pre-FX)—for example, you might have effects inserted directly into the media items themselves. If your DAW offers you a better method (such as channel splitting), by all means use it if you wish.

1. We want to start this example with a "clean" project file that has no existing reverb from any previous exercise. Open the file Whiskey80 and save it as Whiskey84.

2. Create a loop from about 1 min 8 sec to about 2 min 56 sec. This will give you a representative sample of the song suitable for this example.

3. Create duplicate tracks of both the male vocal and female vocal tracks. Give them suitable names (for example, Vocal M Copy and Vocal F Copy). Remove all plug-ins from the FX bins of these new tracks. You should also make sure that both your new tracks are routed to the same submix (post-FX, post-faders) as the original two vocal tracks. Depending on exactly how your DAW implements routing, these sends may or may not have been automatically created when you duplicated the original tracks.

4. Insert an EQ plug-in into the FX bin of the Vocal F Copy track. Create a band-pass filter about 2 octaves wide (Q approx 0.67). Play the song with this track soloed and sweep the higher frequencies to find a spot where you hear mostly sparkle and clarity. This will probably be somewhere around 5,000 Hz to 6,000 Hz.

5. Now add a reverb plug-in of your choice after the EQ. Select a fairly "safe" preset, such as a warm plate or a medium-sized room. You can change it later if you wish.

6. Add a compressor after the reverb. Set a ratio of about 16:1, a fairly soft knee, and threshold, release, and (if available) RMS levels that will ensure the threshold is gently engaged most of the time the singer is singing.

7. Lower the track fader to about −7.0 dB. Solo both female vocal tracks and play them. You should hear the reverb shimmer trailing behind the vocal. Unsolo the tracks and make adjustments to your reverb parameter settings as you wish. Save the file.

8. Now apply the same principle to the Vocal M Copy track. Strip out all existing plug-ins and use a band-pass EQ to identify where the voice seems to have the most body. This is likely to be somewhere around 300 Hz to 400 Hz. Add a similar reverb to that which you used in Step 5. Adjust its settings to create a slightly longer reverb tail than before. Compress the reverb output, adjust the volume between the two vocal tracks as you see fit, and then play the song.

9. Save the file.

10. If you want to experiment some more, try changing the EQ on the female vocal from band-pass to high-pass, adjusting the frequency and output gain

accordingly. This should create a more haunting effect. As another variation, try using GlaceVerb as your reverb plug-in. (Download details can be found in Chapter 1, Table 1.2.) You might find it adds more shimmer. If the shimmer seems to be getting away from you, you can also try compressing it.

11.   One lesson you should take away from this is that different synthetic reverb plug-ins most definitely color your sound in different ways. This is in no small measure due to the different algorithms they use to create their artificial environments. It probably will take a fair amount of time and experimentation before you work out which reverb you prefer in which particular sets of circumstances.

More about Gated Reverb   In Tutorial 8.3, among other things you applied gated reverb to a snare. However, what should you do if the reverb plug-in that you consider best for your snare does not include any gate controls?

One solution can be to create a separate track or send for your reverb (such as in Tutorial 8.4) and then simply place a noise gate immediately after the reverb plug-in on that track.

The Impossible Environment   In Tutorial 8.4, you used reverb in combination with equalization and compression to mold vocals into a sound that could never be created naturally. By playing around with various reverb parameters, you can place an instrument or even a whole song in an environment that simply cannot exist in the real world. For example, you can try a very small room size with very long reverb delay and slow decay.

It gets interesting. The more your reverb is set up to contradict any environment your listeners could possibly have encountered, the more that reverb is likely to have an unsettling effect on those listeners. Handled carefully, this can help to make an instrument or even a whole mix edgy or tense.

Convolution Reverb

All of the examples that you have encountered so far have used synthetic reverb. By now you should be developing a good idea of the potential capabilities of synthetic reverb, but you might also be pondering its limitations. For example:

■   Unlike, say, compression and equalization, which behave pretty much according to definable scientific laws, the process that goes into generating synthetic reverb includes a fair amount of assumption, oversimplification, and potential error.

■   The environments that you are attempting to create artificially are still likely to finish up accurately representing nothing that actually exists. For example, suppose that you are creating a small hall. Which one? Every small hall you know is different. What about its shape, its dimensions? What about the listener's position? Front row? Back row? Center? Left? Right? I could go on and on, but I'm sure you get the point.

This is where convolution reverb comes in. In short, convolution reverb attempts to reproduce an actual environment rather than create an artificial one. It does so by combining a dry signal (such as your audio material) with a previously recorded impulse response or set of impulse responses. This brings us to the obvious question, "What is an impulse response?"

You'll find it easier to understand the answer to that question if you start by looking at and listening to a selection of wave files, each containing a single impulse. Table 1.2 in Chapter 1 lists a number of sites from which you can download free sample reverb impulse files. If you take a small selection of these and insert them as individual tracks in a new DAW project file, you will get something similar to Figure 8.11.

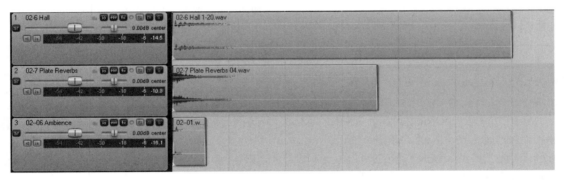

Figure 8.11   Three examples of impulse wave files, each inserted as a track in a DAW project file. From top to bottom, we have examples of hall reverb, plate reverb, and ambience reverb.

Tutorial 8.5: Understanding Convolution Reverb

In this next tutorial, you will do just that. Of course, you would not normally insert impulse files into your project in this way. The purpose of this exercise is purely to help you understand what convolution reverb is.

1.   Create a new DAW project file and save it as Impulse85.

2.   Import three or four different impulse reverb files into this project, each as a new track. After doing this, your track layout should be *similar* to that shown in Figure 8.11.

3.   Play each of the impulses in turn, each time soloed.

4.   Save the file.

Each of the examples that you have listened to represents the sonic signature of a particular environment, such as a particular position in a hall, or an actual reverb plate.

Typically, this consists of a very short transient containing all of its frequencies, rather like white noise.

Convolution reverb software works by combining the reverb impulse with the audio material in a particular way. Without getting bogged down in too much mathematical theory, the process essentially consists of sending both audio sources through a number of FFT (*Fast Fourier Transform*) algorithms and then playing back the result. The real point here is that this method enables us to much more closely create the illusion that our audio material was recorded in a particular environment, be it a basement nightclub or a grand concert hall. If you need more technical background information, you can find plenty on the Internet—but don't worry if you don't understand it! You don't need to.

D.I.Y. Reverb Impulses Here's something you might find interesting. It isn't too difficult to create your own reverb impulses if you wish to. It does, however, require a lot of attention to detail. Creating your own impulses really takes us outside the scope of this book, but you can learn more from a number of websites, including emusician.com/tutorials/emusic_acting_impulse.

Experimenting with Impulses Here's another idea that you might find interesting. Depending on the style of music and the effect you are aiming to achieve, you can try experimenting with all sorts of sounds as the impulse files used with convolution reverb. Try using vocal oohs or aaahs as an impulse file for a lead vocal, or the sounds of a chainsaw with a distorted electric guitar, or a bell with a flute or other wind instrument.

Tutorial 8.6: Using Convolution Reverb

This tutorial uses the HybridReverb2 plug-in from Christian Borss. Download details can be found in Table 1.2 in Chapter 1. As with other convolution reverb products, the interface includes a number of additional controls (which by now should be mostly familiar!) that can be used for fine-tuning the effects of the reverb.

1. Open the file Mud80 and save it as Mud86.

2. Mute the RoomMic track. We don't need it for this exercise.

3. Select the harmonica track. For the sake of this example, set to bypass any delay and EQ plug-ins that may be there from earlier tutorials. Lower the track volume fader by about 3 dB.

4. Add a bus called Main Reverb and insert an instance of HybridReverb2 into this bus.

5. Create post-FX, post-volume sends to this bus from every track except the RoomMic.

6. Use the preset selector to choose a position near the front for listening to music in a small concert hall, 2 m distance. This will produce the settings shown in Figure 8.12.

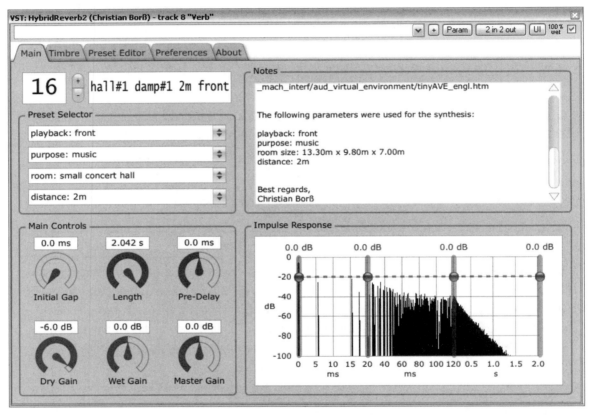

Figure 8.12   The main interface screen for the Christian Borss plug-in HybridReverb2.

7. Adjust the output level on the fader and the levels of the six sends until the reverb sounds about right. Your adjustments will probably want to include lowering the sends on the guitar tracks relative to the others, especially if you have any delay there from an earlier tutorial.

8. Save the work. You should notice now that with the reverb enabled, the music has a much more live feel.

9. Fade the pre-delay control up to about 60 ms. The impulse response graph will give you visual feedback.

10. Compare these two options. The 60 ms pre-delay may increase the clarity without detracting from the live feel at all. If you wish, use headphones when checking these.

11. Display the HybridReverb2 timbre settings page and roll off some of the top end, as shown in Figure 8.13. This should make the sound a little mellower, but without adversely impacting either the clarity or the live feel.

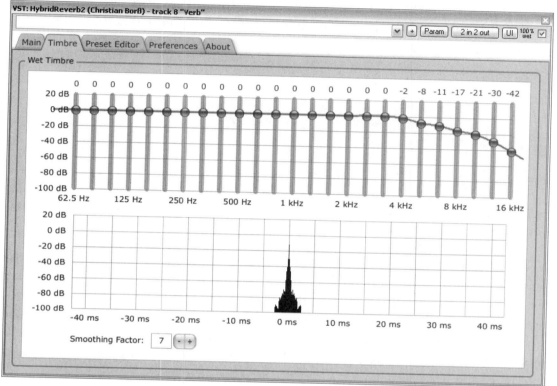

Figure 8.13 The timbre interface screen for the Christian Borss plug-in HybridReverb2.

12. Purely as a point of interest, display the HybridReverb2 preset editor page. You will see that each preset is in fact created using a combination of four separate impulse files, which together re-create the impression of space.

13. Save the file.

Checkpoint 1

Save as Mud86a the file that you created in Tutorial 8.6. Experiment with different impulse reverb files and parameter settings for this file. Pay attention to the differences—some subtle, some more obvious—that different options will create.

Reverb Effects Chains

The topic of effects chains has been steadily evolving throughout this book from just about Chapter 3 onward and will continue to do so all the way through to Chapter 14 and beyond. This is because there is virtually no limit to the number of different ways that you can combine effects and obtain substantially different outcomes.

Already in this chapter, in almost every tutorial you have built effects chains that included reverb. We'll now explore this concept a little further, including the use of more than one reverb effect on the same material. As with other effects, this can be done in serial or in parallel, with each of these options producing different results. Figure 8.14 illustrates the difference between applying two separate reverb effects in parallel (left) and in serial (right).

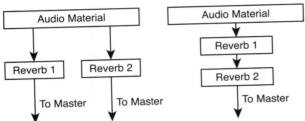

Figure 8.14   These two flow diagrams illustrate the differences in how parallel reverb (left) and serial reverb (right) are applied to an audio stream.

In short, the difference between parallel and serial reverb is that with parallel reverb both effects are applied at the same time, whereas with serial reverb one is applied *after* the other. In the first example (parallel), the signal is split into two, with each signal being independently processed before being sent to the master track. This can produce almost the effect of having two different instruments (or voices) playing (or singing) together. Depending on how far you wish to push this, it can be used to add edge or tension to the particular track.

In the second example (serial), the signal is fed first through one reverb effect before then being passed through the other. This tends to create a warmer and more unified feel. As always, it will help if you work through a couple of examples.

Tutorial 8.7: Using Reverb Chains

This tutorial comes in two parts. First you will be working with the *Mud Sliding* project, adding some parallel reverb to the percussion. Then you will be working with the *Now Is the Time for Whiskey* project, creating serial reverb for the vocals. In each case, you will need to retrieve one of the files that you created earlier in this chapter. In each case, you also will be encouraged to explore possible options for yourself rather than being given detailed instructions.

1. Open the file Mud86 and save it as Mud87.

2. Modify the sends from both the kick and the snare to the reverb bus so that they are both pre-FX. This ensures that the reverb you are about to add to each of these tracks will be processed in parallel with the reverb on the reverb bus.

3. Insert a reverb plug-in into both the kick and the snare FX bins. If you are uncertain about which parameters to use as your starting point, try something

similar to Steps 4 to 11 in Tutorial 8.3 as a model. If you wish, you can also use EQ to shape the sound of either track. Remember that the EQ will not be included on the signal sent to the reverb bus.

4. Aim to adjust the track settings so that with the FX bins on these tracks engaged, your snare sounds just a little more urgent in the mix, and the bass sounds just a little punchier.

5. Save the file.

6. Now open the file Whiskey84 (in which you duplicated both vocal tracks and added some reverb to both duplicate tracks) and save it as Whiskey87.

7. Set the delay on the male vocal track to bypass. Instead of this, we are going to use some additional reverb.

8. Create a new bus and call it Reverb. Add an instance of HybridReverb2 (or another convolution reverb of your choice) to this bus. The next step will be to create your post-FX, post-fader sends to this bus.

9. Add a send from the Shakuhachi track to this bus.

10. If your DAW routing allows, add sends from both your vocal submix and your guitar submix to this bus. If your DAW does not allow direct sends from one bus to another, instead add sends from each of the four individual vocal tracks and the four individual guitar tracks to this bus.

11. Play the song. Select the reverb bus. Choose an impulse file representing something like a nightclub or a small hall. Adjust the various sends to this bus so that the balance seems about right. Adjust the controls of the reverb plug-in to suit. For example, you might wish to add a little extra pre-delay to increase clarity. You might also wish to adjust the wet/dry balance.

12. Fade the output of the reverb bus back in the mix so that you have just enough reverb to add some warmth and bind the mix together. You might also need to make some adjustments to the different track and bus output levels.

13. Save the file.

Checkpoint 2

This consolidation exercise will help to reinforce much of what you have learned in this chapter.

Open the file Alone80 that you created earlier in this chapter and save it as Alone88.

Add reverb to this project to create the impression of a fairly laidback, intimate environment, with the lead guitar pushed back just a little behind the rhythm guitar. If you wish, use other effects with the reverb to help you achieve this. There are several different valid ways in which you could approach this—you only need come up with one!

Save the file when you're finished.

Project Files Log

If you have completed all of the examples and tutorials in this chapter, you should have created the following files:

Preparation: Foggy80, Lying80, Mud80, Whiskey80

Tutorial 8.1: Lying81

Tutorial 8.2: Whiskey82

Tutorial 8.3: Foggy83

Tutorial 8.4: Whiskey84

Tutorial 8.5: Impulse85

Tutorial 8.6: Mud86

Checkpoint 1: Mud86a

Tutorial 8.7: Mud87, Whiskey87

Checkpoint 2: Alone88

Your complete project file log should now be as follows:

Alone00, Alone70, Alone76, Alone80, Alone88

AudioExperiment21, Impulse85

Foggy00, Foggy41, Foggy42, Foggy43, Foggy44, Foggy50, Foggy52, Foggy53, Foggy60, Foggy61, Foggy62, Foggy64, Foggy66, Foggy69, Foggy70, Foggy73, Foggy75, Foggy80, Foggy83

Lying00, Lying23, Lying43, Lying50, Lying51, Lying52, Lying54, Lying60, Lying61, Lying62, Lying80, Lying81

Mud00, Mud40, Mud41, Mud60, Mud63, Mud65, Mud70, Mud74, Mud80, Mud86, Mud86a, Mud87

Whiskey00, Whiskey22, Whiskey30, Whiskey31, Whiskey32, Whiskey33, Whiskey60, Whiskey65, Whiskey67, Whiskey68, Whiskey70, Whiskey71, Whiskey72, Whiskey76, Whiskey80, Whiskey82, Whiskey84, Whiskey87

9 Time Modulation, Pitch Shifting, and More

The effects that we have examined up to now have by and large been effects that have a broad variety of potential uses and applications. This is the case, for example, with equalization, compression, and reverb. However, as computer technology has developed, a growing number of software effects have appeared (and are appearing) whose purpose is essentially to imitate the behavior of various highly specific hardware effects pedals, such as tremolo, distortion, flanging, or pitch shifting. These together will be the subject of this chapter. In a sense, they represent a slight departure from the "bigger picture" approach taken up to now.

Because these effects are so different in their application from those covered in earlier chapters, the approach taken in this chapter will also be different. We'll simply spend a short amount of time looking at a selection of these and then move on.

Introduction

In this chapter, you will examine a number of software "pedal effects" before looking at some examples of how they might be chained together.

- Phasing
- Flanging
- Tremolo
- Vibrato
- Ring modulation
- Vocoders
- Distortion
- Guitar amp
- Pitch shifting
- Pitch correction
- Chained FX
- Various bonus FX

Preparation

Throughout this chapter you will be working mostly with the sample project *Alone Again,* although I'll also show you a few surprises using the *Foggy Desperation* project. It should take you only a couple of minutes to prepare the necessary sample files.

Preparation: Preparing the Project Files

In each case, the only preparation required will be to open the specified version of each project, in one case make some simple changes, and then save it to the new name required for these tutorials.

1. Open the file Alone80 that you created earlier and immediately save it as Alone90. Remove any existing plug-ins. Add a bus called Rhythm FX with a send from the rhythm track and a bus called Lead FX with a send from the lead track. Both sends should be post-FX, post-fader. Add to each bus a utility limiter with output set to −1.0 dB to the master. Save the file.

2. Open the file Foggy76 that you created earlier and immediately save it as Foggy90.

Most of the effects covered in this chapter could in fact be added directly to the track's FX bin. In most examples, however, a bus will be used because this gives you more flexibility.

Phasing

With phasing, the audio signal is split into two streams. One stream is left unprocessed, while the other is fed through a series of phase shifts under the control of a low-frequency oscillator (LFO). Figure 9.1 illustrates this concept. The variations in the degree to which each stage is out of phase with the original signal combine to produce a continuous and repeated change in the sound. Psychologically, this results in a sound that is more distant and less immediate.

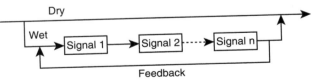

Figure 9.1   This diagram represents a simplified view of the route taken when an audio signal is passed through a phaser.

Table 9.1 summarizes the core parameters used to control phasing. As with chorus, delay, and reverb, you may find that individual phasing plug-ins might include some additional features of their own.

Table 9.1	Summary of Typical Phaser Parameters
Name	**Description**
Gain	Used to add gain to the incoming or outgoing signal.
Stages	This determines the number of all-pass filters that are used to create the phased signal (typically up to 32). The more stages, the more notches and peaks are created, hence the more pronounced the effect.
Depth	The greater the depth, the greater the phase change that occurs at each stage will be.
Rate	This determines the speed at which each individual phased cycle is completed.
Feedback	As with delay, this control determines how much of the phased signal is fed back to itself—and also as with delay, it needs to be handled with caution. If necessary, refer back to Table 7.1 (and the comments that immediately follow it) to review this.
Dry/wet	One or more controls may be available to control the proportions in which the dry (unprocessed) and wet (phased) signals are mixed.
Shape or LFO	As with chorus, this setting determines the shape of the oscillator used to create the wet signal. If necessary, refer back to Table 7.2 to review this.
Stereo	When present, this controls the degree of stereo spread that will apply to the phased signal.

Tutorial 9.1: Using a Phaser

In this tutorial you will use Blue Cat's Phaser plug-in (see Figure 9.2) to enhance the sound of one of your electric guitar tracks. Experiment extensively throughout this exercise. Download details can be found in Table 1.2 in Chapter 1.

Figure 9.2   Blue Cat's Phaser plug-in is available for both the PC and the Mac.

1. Open the project file Alone90 and save it as Alone91.

2. Add to the FX bin of the Rhythm FX bus (before the limiter) Blue Cat Audio's Phaser. Set the limiter output at −1.0 dB. This is a precaution against excessive feedback.

3. Solo the Rhythm FX bus and play the song. Select the Classic Flange preset. As you work through this example, be prepared to frequently toggle the solo status of the rhythm FX bus.

4. Select the preset No Effect as your starting point.

5. Set the dry output to 0% and wet output to 100%. This will give you a completely wet signal.

6. Set the number of stages to 5.

7. Adjust the depth and rate to create a definite but unchaotic phase effect. Try a depth between 60% and 75% and a rate within the range of 3 Hz to 5 Hz.

8. Increase the stages slowly, first to 10 and then to 15. Notice how this creates a more urgent, even agitated, effect. Return this fader back to 5.

9. Try each of the two different LFO settings. Notice how each shapes the sound differently. Decide which you prefer.

10. Unsolo the track and adjust the volume faders of the tracks and busses until you are happy with the balance.

11. Save the file. If you wish, explore the various presets supplied with this plug-in and experiment with creating your own variations.

Flanging

Flanging was developed a little later than phasing. Today's digital flangers aim to reproduce and enhance this effect, originally created at EMI's Abbey Road Studios in the 1960s. The technique used was to record audio simultaneously to two tape machines and then mix back their combined output to a third machine. Very small differences in timing (considerably less than 20 ms) between the two tape decks would create a phasing effect, to which flanging was added by using the finger to place gentle pressure on the rim (also known as the *flange*) of one of the tape reels to slow playback on that machine ever so slightly.

If you wish to make a mental comparison between flanging and chorus, it might help to keep these points in mind:

■ Chorus generally uses longer delay times than flanging does.

- Unlike chorus, today feedback is often used with digital flanging to create a kind of warbling echo effect. This effect was not obtainable in the pre-digital days of tape flanging.

Expressions that you may have heard used in conjunction with phasing include *the jet plane effect* (which attempts to describe the nature of the effect) and *comb filtering* (because when a flanged frequency response is plotted on a graph, it vaguely resembles a comb).

Table 9.2 summarizes the core parameters used to control flanging. By now you should be familiar with many of them from what you have already learned, especially about chorus and phasing. However, as with chorus, delay, and reverb, many of today's digital flanging software plug-ins add their own individual characteristics and features.

Table 9.2 Summary of Typical Flanger Parameters

Name	Description
Gain	Used to add gain to the incoming or outgoing signal.
Delay	This is the time difference that occurs between the playback of the first and second signals. Where the software allows for a negative delay setting, this can be used to produce an interesting ambient effect.
Depth	The greater the depth, the greater the pitch shift that occurs between the two signals will be, and the greater the warbling effect.
Width	This works in conjunction with the depth setting. The lower the width setting, the less time the processed signal will take to travel between its peaks and its troughs.
Rate	This determines the rate at which each individual flange cycle is completed.
Feedback	As with delay, this control determines how much of the flanged signal is fed back to itself—and also as with delay, it needs to be handled with caution. If necessary, refer back to Table 7.1 (and the comments that immediately follow it) to review this.
Shape or LFO	As with chorus, this oscillator setting determines how the flanged signal is shaped. If necessary, refer back to Table 7.2 to review this.
Dry/wet	One or more controls may be available to control the proportions in which the dry (unprocessed) and wet (flanged) signals are mixed.
Stereo	When present, this controls the degree of stereo spread that will apply to the flanged signal.

Tutorial 9.2: Using a Flanger

In this tutorial you will use Blue Cat's Flanger plug-in (see Figure 9.3) to enhance the sound of one of your electric guitar tracks. Download details can be found in Table 1.2 in Chapter 1. Experiment extensively throughout this exercise.

Figure 9.3   Blue Cat's Flanger plug-in is available for both the PC and the Mac.

1. Open the project file Alone90 and save it as Alone92.

2. Add to the FX bin of the Rhythm FX bus (before the limiter) Blue Cat Audio's Flanger. Set the limiter output at −1.0 dB. This is a precaution against excessive feedback.

3. Solo the Rhythm FX bus and play the song. Bring the dry fader up to 100%. As you work through this example, be prepared to frequently toggle the solo status of this bus.

4. As a rule, you would expect flange to make significant use of feedback. Set the Fback and FFwd settings both to about 60% to 80%. FFwd is used to feed the flange effect back to the signal ahead of itself!

5. Slowly increase the delay from 0 ms to 7 ms or more. Notice that as you do, the sound becomes ghost-like, and the basic structure of the tune becomes overwhelmed by the flange effect. Turn it down to about 1 ms.

6. Set the depth at 50% and then gradually fade up to 90%. As you do so, the flange effect will be more prominent, but the integrity of the tune will be preserved. Find a level you like somewhere between 60% and 70%.

7. Set the rate up all the way to 20 Hz. Notice the signal appears much "wobblier." Fade it back down to somewhere close to 1. Experiment with selecting each of the two settings in turn.

8. If you temporarily raise both the depth and rate levels, the difference between each of the two shape settings should be easier to detect. Fade them back to about 65% and 1, respectively, when finished.

9. Unsolo the bus. Make any adjustments you need to track and bus volumes and then save the file. If you wish, experiment with panning the FX bus away from the main rhythm guitar track.

Flanged Vocals Effects such as flange are most commonly associated with guitars, but their potential applications don't stop there. Added to vocals, for example, flange can be used to create an edgy effect.

If you'd like, you can try this with the *Foggy Desperation* project.

Open the file Foggy90 and save it as Foggy92. Make a duplicate copy of the lead vocal track and remove any existing effects from the FX bin of this copy track. Insert a flanger plug-in and adjust the parameters and track levels to suit. You should find that by doing this, you can modify the voice in any number of interesting ways.

Save the file when you're finished.

Tremolo

Tremolo is a shivering, stammering, or shuddering effect that is brought about using a repeated pattern of variations in the volume of a note or chord. This pattern is created by applying a low-frequency oscillator to the signal. The effect can be created using three basic controls, which are depth, rate, and shape (see Table 9.3). As with other such effects, you will often find that a particular plug-in or device will include extra controls that may allow you more sophisticated options.

Table 9.3 Summary of Typical Tremolo Parameters

Name	Description
Depth	This sets the ratio of dry and wet signals used for output. The greater the depth, the louder the tremolo effect in the mix will be.
Rate	This determines the speed of the low-frequency oscillator.
Shape or LFO	This setting determines the frequency and shape of the oscillator. The larger the setting, the slower it moves; the smaller the setting, the quicker it will move, and as a consequence, the more "warbled" the sound will be.
Phase difference	This can be used to modify the phase relationship between the left and right channels.

Tutorial 9.3: Using Tremolo

This tutorial uses MeldaProduction's MTremolo plug-in (download details are included in Table 1.2 in Chapter 1), but you may use different software if you wish. The Melda plug-in includes a number of other optional parameters that you can explore at your leisure if you wish.

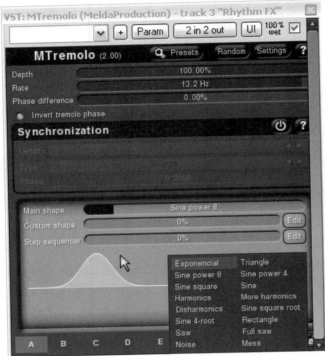

Figure 9.4   MeldaProduction's MTremolo plug-in offers a good selection of built-in LFO shapes, any of which can be customized.

1. Open the project file Alone90 and save it as Alone93.

2. Add to the FX bin of the Rhythm FX bus (before the limiter) MTremolo (or a different tremolo plug-in). Set the limiter output at −1.0 dB. This is a precaution against excessive feedback.

3. Solo the Rhythm FX bus and play the song.

4. Select a sine shape. In the example shown in Figure 9.4, this was done by right-clicking over the graph and choosing Sine Power 8.

5. Experiment with the depth setting. The higher you make this, the more "stuttered" will the effect be. Leave this close to or at 100%.

6. Experiment with the rate control. In general you will find that at low values the effect will be barely noticeable, at high values a consistent and regular stammer

is produced, and there is a significant area between these where the sound will drop out altogether before returning. Leave this at about 14 Hz.

7. Save the file. Unsolo the bus and make such adjustments as you think appropriate to the different track faders.

8. If you wish, explore the other various shape options to see how they change the tremolo sound.

Vibrato

Vibrato is an effect that can be used to add an almost vocal-like quality to a musical instrument (usually a guitar). It does this by using regular slight variations in pitch to add depth and sustain to the sound.

A comparison of Figure 9.5 to Figure 9.4 suggests that vibrato and tremolo appear to be very similar effects. Although this is true in many respects, it is important that you understand the one important difference: Tremolo works by creating variations in the amplitude (volume) of the audio signal, whereas vibrato uses variations in pitch (frequency). Table 9.4 summarizes the functions of controls typically used in connection with vibrato.

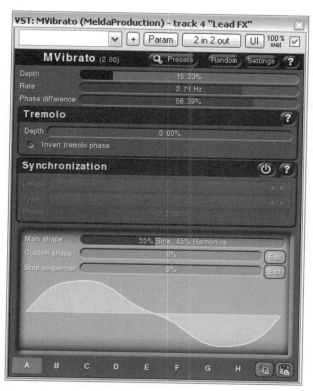

Figure 9.5   MeldaProduction's MVibrato plug-in. Like MTremolo, it offers a good selection of built-in LFO shapes, any of which can be customized. Refer back to Chapter 7 if you need to refresh your memory on the main different shapes and their characteristics.

Table 9.4 Summary of Typical Vibrato Parameters

Name	Description
Depth	This determines the amplitude (volume) of the variation. At its minimum setting (zero), no effect is added to the sound at all.
Rate	This determines the frequency of the variation. Typically, this will be set within the range of about 1 Hz to 5 Hz (or, for a more extreme effect with faster repetitions, even higher).
Shape or LFO	This setting determines how the oscillator or LFO (vibrato) signal is shaped.
Phase difference	This can be used to modify the phase relationship between the left and right channels.

Tutorial 9.4: Using Vibrato

This tutorial uses MeldaProduction's MVibrato plug-in (download details are included in Table 1.2 in Chapter 1), but you may use different software if you wish. The Melda plug-in includes a number of other optional parameters that you can explore at your leisure if you wish.

1. Open the project file Alone90 and save it as Alone94.

2. Add to the FX bin of the Lead FX bus (before the limiter) MVibrato (or a different vibrato plug-in). Set the limiter output at −1.0 dB. This is a precaution against excessive feedback.

3. Solo this bus and play the song.

4. Start with depth at 0%, rate at 2 Hz, phase difference at 0%, and a sine-shaped LFO.

5. Slowly increase the depth to 100%. At this setting the effect is clearly overdone. Fade it back to somewhere between 10% and 30%. The effect should still be noticeable but not overpowering.

6. Fade up the phase difference to somewhere within the range of 30% to 50%. This should add more body and sustain to the sound.

7. Unsolo the bus and adjust the various track and bus volume faders until you are satisfied with the relative levels. Save the file.

8. Experiment with making changes to these settings, including the LFO shape.

Ring Modulation

Ring modulation is an effect created as a result of using two signals (at different frequencies) and multiplying them together to create a new signal that produces notes at the frequencies represented by both the sum and the differences between the two original signals. The resulting effect can be quite gong-like, but also be aware that the more these frequencies are non-harmonic, the more the sound will tend to sound dissonant.

Figure 9.6 shows the MRingModulator. It uses two separate oscillators (set to different frequencies and possibly different shapes) to produce the two sounds. Each oscillator has its independent depth, frequency, phase, and shape controls. Table 9.5 summarizes the functions of the various controls typically found in a ring modulator.

Figure 9.6   MeldaProduction's MRingModulator plug-in. Like others in this series, it offers a good selection of built-in LFO shapes, any of which can be customized.

Tutorial 9.5: Using Ring Modulation

This tutorial uses MeldaProduction's MRingModulator plug-in (download details are included in Table 1.2 in Chapter 1), but you may use different software if you wish. The Melda plug-in includes a number of other optional parameters that you can explore at your leisure if you wish.

1.   Open the project file Alone90 and save it as Alone95.

2.   Add to the FX bin of the Lead FX bus (before the limiter) MRingModulator (or another equivalent plug-in). Set the limiter output at −1.0 dB. This is a precaution against excessive feedback.

Table 9.5 Summary of Typical Ring Modulator Parameters

Name	Description
Depth	For each oscillator this determines the strength of the modulated signal. The higher the setting, the greater the proportion of the wet signal in the mix.
Frequency	This determines the speed of the variation. The higher the frequency, the faster the speed.
Phase	Where a phase control is available, it can be used to control the phase relationship between the left and right channels.
Shape or LFO	This oscillator setting determines how the vibrato signal is shaped.

3. Solo this bus and play the song. Make sure both oscillators are enabled.

4. Set the shape of both oscillators to Sine. This will produce a reasonably smooth effect. If you later wish to experiment with harsher shapes, such as saw, triangle, or square, please do so.

5. Set the depth of both oscillators to 100% and specify a 10% phase shift.

6. Specify a frequency of 400 Hz for the first shape and 1,000 Hz for the second one.

7. Unsolo the bus. Save the file.

8. Adjust the levels of the volume faders on the tracks and busses to obtain a suitable balance.

Vocoder

Another effect that deserves a mention here is the Vocoder. One of its main applications is to create an artificial, robotic sound on vocals, but it can also be applied to a range of musical instruments with varied and various results, often to make the instrument sound mesmerizing or haunting. An example is the mda Vocoder, shown in Figure 9.7.

The effect is created using a recorded vocal or instrument track in conjunction with the output of a second track whose audio stream is generated by a synthesizer. The vocal (or instrument) track is known as the *carrier* and the synthesizer track as the *modulator*. Each of these is routed (post-FX but pre-fader), with the carrier usually panned 100% hard left and the modulator 100% hard right. The volume faders on both tracks are

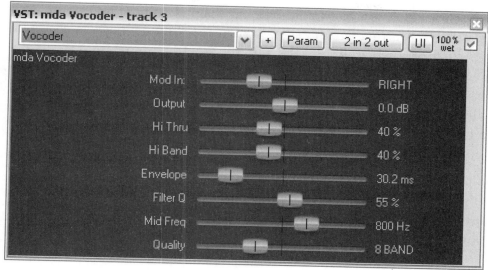

Figure 9.7   Shown here is the mda Vocoder, included in the mda plug-ins pack. Download details can be found in Table 1.2 in Chapter 1.

then taken all the way down to −inf. The Vocoder is then placed in the FX bin of this bus as the first effect.

The use of synthesizers is outside of the scope of this book, but if you are adept at their use, it should not prove too demanding a task for you to set up an example using one of the vocal tracks from one of the supplied projects and a synthesizer of your choice. For best results, use chords rather than individual notes, keep the volume level fairly even, and select synth patches with a reasonably lengthy sustain.

The Vocoder parameters include a number of filter controls (which are applied to the carrier), an envelope control (which is applied to the modulator), and a quality control, which determines the number of bands used in each case (usually 8).

Modulated Vocals   Earlier in this chapter, we looked at an example that applied a flanging effect to a vocal track. Keep in mind that if you want to add an unnatural robotic, synthetic, or electronic sound to a vocal track, then many of the effects discussed in this chapter can do that. Try applying ring modulation or phasing and see how it sounds.

For certain styles of music, the same also applies to other effects, such as distortion or guitar amp simulation, which are discussed in the two sections immediately following this.

Distortion

Distortion (or overdrive) is an effect usually applied to a guitar, but it can also be used with other instruments (such as the harmonica). With some styles of music, distortion can also be applied to vocals. It works by compressing a signal and then pumping it up to create clipping—that is, cutting off the signal when the volume exceeds a certain level. The degree of distortion created (and the way the sound is shaped) is largely determined by the degree of clipping. The trick is often to set the distortion parameters so that the average signal is just loud enough to create the barest amount of clipping (soft clipping). This will ensure that when the notes are played harder, the clipping will intensify. Conversely, when the strings are plucked more softly, the sound will be clean (without clipping taking place).

Digital distortion plug-ins aim to imitate the effects created by various types of distortion pedals. These vary widely in their construction, from just a couple of simple rotary faders to a much more sophisticated arrangement with tone shapers and more. The essence of distortion is relatively straightforward, requiring just a gain control and some sort of hard/soft control (see Table 9.6).

Table 9.6 Summary of Essential Distortion/Overdrive Parameters

Name	Description
Gain	This determines the extent to which the volume of the audio signal will be "pumped up."
Harshness	This determines how soft or hard the distortion will be applied.

Tutorial 9.6: Using Distortion

This tutorial uses the JS Guitar/distortion plug-in, which is included on your DVD. A general introduction to this group of plug-ins (including install instructions) can be found in Chapter 1. Of course, you may use a different plug-in if you wish.

1. Open the project file Alone90 and save it as Alone96.

2. Solo the Lead FX bus. Insert an instance of ReaJS into its FX bin (before the limiter) and then load JS:Guitar/distortion (see Figure 9.8) into ReaJS. Play the song.

3. This particular plug-in includes a channel mode. Set it to stereo (but experiment with the other two options if you wish).

4. Fade the hardness control all the way left. The distortion will become very soft. As you fade it back up, it becomes harsher. Find a level you like, perhaps around 7.0 or 8.0.

5. Fade the Gain control down to about 5 dB. The distortion should now be applied only to the occasional louder note. As you fade it up to 40 dB, it becomes engaged all the time. Fade it back down to get the degree of distortion that (for

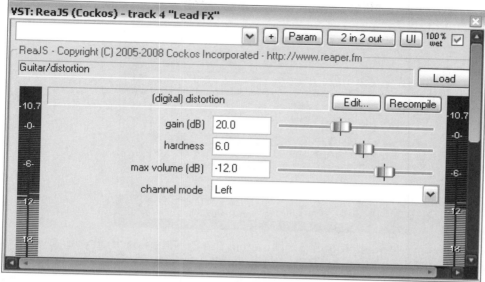

Figure 9.8 The JS Guitar/Distortion plug-in is included in the ReaPlugs pack on your DVD. It can be loaded into a track's FX bin using the VST plug-in ReaJS.

this example) sounds best to you. This is likely to be somewhere between 16 dB and 24 dB. Unsolo the bus and make such adjustments as you like to the various track and bus volume faders.

6. Now apply distortion also to the Rhythm FX bus, using the same technique to arrive at your preferred settings.

7. Save the file.

Guitar Amp

Using a guitar amp plug-in, you can take an electric guitar track that has been recorded in-line and make it sound as if it has been recorded using a miked-up guitar amp. Guitar amp plug-ins can be used to emulate the sound of specific models, and they come with an eclectic variety of individual controls. Figure 9.9 shows the JS plug-in Guitar/Amp-Model, one of two such plug-ins included on the DVD accompanying this book.

Guitar amp plug-ins essentially work by filtering the recorded audio stream through a sample WAV file, which captures the characteristics of the amplifier.

Tutorial 9.7: Using a Guitar Amp Plug-In

This tutorial uses the JS Guitar/Amp-Model plug-in, which is included on your DVD. A general introduction to this group of plug-ins (including install instructions) can be found in Chapter 1. Of course, you may use a different plug-in if you wish.

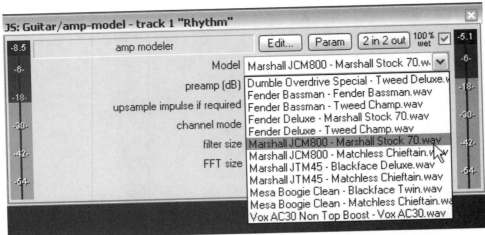

Figure 9.9   The JS Guitar/Amp-Model plug-in is included in the ReaPlugs pack on your DVD. It can be loaded into a track's FX bin using the VST plug-in ReaJS.

1.   Open the project file Alone90 and save it as Alone97.

2.   Solo the Rhythm Guitar track (rather than the FX bus). Insert an instance of ReaJS into this track's FX bin and then load JS:Guitar/Amp-Model into ReaJS. If there is no limiter in this track's FX bin, insert one after the guitar amp and limit its output to −1.0 dB.

3.   Play the song. Mute the two busses and solo the rhythm guitar track. In the amp-model plug-in, select the Marshall JCM800 Marshall Stock 70. This will cause the appropriate values for the two items' filter size and FFT size to be set automatically.

4.   Unsolo this track. Adjust the preamp level to achieve the best available sound. Set the channel mode to stereo-stereo.

5.   Save the file.

Don't think that the guitar amp is only suitable for use with a guitar. In the *Mud Sliding* series of projects, for example, the harmonica was recorded through an actual guitar amp.

Playing with Pitch

Before moving on to look at some examples of how the various effects covered in this chapter can be chained together, we'll take a brief look at two more special types of plug-in, pitch shifting and pitch correction. Both of these effects are most commonly associated with vocals, but there's no reason why you can't experiment on various instruments as well.

Pitch Shifting

Pitch shifting is an effect that can be used not only to fatten a voice or instrument, but also to change its sound in a way somewhat similar to that which might be achieved by flanging and (as you are about to discover) somewhat different. One simple technique is to make two copies of an original track and then pitch shift each of the copies—one up and the other down. This can be used, for example, within a mix to help emphasize key words or phrases, or within a chorus.

Tutorial 9.8: Using a Pitch Shift Plug-In

This tutorial uses the JS Pitch/Superpitch plug-in, which is included on your DVD. A general introduction to this group of plug-ins (including install instructions) can be found in Chapter 1. Of course, you may use a different pitch shift plug-in if you wish.

In this example, we will create the desired effect using multiple tracks. Your software's routing architecture may allow for more efficient methods, such as track or channel splitting, but for the sake of the example, it will probably be easier if you use the method outlined here.

1.   Open the project file Foggy90 and save it as Foggy98.

2.   Mute the vocal harmony track. This will help you hear more clearly the effect that you will be creating by pitch shifting. Play the song.

3.   Create two new tracks immediately below the lead vocal track and copy the lead vocal media item to both of these tracks. Label these tracks Pitch Up and Pitch Down, respectively. Neither of these new tracks should at this point have any effects in their FX bin.

4.   If you are using Superpitch, add an instance of ReaJS to each of these two tracks and then load Superpitch (see Figure 9.10) into each of these. If you wish, use a different pitch shift plug-in instead.

5.   Use the semitone fader to raise the pitch of the first of these tracks a full semitone.

6.   Use the semitone fader to lower the pitch of the second of these tracks half a semitone.

7.   Pan the Pitch Up track about 35% to 40% left, the Pitch Down track a similar amount right, and the lead vocal track dead center. Lower the volume of the two pitch shift tracks to about −10 dB to −15 dB each. The exact preferred level will depend largely on your other volume settings. Figure 9.11 shows an example of this in one particular DAW. Your screen should look similar, though of course not identical to this.

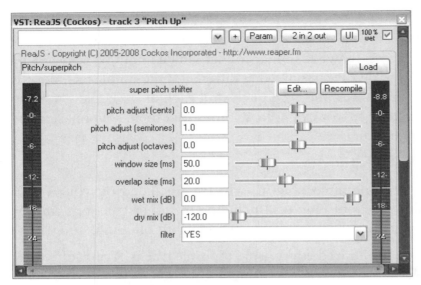

Figure 9.10   The JS Pitch/Superpitch plug-in is included in the ReaPlugs pack on your DVD. It can be loaded into a track's FX bin using the VST plug-in ReaJS.

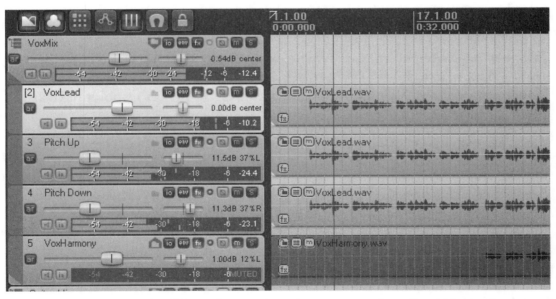

Figure 9.11   An example of how the vocal tracks in your project should look after completing Tutorial 9.8.

8. Save the file.

9. Play the song, making any adjustments you think necessary. You should find that the pitch shift tracks create a double-tracking effect as well as giving a rough, gravelly edge to the vocal.

Pitch Correction

Pitch correction differs from pitch shifting in that whereas pitch shifting is primarily an *effect*, pitch correction is essentially a *corrective tool* (as indeed its name implies!) used to rectify errors in pitch, usually on vocal tracks. Most good DAW hosts include some sort of pitch correction software as standard. For those that don't (and even for those that do), third-party plug-ins such as Melodyne are available. Another is GSnap, included in the GVST package. You can find details of where to download this in Table 1.2 in Chapter 1.

Most pitch correction software can be used in automatic or manual mode. With the former, the software aims to identify those notes that are off pitch and correct them for you. With the latter, you manually make each adjustment to individual notes. Be careful about how you use pitch correction software. You should not regard it as a silver bullet that will give you a solution to all your vocal pitch problems. There is no substitute for singing correctly. Pitch correction software works best when used only to pull occasional minor deviations and errors back into line, not for the wholesale realignment of a bad performance.

Largely because different pitch correction products have significantly different interfaces and controls, there's no formal tutorial included in this section, just a general overview. If you like, insert an instance of GSnap (see Figure 9.12) into the FX bin of your lead vocal track in the file Foggy98. It should go immediately after any noise gate. Play the song.

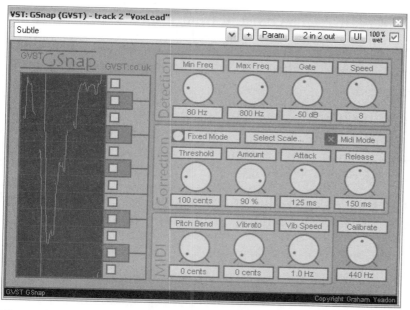

Figure 9.12   Good freeware pitch correction is hard to come by. Shown here is GSnap, which is a notable exception. Its main limitation is that it can be used in automatic mode only.

As you play the song, GSnap will attempt to correct any pitch errors it finds in real time.

The four detection parameters in the top row allow you to limit the frequency range within which the pitch correction will be applied. The four correction parameters in the second row together set the degree of precision applied to the correction and how these are transitioned. They work according to similar principles that govern threshold, attack, and release controls on other effects, such as compressors. Too aggressive of levels here can make the correction too perfect, and as a result it may sound unnatural and artificial. Make them too subtle, and the software won't be able to do its job. The controls in the third row (MIDI) do not apply to audio media items.

I'll just finish by repeating what I said before. Singing correctly in pitch will give you better outcomes than you will get by using pitch correction software!

Chained FX

Quite often, the whole point of using effects such as those discussed in this chapter is so that they can be chained together to create a special sound. There are no hard-and-fast rules for the order in which you should place them. The only rule is that the order that gives you the sound you want is the best order! However, there are a few guidelines that you might find helpful. At the very least, understanding these can save you a lot of time wasted by thrashing around using trial and error.

Table 9.7 outlines a suggested order in which various effects are likely to be used when chained together. This table needs to be read with the following in mind.

■ The table includes the word "Guitar" in its heading, but the reasoning it contains is equally applicable when effects are used on other instruments.

■ Depending on which combination of effects you are using, the order in which they are applied may have a greater or lesser effect on the sound that is produced. The next tutorial will demonstrate this.

■ The order of effects suggested in this table is not set in stone, nor is it gospel. If you have no idea where to begin, it offers you a sensible starting place. This does not mean that you should not experiment. For example, you might find that placing EQ effects ahead of compression works well for you.

■ Outcomes described in Table 9.7 as generally "unpredictable" or "undesirable" might in some circumstances be exactly what you want—for example, with some types of electronic music.

Table 9.7 Guidelines for Placing Effects in a Guitar FX Chain

Category	Comments
Compression	Putting a compressor (if used) as the first item in your guitar FX chain makes sense because it makes the behavior of other effects more predictable. Suppose, for example, that you are also using a flanger or phaser effect. You might get that sound just right, only to find that adding compression after it damages the effect.
EQ	EQ-based effects, such as wah wah, work by sweeping a narrow frequency range up and down. It is harder to obtain a consistent sound from this kind of effect if it comes after, say, chorus or flanging. Incidentally, a wah effect is included on your DVD—see Figure 9.13 and Table 9.8.
Drive	Overdrive, distortion, and fuzz effects all add substantial gain to an incoming signal. Using any of these before (rather than after) modulation effects helps prevent boosting unwanted noise.
Modulation	Phasers, flangers, and chorus all work by splitting a signal and making some change (such as delay or pitch change) to one (wet) stream, which then gets mixed back with the other (dry) stream. Placed too early in the effects chain, their impact can be weakened by other effects that are placed after them. This is about the place in the chain where you would also be inclined to insert such effects as vibrato or tremolo if used.
Time based	Effects such as delay and reverb generally repeat a signal without changing its basic qualities to any great extent (other than perhaps applying a high- or low-pass filter). Using one of these before any other effects that modify the shape of the waveform is likely to produce unpredictable and uncomfortable results.

Tutorial 9.9: Using Chained Guitar Effects

This tutorial will explore one or two examples of how some of the effects introduced in this chapter can be used with each other and with compression. You will probably find the exercises easier if you use exactly the same plug-ins as in the example, but you may substitute other equivalent items if you wish.

1. Open the project file Alone90 and save it as Alone99.

2. Insert the JS Wah plug-in at the start of the Rhythm FX bus (before the limiter). Unless you are using REAPER as your host, you will need to do this by first inserting ReaJS and then loading it into that. Play the song and solo this bus.

3. The two resonance controls determine the frequency range to which the effect will be applied. Set these to 0.72 (top) and 0.1 (bottom). Set the filter distortion

to about 0.08. Adjust the position fader to obtain the required effect. This will probably be somewhere between 0.50 and 0.80.

4.   After the wah plug-in, add the Blue Cat Audio Flanger. For the sake of this example, choose the classic flange preset.

5.   Experiment with changing the order of these two effects. You should find that the difference, though noticeable, is probably not critical, especially when you unsolo the FX bus.

6.   Now solo the Lead FX bus. Insert before the limiter, and in this order, the JS Guitar/Distortion effect (via ReaJS unless you are using REAPER as your host), the Blue Cat Audio Phaser, and the MeldaProduction MVibrato. Set the latter two to bypass.

7.   Create a reasonable level of distortion by lifting its gain control to about 25 or 30, its hardness control above 7, channel mode to stereo, and max volume to about −10.0 or −12.0.

8.   Engage the phaser effect. For the sake of this example, select the mod preset. You can adjust these settings later if you wish.

9.   Engage the vibrato effect. Select the default preset and then lower the vibrato depth level to about 20%.

10. Continue to play the song. Move the distortion effect so that is third in the chain, after the vibrato. You should notice that this "sledgehammer" effect just about ruins the vibrato and phaser effects. Return the distortion to the top of the FX chain.

11. Now add a compressor of your choice (such as ReaComp) after the vibrato effect. Set the ratio to about 6:1 and adjust the threshold so that the compressor is significantly engaged all of the time. This will take much of the "twang" off the combined phaser/vibrato effect.

12. Now move the compressor to the very beginning of this FX chain. You may need to lower the threshold to ensure it is engaged. You should now notice that the guitar signal is much cleaner, with the phaser and vibrato effects better preserved.

13. Unsolo the Lead FX bus and make such adjustments to the volume of each track and fader as you see fit. Save the file.

Parallel Chained FX   Some examples of the use of parallel FX chaining have already been introduced in this book—for example, with respect to compression and reverb. Chapter 14, "Chaining the Chain Gangs: Parallel FX Processing," will deal with this subject in more depth. In the meantime, keep in mind that any type of audio effect can be used with other effects in serial, in parallel, or both. It's just a question of creating the sound that you want to hear.

The method you should use for setting up parallel FX chains will depend on the capabilities, features, strengths, and limitations of your particular host DAW. If your DAW supports it, channel splitting is likely to be your preferred option. The entire parallel chain is built on the one track (conserving screen space), and all of the FX can be accessed and managed from a single window (efficient workflow). Other possible methods include duplicating the original track and/or using a bus or busses.

Now would be a good time to experiment with this. Open the file Alone90 and save it as Alone99P. Explore the possibility of using two effects in parallel on one of the guitar tracks—for example, a dry track in parallel with two different pitch-shifted tracks or a flanged track in parallel with a chorused one. Only by discovering for yourself what *sounds* right for you will you really learn how to use audio effects to their best advantage.

Bonus Plug-Ins (Overview)

The DVD supplied with this book includes a variety of JS plug-ins of the general type introduced in this chapter. None of them is difficult to use, and their quality ranges from good to excellent. If you take a little time to explore these for yourself, you will surely uncover at least the odd gem or two.

Table 9.8 summarizes many of the most interesting of these, including some that have been used in earlier tutorials, and Figure 9.13 illustrates a selection of these.

Table 9.8 Summary of JS Modulation and Similar Plug-Ins

Name	Description
Guitar/Amp-Model	Simulates the effect of a guitar having been recorded using any of a number of popular amps, including Fender and Marshall.
Guitar/Amp-Model-Dual	Simulates the effect of a guitar having been recorded using two different amps, selected from a range that includes Fender and Marshall.
Guitar/Chorus	An easy-to-use chorus effect that allows for a maximum of eight voices.
Guitar/Distort/Fuzz	Simulates the effect created using a fuzzbox pedal, with its amplifier and clipping circuit (see Figure 9.13).
Guitar/Distortion	Creates digital distortion modeled on modern stomp boxes.

(Continued)

Name	Description
Guitar/Flanger	An easy-to-use use but effective flanger. Its most unusual characteristic is that it allows delay time up to 200 ms.
Guitar/Phaser	A four-stage (all-pass filter) phaser, very easy to use and very effective.
Guitar/Tremolo	A basic tremolo effect, especially good for adding subtle touches of tremolo.
Guitar/Wah	Simulates the effect created using a wah wah pedal, with just four simple controls. Creates the impression of adding almost a human voice–like quality to a guitar (see Figure 9.13).
Misc/Tonifier	An ingenious frequency-shifting device capable of creating a series of interesting and unusual effects.
Misc/Tonifier2	A variation of the Tonifier with added amplitude modification.
Pitch/FFT-PS	Creates unusual and experimental pitch-shift effects based on a combination of FFT size, linear slide, semitone shift (up or down), and peak width.
Pitch/MDCT-Shift	Creates unusual pitch-shift effects based on MDCT (*modified discrete cosine transformation*) algorithms. In brief, this essentially works not by applying the effect to the signal directly, but by using a series of filter bands.
Pitch/Octavedown	A more interesting effect than its name implies. Splits the signal into two streams and lowers one stream by a single octave. Its chunk size and overlap controls, together with wet/dry mix, make it possible to achieve very interesting effects very easily, including a "wobulator" type of sound.
Pitch/Octaveup	A more interesting effect than its name implies. Splits the signal into two streams and raises one stream by a single octave. Its chunk size and overlap controls, together with wet/dry mix, make it possible to achieve very interesting effects very easily, including a "wobulator" type of sound.
Pitch/Pitch2	More than just a pitch-lowering plug-in (up to six octaves) with a comparatively low CPU overhead. Its subdivide and mix parameters can be used to create a range of interesting sounds (see Figure 9.13).
Pitch/Pitchdown	Similar to Pitch2 but simpler.
Pitch/Superpitch	A genuine fully functional pitch-shift plug-in (up or down up to 12 octaves) with window size, overlap size, and mix controls that can create some impressive sounds.

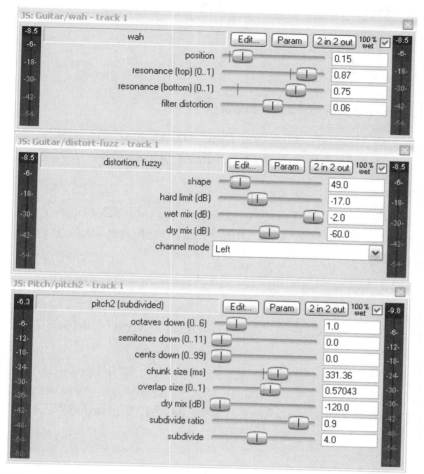

Figure 9.13   From top to bottom, Wah, Distort-Fuzz, and Pitch2—just three of the many interesting JS plug-ins included on your DVD.

Project Files Log

If you have completed all of the examples and tutorials in this chapter, you should have created the following files:

Preparation: Alone 90, Foggy90

Tutorial 9.1: Alone91

Tutorial 9.2: Alone92, Foggy92

Tutorial 9.3: Alone93

Tutorial 9.4: Alone94

Tutorial 9.5: Alone95

Tutorial 9.6: Alone96

Tutorial 9.7: Alone97

Tutorial 9.8: Foggy98

Tutorial 9.9: Alone99, Alone 99P

Your complete project file log should now be as follows:

Alone00, Alone70, Alone76, Alone80, Alone88, Alone90, Alone91 Alone92, Alone93, Alone94, Alone95, Alone96, Alone97, Alone99, Alone99P

AudioExperiment21, Impulse85

Foggy00, Foggy41, Foggy42, Foggy43, Foggy44, Foggy50, Foggy52, Foggy53, Foggy60, Foggy61, Foggy62, Foggy64, Foggy66, Foggy69, Foggy70, Foggy73, Foggy75, Foggy80, Foggy83, Foggy92, Foggy98

Lying00, Lying23, Lying43, Lying50, Lying51, Lying52, Lying54, Lying60, Lying61, Lying62, Lying80, Lying81

Mud00, Mud40, Mud41, Mud60, Mud63, Mud65, Mud70, Mud74, Mud80, Mud86, Mud86a, Mud87

Whiskey00, Whiskey22, Whiskey30, Whiskey31, Whiskey32, Whiskey33, Whiskey60, Whiskey65, Whiskey67, Whiskey68, Whiskey70, Whiskey71, Whiskey72, Whiskey76, Whiskey80, Whiskey82, Whiskey84, Whiskey87

10 Channel FX: Auto-Pan, De-Essers, De-Poppers, and More

This chapter will focus on a selection of what I sometimes call *tailored effects*, or effects that are designed to perform a specific function. An example might be the use of special plug-ins to improve the sound of vocals by removing sibilance or plosives. Such plug-ins are sometimes referred to as *channel effects*. The one thing that most of these effects have in common is that they usually consist of some other generic effect or control (such as an equalizer or a compressor) that has been adapted or modified to be targeted at a particular task. Sometimes, as you will see when we look at vocal strips and channel strips, they are made up from a number of other effects chained together.

You might like some, and you might find some convenient, whereas there are others that you probably won't need and can better manage without. In some cases, you might find that you can just as (or more) effectively obtain equally good (or better) results using one or more of the items that you already have in your audio toolkit. Indeed, going back to the generic effect(s) on which a tailored plug-in is based can often offer you more flexible options. The main reason for including a selection of these items here is to help you decide for yourself when you are likely to find such effects useful and when you might prefer to manage without them.

The tutorials in this chapter will give you an introduction to a variety of effects and show you examples of how they can be used. That doesn't mean that you should be constrained by these examples; rather, you should regard each of them as a gateway through which you can step to learn more by further experimentation.

Introduction

In this chapter, you will examine and experiment with using the following audio effects.

- Auto-pan
- De-essers
- De-poppers
- Exciters
- Vocal strips and channel strips

- Tape and tube saturation
- Various bonus FX

Preparation

Throughout this chapter, you will be working with the sample project *Foggy Desperation*. The preparation required should take you only a few moments.

Preparation: Preparing the Project Files

1. Open the file Foggy90 that you created earlier and immediately save it as Foggy100.

2. That's all!

Auto-Pan

Auto-pan is a fun effect that allows you to constantly change the panning of an instrument or vocal track according to a specified pattern. Several interesting transient-driven auto-pan plug-ins are included with the JS effects on your DVD. These plug-ins adjust the track's pan position in synch with its transients (peaks), thus ensuring that the left-right movements across the panning spectrum follow the song's tempo.

Another example is MeldaProduction's MAutopan, which uses an LFO oscillator to determine the panning pattern (see Figure 10.1). Used sparingly and within reason, adding auto-pan to one or two instruments can help to add a live feel to the song.

Figure 10.1 MeldaProduction's MAutopan is an example of one of many plug-ins that are available for making a variety of tasks easier.

Plug-ins of this nature tend to be highly specialized and customized. For example, there are other auto-pan effects that are time-based. It simply is not possible to summarize exactly what controls you are likely to find on an auto-pan plug-in, other than to say that their three main tasks are likely to be to control the rate at which the panning changes, the extent to which it changes, and the pattern that these changes follow.

Tutorial 10.1: Using Auto-Pan

In this tutorial you will explore an example of how you might use the MAutopan plug-in on an instrument.

1. Open the project file Foggy100 and save it as Foggy101.

2. Solo the mandolin track and change the pan setting to dead center. Play the song.

3. Insert the MeldaProduction MAutopan into the FX bin for this track, before any other plug-ins (such as EQ) that might be there from previous tutorials.

4. Right-click over the graph and select for your oscillator the triangle shape (see Figure 10.1).

5. The higher the depth setting, the more extreme the panning differences created will be. For now, set this somewhere between 50% and 60%.

6. The rate determines the speed at which the oscillator operates. Too high a setting will produce an unsettling, stuttering effect. As a starting point, try somewhere close to 0.5.

7. Too high a pan law setting will cause too much compensation for loss of gain as the signal is panned. This can sound unnatural and unsettling. Try a level of about −3.0 dB at first.

8. Unsolo the track. One result of the auto-pan might be to make this instrument too noticeable in the overall mix. If this is the case, lower the volume fader.

9. Experiment with adjusting the main shape fader to smooth the panning a little.

10. Save the file.

11. Next comes an interesting experiment. Pan the mandolin back out to about 75% right and decrease the depth setting on the auto-pan to somewhere between 0.40 and 0.55.

12. Copy the plug-in (with the same settings) to the electric guitar track, after any existing effects in that track's FX chain. Save the file.

13. Play the file, adjusting the depth setting on the auto-pan plug-ins if you wish. The subtle shifts in the left-right movement of these two instruments panned against each other will help to generate a "live" feel to this track. Save the file when finished.

In theory, there may be nothing you can do with auto-pan that you could not do yourself with pan automation envelopes. In practice, however, the amount of time you would need to take to do this would likely be prohibitive. Moreover, with auto-pan plug-ins you can explore many possible options quickly and easily. If auto-pan is an effect that you are likely to want to use even occasionally, it's definitely worth keeping one or two auto-pan plug-ins somewhere in your toolkit.

De-Essers

De-essers are special plug-ins that are used to remove sibilance from vocal tracks. They essentially work by first identifying the frequency range containing the unpleasant hissing sounds and then compressing those frequencies as heavily as is required.

If your host DAW includes a de-esser, or if you have already purchased some third-party product, such as the Waves RDeEsser, shown in Figure 10.2, then by all means use it. However, if you do not already possess such software, you should be able to construct your own de-esser using any multiband compressor.

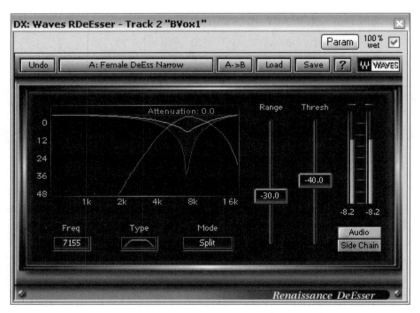

Figure 10.2   The Waves RDeEsser is an example of a de-esser plug-in.

Figure 10.3 shows an example of this. The trick is to first identify the frequency at which the sibilance occurs. This can be at its worst in the vocal itself or somewhere in the harmonics. You can find it by sweeping the track with an EQ band-pass filter, a technique explained in Chapter 5. You should find that the sibilance mostly occurs within a fairly narrow band. The key frequency range will vary with the singer, but typically you should start looking around 4,000 Hz to 6,500 Hz for male vocals and around 5,500 Hz to 10,000 Hz for female vocals.

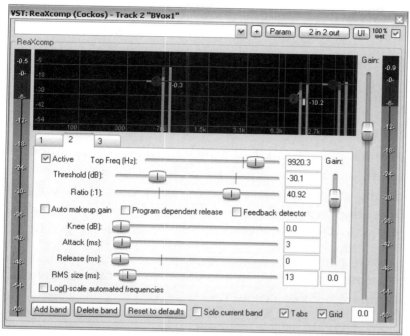

Figure 10.3 Almost any multiband compressor can be configured to act as a de-esser. Shown here is ReaXcomp, included on your DVD.

Despite their different appearances, a custom de-esser (such as that shown at Figure 10.2) and a multiband compressor (such as that shown in Figure 10.3) are operated by the same core controls.

Table 10.1 Summary of Typical De-Esser Parameters

Name	Description
Frequency	This is the frequency that will be targeted by the de-esser. This can be set either by selecting a specific center frequency and then determining how narrow or wide a range should surround it (as in Figure 10.2) or by specifying the lower and upper limits of the range (as in Figure 10.3).
Threshold	This determines the decibel level above which the compression will be applied.
Ratio	This determines the compression ratio that will be applied to the selected frequency range. Notice that with some de-essers, this is calculated automatically.
Sidechain	This option allows you to hear by itself the "sss" that is being removed from the main signal rather than the vocal track itself. This can help you find the best frequency. Sidechain is sometimes labeled *listen* or *effect only*.

Of course, in some cases you are likely to find additional controls. For example, the knee, attack, and release parameters in ReaXcomp work in exactly the same way as do these single controls in any other compressor (except, of course, that they are only applied to the specified frequency range). These were examined in great depth and detail in Chapter 6.

Tutorial 10.2: Using a De-Esser

Sibilance in recording can come about as a result of problems in any of a number of areas, such as singing techniques, microphone selection, and microphone placement. These issues are well outside the scope of this book, but it is nevertheless worth observing that prevention is better than cure. Using a windshield, making sure the singer does not stand too close to the microphone, and lowering the microphone position a little can all help.

Included on your DVD is a JS Liteon de-esser plug-in. However, in this tutorial you will learn how to use a multiband compressor as a de-esser.

1.   Open the project file Foggy101 and save it as Foggy102.

2.   Solo the VoxLead track and select the region from about 0 min 27 sec to about 1 min 6 sec. Play the song with this region looped. You should notice just a touch of sibilance. Some engineers would not consider an amount such as this to be a problem, but for the sake of this exercise, we are going to assume that it is.

3.   If you completed all of the exercises in Chapter 9, there may be a flanger at the end of the FX chain for this track. If so, remove it. For the time being, set all other plug-ins in this track to bypass.

4.   Insert an instance of ReaEQ immediately after the noise gate. If there is no noise gate, insert ReaEQ at the start of the FX chain. Create a band-pass filter of half an octave and sweep the higher frequencies as you play the song. You might notice some slight sibilance around 6,500 Hz.

5.   Remove the ReaEQ and in its place insert an instance of ReaXcomp. By default, this will have four bands. We only really need three. Select the Band 4 tab, then click the Delete Band button to remove it.

6.   Select the Band 3 tab and drag the top frequency fader all the way to the right. Make sure auto makeup gain is disabled.

7.   Select the band 2 tab and set the top frequency to about 6,750 Hz. Make sure auto make-up gain is disabled.

8.   Select the Band 1 tab and set the top frequency to about 4,750 Hz. Make sure auto make-up gain is disabled.

9. Now select the Band 2 tab. This will be our de-esser. Set the ratio to about 30 or 40 to 1. Lower the threshold so that the compressor band is engaged during the "ss" sounds. In Figure 10.4, this is at about −40 dB.

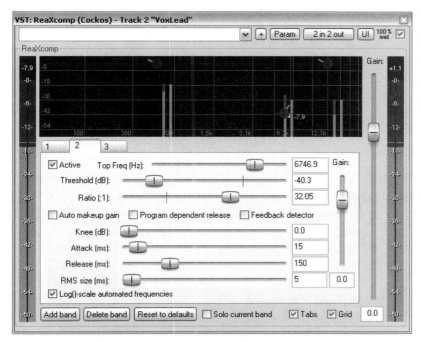

Figure 10.4 Shown here are suggested possible multiband compressor settings for the de-esser in Tutorial 10.2.

10. Re-engage the other plug-ins in this track. Unsolo the VoxLead.

11. Save the file.

There's one more very important point that you need to understand about de-essers. It's so important that I've left it until the very end of this section.

De-esser plug-ins (or multiband compressors set up to act as de-essers) cannot provide a "silver bullet" solution to your problems. No matter how careful you are in trying to target them at the exact frequency that you want to attenuate, there will be side effects. In the example you have just completed, applying a de-esser does not only attack the sibilance—it also affects the "good" sounds that are present around those frequencies. In some cases you may find that the collateral damage done to a mostly good vocal track makes it simply not worth it.

The lesson here is that there will often be times when a solution that avoids using an audio effect may turn out to be the best one. Unlike with our earlier auto-pan example, in this case a simple volume envelope, lowered around the sibilance, just might turn out to be your preferred option. Figure 10.5 shows an example of this being done in one DAW host program.

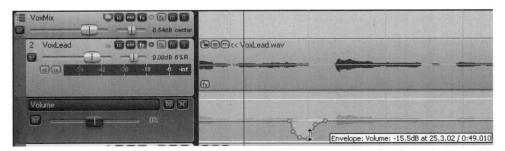

Figure 10.5   An example of using a volume envelope to lessen the effect of sibilance. Sometimes this can be a better solution than using a de-esser.

De-Poppers

Plosive sounds (such as "bbb" and "ppp") can also be tackled using a multiband processor, in a similar fashion to the approach taken by de-esser software. The main difference is that the problem area here is at the lower end of the frequency. Figure 10.6 shows a possible starting point for your settings when you are using a multiband compressor to remove these plosives (as they are often called).

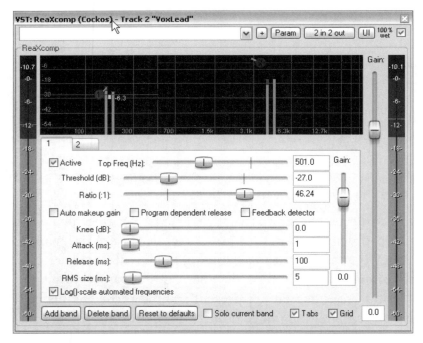

Figure 10.6   An example of the kind of settings that you might apply when using a multiband compressor to deal with vocal plosives.

However, as with sibilance, two golden rules apply. Prevention is better than cure. By using of a pop filter, taking care with microphone placement, and applying correct vocal techniques, you should be able to eliminate the problem at source. Even then, for the odd "ppp" or so that gets through, a simpler solution than compression will often work better.

Take a look at Figure 10.7. Where plosives occur, they can usually be identified quite easily in the waveform by a telltale sharp V shape (see position of mouse pointer in the top picture). By splitting the item at this point and then fading down from the first track and back up from the other, the plosive will usually be eliminated. Alternatively, you could use a volume envelope, as we did with sibilance in the section immediately before this one.

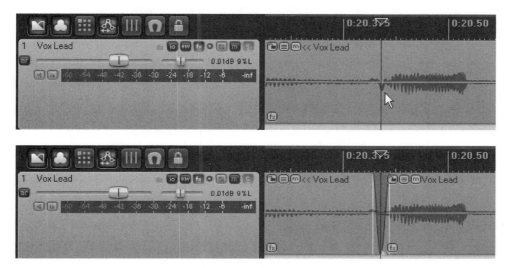

Figure 10.7   A better way to deal with plosives can be to simply split the media item at the telltale V pattern and then fade down from the first item and back up into the other.

This approach brings with it at least one important advantage. It can remove the un-wanted sounds without affecting the dynamics of the recording. It is another example of an audio effect being available but not necessarily being the best solution.

Exciters

A high-end exciter can be used to add a little extra top end to a track, bus, submix, or mix. More often than not, when working with individual tracks, you would be likely to use an equalizer with a high-shelf filter for this purpose. However, an exciter can be a quick and easy way of brightening up and adding a little extra sparkle to a submix.

Figure 10.8 shows two JS exciter plug-ins that are included on your DVD. Although the controls appear to be slightly different, they are in essence very similar. The frequency control determines the frequency above which the high-shelf filter will be applied. The drive or boost control determines how much high-shelf gain will be added. Notice that the second of these two exciters has a rather handy additional control that allows you to specify how much of the late harmonics you would also like added.

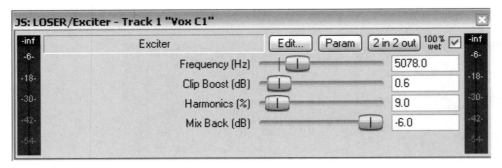

Figure 10.8   Two examples of exciter plug-ins, both included on your DVD. Although each has a slightly different set of controls, both essentially perform the same task.

Tutorial 10.3: Using an Exciter

This exercise uses the JS LOSER Exciter plug-in to brighten up a guitar submix. However, you can use a different plug-in of your own choice if you prefer.

1. Open the project file Foggy102 and save it as Foggy103.

2. Play the song with your guitar submix soloed. Add an instance of LOSER's exciter to the FX bin for this bus. Unless you are using REAPER, you will need to load this via the ReaJS plug-in.

3. Solo the submix bus. Set the frequency at about 4,000 Hz and raise the clip boost to about 2.0 dB or 3.0 dB. Leave the mix back setting at its default level and set the harmonics fader at around 15% to 25%.

4. Compare how the guitars sound with this effect enabled and then bypassed. Enable it and unsolo the bus.

5. Make any further adjustments to your exciter's parameters that you feel improve the sound. You might also wish to adjust the volume output fader for this bus.

6. Add one of the exciter plug-ins to the vocal submix bus. Adjust its parameters to brighten up the vocals a little.

7. Save this file.

Having completed this exercise, you should be able to answer for yourself the question of whether there is much point to using an exciter plug-in. My own view is that although you could probably live quite comfortably without one, it is an easy and handy little tool to have available when all you want to do is add a little top end.

Channel Strips, Vocal Strips, and More

At their simplest, channel strip plug-ins consist of various commonly used audio effects (such as a noise gate, equalizer, and compressor) bundled together in one handy interface. The elements are designed to work smoothly with each other and offer you the advantage of sharing a common window. This means, for example, that when you are making adjustments to any one element, the entire FX chain remains in view. This makes it very easy for you to switch back and forth between tweaking, say, the equalizer and the compressor. TrackPlug from Wave Arts (see Figure 10.9) is an example of such a plug-in. At any one time, you can engage as many or as few as you wish of its various elements.

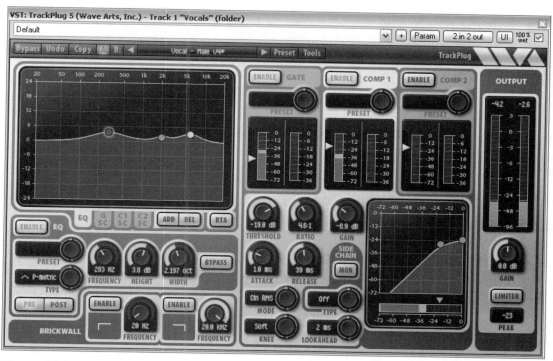

Figure 10.9   The Wave Arts TrackPlug plug-in includes a noise gate, an equalizer, two compressors, and a limiter, all combined in one interface.

The first thing you should note about plug-ins like this is that they bring nothing that you could not create yourself by putting together your own FX chain from the various individual effects. Arguably (but also debatably), you might also get some benefit from analyzing some of their presets.

In some cases, however, they may also exhibit a serious limitation if the order in which the different effects are routed cannot be customized by the user. You have already encountered numerous examples in this book where changing the order in which different effects are placed in a chain will significantly change the outcome. Equalization, for example, is more often than not preferred before compression, but there are any number of circumstances in which you might wish to reverse this order.

Some of the more recent plug-ins of this type overcome this limitation by allowing the user to route the various elements in whichever order they prefer for each instance. Examples of this are Cakewalk's percussion strip and vocal strip (see Figure 10.10). Being able to do this lifts them, in my view, to a whole new level, making them potentially extremely useful.

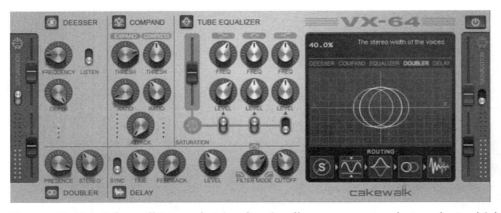

Figure 10.10   Cakewalk's vocal strip plug-in allows you not only to select which elements you wish to use (and, of course, to adjust their parameters) but also to determine the order in which they are routed.

There'll be more about chaining audio effects in Chapters 13 and 14, but for the time being keep this point in mind. You've already seen that even a single effect, such as an equalizer or a compressor, can do a fair amount of damage if it isn't used wisely. How much more would this be the case with any of these composite channel plug-ins?

Tape and Tube Saturation

One more group of effects that deserves a mention here is *saturation*. Saturation effects fall into two main groups—tape saturation and tube saturation. Both types share a common goal, which is to use digital technology to emulate the behavior of analog tape in the real world. It can be used to produce a form of distortion that can be considerably subtler than the overdrive distortion discussed in Chapter 9. If you take a careful look back at Figure 10.10, you will see that Cakewalk's vocal strip plug-in includes saturation faders whose purpose is to do just this.

When 24-track 2-inch tape is used for recording, a natural compression of higher frequencies will occur when the audio signal is particularly hot (strong). This results in a kind of harmonic distortion that can itself lead to the bottom-end (bass) sounds appearing somewhat fuller and warmer. Thus, those who assert that analog recording produces a more accurate representation of the sound are, in fact, wrong. However, they may well be right in asserting that it can produce a more *pleasing* sound.

One example of such a plug-in is Cakewalk's FX2 Tape Sim, shown in Figure 10.11. Tape simulation plug-ins can often be used effectively with vocal tracks or in the final mix. We'll look at the use of effects in a final mix in more detail in Chapter 15, "Multiband Compressors, Mastering Limiters, and More."

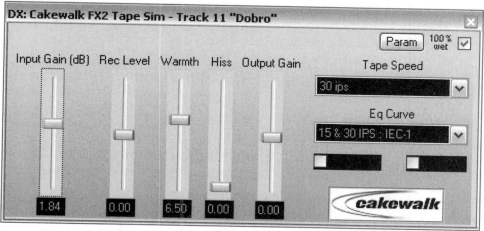

Figure 10.11   Cakewalk's FX2 Tape Sim (included with its flagship DAW SONAR) can be used to emulate the sound of material having been recorded to analog tape rather than digitally.

Bonus Plug-Ins (Overview)

The DVD supplied with this book includes a variety of JS plug-ins of the general type introduced in this chapter, as well as a few more. None of them is difficult to use, and their quality ranges from good to excellent. If you take a little time to explore these for yourself, you will surely uncover at least the odd gem or two.

Table 10.2 summarizes several of the most interesting of these, including some that have been used in earlier tutorials.

Project Files Log

If you have completed all of the examples and tutorials in this chapter, you should have created the following files:

Preparation: Foggy100

Tutorial 10.1: Foggy101

Tutorial 10.2: Foggy102

Tutorial 10.3: Foggy103

Table 10.2 Summary of JS Track, Bus, and Similar Plug-Ins

Name	Description
Liteon/deesser	A de-esser whose parameters include mono/stereo processing options and a choice of high-pass or band-pass filter, as well as the expected frequency, bandwidth, threshold, and ratio controls.
LOSER/compciter	A combined compressor and high-frequency stimulator (exciter).
LOSER/exciter	A high-frequency stimulator (exciter).
LOSER/ppp	An easy to use ping-pong auto-pan effect with just two controls—frequency (or rate) and width.
LOSER/saturation	A simple but effective tube saturation effect, complete with graphical interface.
LOSER/timedifferencepan	Another auto-pan plug-in.
Misc/reverseness	This effect reverses segments of the recoded material. Its controls include a length fader to determine the length of each segment and wet/dry mix faders. See Figure 10.12.
SStillwell/exciter	Another easy-to-use exciter plug-in.
SStillwell/ozzifier	This plug-in deserves a special mention (see Figure 10.13). It is a pitch-delay doubler, allowing up to a maximum of eight voices. It uses a combination of pitch shift and delay to create a doubling or chorus effect. If you want to test it out, try it on the lead vocal of one of your *Foggy* project files, with other vocal FX set to bypass.
Till/Transient-driven Auto-Pan	A series of auto-pan plug-ins driven by transients in the audio signal.

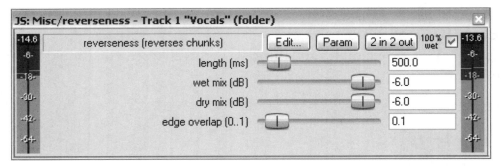

Figure 10.12 The JS reverseness plug-in is included on your DVD and can be loaded into the VST plug-in ReaJS.

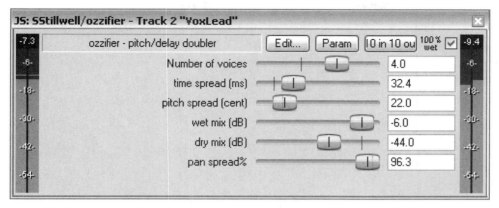

Figure 10.13   The JS SStillwell/ozzifier (included on your DVD) can be used on vocals to create doubling effect. Load it into the ReaJS plug-in.

Your complete project file log should now be as follows:

Alone00, Alone70, Alone76, Alone80, Alone88, Alone90, Alone91 Alone92, Alone93, Alone94, Alone95, Alone96, Alone97, Alone99, Alone99P

AudioExperiment21, Impulse85

Foggy00, Foggy41, Foggy42, Foggy43, Foggy44, Foggy50, Foggy52, Foggy53, Foggy60, Foggy61, Foggy62, Foggy64, Foggy66, Foggy69, Foggy70, Foggy73, Foggy75, Foggy80, Foggy83, Foggy92, Foggy98, Foggy100, Foggy101, Foggy103

Lying00, Lying23, Lying43, Lying50, Lying51, Lying52, Lying54, Lying60, Lying61, Lying62, Lying80, Lying81

Mud00, Mud40, Mud41, Mud60, Mud63, Mud65, Mud70, Mud74, Mud80, Mud86, Mud86a, Mud87

Whiskey00, Whiskey22, Whiskey30, Whiskey31, Whiskey32, Whiskey33, Whiskey60, Whiskey65, Whiskey67, Whiskey68, Whiskey70, Whiskey71, Whiskey72, Whiskey76, Whiskey80, Whiskey82, Whiskey84, Whiskey87

11 Harnessing the Power of Automation

No matter how good your audio effects are, your ability to get the very best from them will to a considerable extent be determined (and perhaps limited) by the features that your host DAW makes available to you for using, applying, managing, and organizing those effects. I'll have more to say on this subject and its various aspects in the concluding chapter of this book, Chapter 16, "Where To From Here?" This chapter will focus on one of these aspects—the one that is at least one of the most important: the ability to use automation envelopes with your various FX plug-ins and their parameters.

Being able to create automation envelopes for FX parameters is one thing. However, unless a software host also gives its users the facilities and features that are needed to edit, manage, and modify those envelope, their usefulness will be limited, to say the least. Toward the end of this chapter, there is a table listing some of the basic essential automation features that I believe DAW users today are entitled to expect from their host software.

Introduction

There have already been a handful of places in this book where automation envelopes have been briefly discussed, including a couple of times when their use has been suggested. This chapter assumes that you are familiar with the general concept of what automation is and how to apply that concept on your host DAW.

Most DAWs provide you with a number of different ways to create and edit your automation envelopes. Typically, at the very least these should include:

- Creating automation curves by manually adding envelope points with your mouse and then clicking and dragging to adjust the shape of the curve (typically to increase or decrease the value of some parameter as the song is played).

- Recording fader movements from the screen onto an automation envelope. Typically, this means that adjustments you make with your mouse to a parameter's value as the song is played back are recorded and written to an automation envelope that can later be played back with the song.

■ Recording fader movements from some external control device (such as a Behringer BCR2000 or a Mackie MCU) onto an automation envelope. Typically, this means that as the song is played back, adjustments that you make physically using that device's knobs and faders are recorded and written to an automation envelope, which can later be played back with the song.

The concept of creating and working with automation envelopes is similar across almost all DAW hosts, but the method of implementation varies widely. Figure 11.1 shows two examples, REAPER and SONAR. I've chosen these two to illustrate a clear example of how a common concept can be implemented using radically different methods in different software.

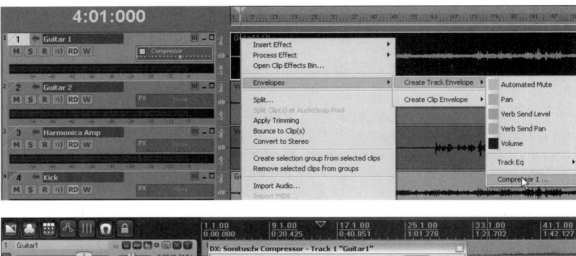

Figure 11.1 Two DAWS, two completely different ways of achieving the same end. To add an FX parameter envelope in SONAR (top), right-click on the track's media and then choose Envelopes > Create Track Envelope > FX Name from the context menu (in this case, Compressor 1). Then select the parameter from a dialog box and click OK. In REAPER, to achieve the same outcome, you click on the parameter control within the FX window and then choose Show Track Envelope from the Parameter menu. Other hosts use other methods.

If you prefer to create your envelopes by recording fader movements, then you will need to know how to switch recording mode on and off, so that when you have finished recording, you can both play back your automated envelopes and make any other adjustments you wish to your various faders and controls for that track without them being recorded. You will, of course, need to consult your DAW's documentation to find out how to do this.

For the sake of simplicity, I'll assume in this section that you will be creating your automation curves by hand, but you can, of course, use whichever method you prefer. You will need to consult your DAW's documentation for details about how to do this with your DAW.

There are four main ways in which you might want to use automation to control your audio effects. Table 11.1 summarizes these.

Table 11.1 Typical Methods of Using Automation with Audio Effects

Method	Description
Simple FX parameter envelopes	This is the method that is probably used the most, and it is the type being applied in Figure 11.1. It can be used, for example, to change the degree of compression applied to a vocal track at different parts of a song or to adjust the EQ of a lead instrument to make it more present during a break.
Dynamic FX parameter modulation	This takes the concept of automating FX parameters to a new level. Rather than having changes in a parameter, such as EQ gain, controlled by a fixed envelope, it is dynamically controlled in real time by some other parameter. An example might be controlling EQ parameters by having the output at specified frequencies on a vocal track automatically lowered and raised as the *actual* volume (rather than the fader level) of that (or any other) track itself rises and falls.
Bypass	This is an on/off setting that can be used to bypass the entire effect for those parts of a song when it is not needed. For example, you might wish to apply an entire set of delay parameters to an instrument for one or two passages only.
Wet/dry mix	Wet/dry mix automation offers you more sophisticated control over how an effect is applied than does a simple bypass envelope. You can vary, as subtly or as intensely as you need, the amount of an effect (such as perhaps reverb) that is applied to a track or bus during different parts of a song.

This chapter will step you through a number of examples, tutorials, and exercises involving the automation of various FX parameter controls. Keep in mind that these examples have been chosen primarily for learning purposes. As always, you should regard them as examples, not models.

Preparation

Throughout this chapter you will be working with the sample projects *Foggy Desperation, Mud Sliding,* and *Now Is the Time for Whiskey.* The preparation required should take you only a few minutes.

Preparation: Preparing the Project Files

In each case, the only preparation needed will be to open the specified version of each project and then save it to the new name required for these tutorials. We will be picking up the projects as they were at the end of Chapter 8 (when reverb was added) and taking them from there.

1. Open the file Foggy83 that you created earlier and immediately save it as Foggy110.

2. Open the file Whiskey87 that you created earlier and immediately save it as Whiskey110.

3. Open the file Mud87 that you created earlier and immediately save it as Mud110.

Simple Parameter Envelopes

There is almost no limit to the number of ways in which automating changes to audio effects parameters can add new creative dimensions to your mixing. That is not to say, of course, that you should go overboard and attempt to create automated changes to every parameter of every effect in sight; rather, it is to say that applied selectively and intelligently, such automation can really breathe more life into your mixes.

Tutorial 11.1: Automating EQ Changes

In this first example, we'll start by looking at using automation envelopes to make adjustments to the equalization of the two vocal parts during the *Now Is the Time for Whiskey* song.

1. Open the project file Whiskey110 and save it as Whiskey111.

2. If you have completed all of the relevant previous tutorials, this project file should include four vocal tracks (VocalM, VocalM Copy, VocalF, VocalF Copy) and a vocals submix. If you did not complete the earlier exercises and have only two vocal tracks (VocalM and VocalF), you should still be able to complete this exercise.

3. The VocalM and VocalF tracks should both contain instances of the Karma FX graphic equalizer. For this exercise, you should first remove these and replace them with instances of a parametric equalizer, such as ReaEQ. In both cases, this should be the first item in the track FX chain.

4. Save the file.

5. For the EQ on the male vocal, add a band at about 150 Hz with a bandwidth of 1 octave (Q approximately 1.4) and a gain of 0.5 dB. For the EQ on the female vocal, add a band at about 3,500 Hz with a bandwidth of 1 octave and a gain of −0.5 dB. You can later adjust these settings to improve the sound if you wish.

6. Create an envelope for the gain control on both of these bands. Edit (modify) these envelopes as follows.

7. For the male vocal, a gain of about 3 to 4 dB during the passages where this is the only vocal and 0.5 dB when singing in harmony.

8. For the female vocal, a gain of about −3 to −4 dB during the passages where this is the only vocal and −0.5 dB when singing in harmony. Figure 11.2 illustrates how these envelopes look in one DAW. Others should be similar.

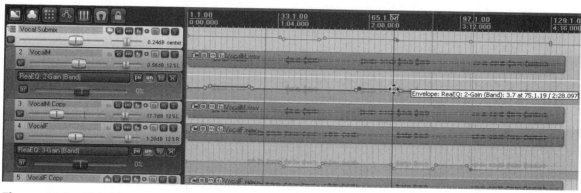

Figure 11.2   This shows the file Whiskey111 with an EQ parameter envelope added to each of the two main vocal tracks. The envelope at the very top is a volume envelope to control the output level of the vocal submix. This should have been added in an earlier exercise; if your file does not include this envelope, you can add it now.

9. Add another band to the male vocal around 3,500 or 4,000 Hz with a single-octave bandwidth and a gain of −3 to −4 dB. No envelope is required for this band.

10. Save the song and play it, making any adjustments you wish to the volume of these tracks and/or the vocal submix.

11. Compare how the track sounds with the EQ engaged and bypassed. With the automated EQ engaged, you should notice more presence during the solo passages and a better harmony when both are singing.

12. We can now turn our attention to the shakuhachi. During an earlier exercise, delay was added to this track's FX bin. If you do not have this, add the Kjaerhus Audio Classic Delay plug-in to this track now and adjust the parameters to create a lingering, haunting effect.

13.   Add an envelope to control the mix parameter. Adjust this envelope so that during the instrumental break from about 2 min 50 sec to about 3 min 20 sec, this is set at about 0.8 (3 o'clock), and at about 0.4 (11 o'clock) the rest of the time. You may also need to fade down the track's volume fader during the instrumental break.

14.   Save the file.

Checkpoint 1

Here are two more examples that you can try, this time using envelopes to control first a compressor and then reverb.

Open the file Foggy110 and save it as Foggy111. This project should include a guitar submix bus. Raise the output volume of this bus by about 3 dB or until the level of this submix is just loud enough to get in the way of the vocals.

Now insert a compressor of your choice into the FX bin for the guitar submix bus. Set a threshold level and add an envelope for the ratio to ensure that during the vocal passages (most of the song), the guitars are compressed slightly to push them back in the mix. During instrumental passages, however, the ratio should be returned to 1:1.

Next, select the Vox reverb bus. The reverb (generated using OmniVerb) is added to the mix of dry signals that are sent to this bus from the VoxLead and Vox Harmony tracks. You can create automation envelopes varying the level of these sends, and hence the amount of reverb that will be generated and added to the mix. Strictly speaking, this is not automating changes to the effect itself, but the outcome is similar. This method is often preferred because it avoids an issue that can occur with some DAW/hardware/plug-in permutations and can lead to a stuttering effect when some parameters in delay-based pug-ins are automated.

Add an automation envelope to the send from the Vox Lead track to the Vox Reverb bus so that the send is raised a few decibels for each instance of the words "foggy desperation" at the end of each main chorus. Figure 11.3 shows an example of how this might look.

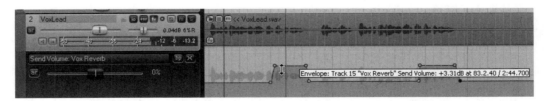

Figure 11.3   This shows the use of a send volume envelope to add an extra touch of reverb to a song at key phrases.

Save the file when you're finished.

This section should have given you a small sample of ideas that show just how useful and effective even simple parameter envelopes like these can be. With practice and experience, you should be able to develop any number of further applications for yourself.

Where Did My FX Parameters Go?   Sometimes when you want to create an automation envelope for use with a particular plug-in, you might follow your DAW's normal procedures, only to find that no parameters are available for your envelopes.

If this happens, don't curse your DAW or rush out to try a different one. Almost certainly it means that the particular plug-in has been written in such a way as to not make its parameters available to the DAW for automation. An example of this is the HybridReverb that we used in Chapter 8.

Dynamic Parameter Modulation

Dynamic parameter modulation is a relatively recent development that, at the time of writing, is only available in one or two DAW programs. It does not require the use of envelopes, but instead works on the principle that a parameter on one track can be controlled and modified by the strength of the audio signal of that track, some other track, or some combination of tracks. The parameter being modified could be a track parameter (such as volume or panning) or an FX parameter (such as EQ gain, compression ratio, or the wet/dry mix in a delay effect).

Figure 11.4 illustrates an example of parameter modulation being used in REAPER. In Chapter 7 (Tutorial 7.4), you applied slapback delay to a harmonica track. In Figure 11.4, parameter modulation has been added to this track so that the harder the harmonica is played, the greater the degree of slapback (wet signal) included in the mix. The result is that the slapback on the harmonica becomes more pronounced during the instrument's louder periods and quieter during its quieter periods. This can help enhance a "live performance" feel.

It is important to understand that this is done without the use of envelopes. You simply set the various controls within the parameter modulation window to get exactly the amount of variation that you require as the song is played back.

Because this feature is not yet standard to most DAWs, it is not really possible to provide a tutorial in this section. Instead, Table 11.2 provides a general overview of how parameter modulation works. It lists and explains only the main controls, without going into too much detail. If you wish to know more about precisely how it is implemented in REAPER, you should consult either the REAPER User Guide or *REAPER Power!* (Course Technology PTR, 2009), or both. If you are using a DAW that supports dynamic parameter modulation, you can try creating the example shown in Figure 11.4 as an exercise. To do so, open the file Mud110 and save it as Mud111.

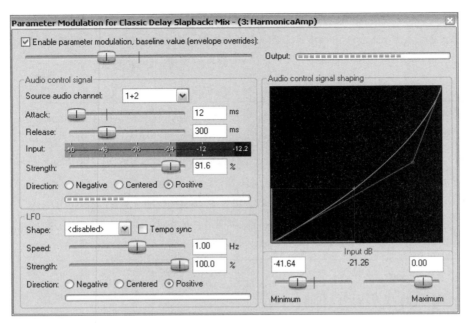

Figure 11.4 REAPER's parameter modulation interface. This example uses parameter modulation rather than compression to tame peaks in volume.

Bypass Automation

A very common practice is to use some audio effect on only part of a track rather than on the whole of the track. Using effects in this way can ensure that a particular instrument will really stand out for those (perhaps brief) periods when you really want it to. It can also help to keep your mix interesting and contribute to the way in which you build your mix to a climax.

If the effect is a very simple one, this can be done reasonably easy with one or two parameter envelopes. This was what you did in Tutorial 11.1 when, for example, you added a single EQ gain envelope to each of two tracks. However, this method is not really convenient if the effect is a complex one, such as delay, with perhaps a half dozen or more parameter envelopes that would need to be adjusted each time you want to turn the effect on or off.

In these circumstances you have four possible solutions:

■ Your DAW host's standard FX interface might include an individual bypass toggle setting for each individual plug-in, which can be automated. If this is the case, then more often than not the simplest solution is to use that. It gives you a common, standard method for managing bypass on any plug-in.

■ Some plug-ins contain their own bypass or enable/disable toggle control. Where this is the case, you can use this.

Table 11.2 How Parameter Modulation Works

Control	Explanation
Source audio channel	Determines whether the parameter's behavior (in Figure 11.4, this is slapback delay mix) is controlled by the track's own volume or that of another track or combination of tracks.
Attack and release	These work in a similar way to attack and release on compressors and other effects. The attack setting determines how quickly the parameter being controlled responds to changes in the source audio signal, and the release setting determines how quickly that change is released.
Strength	This setting determines how aggressively the parameter being controlled will respond to changes in the strength of the source audio signal.
Direction	This determines the nature of the relationship between the parameter being controlled and the source audio used to control it. For example, a negative direction would mean that as the audio signal grows stronger, the parameter value is lowered. A positive setting (as used here) ensures that as the source audio signal increases, the value of the parameter is also increased.
LFO	This group of settings can be used in a similar way to the LFO settings in several modulation effects that we encountered in Chapter 9. It can be used to modify the shape of the way changes to the (in this case) slapback wet/dry mix are applied.
Audio shaping graph	The minimum and maximum controls can be used in conjunction with the shaping handle on the graph (that's the small dot at the point where the two straight lines meet) to restrict the parameter modulation to any specified dB range (in this example, about −40 dB to 0 dB) and to ensure that it responds more strongly at some areas within that range than at others.

■ Less elegant, but workable is to "fudge" it, as we did at Checkpoint 11.1 when we added a compressor to the guitar mix in the file Foggy111. By setting the compressor's ratio setting to 1:1, we effectively ensured that the signal passed through the effect with no compression applied. Of course, this option will not be available for all plug-ins, and even where it is, you may not wish to use it. Remember that even at times when the effect is allowing an unprocessed signal to pass through, it will still be using some of your computer's resources.

■ Provided your host DAW allows you to use audio effects with individual media items (as opposed to a whole track), you can split the item so that the period for which you wish to apply the effect is a discrete item. Where there are several such periods, you can simply add more splits to create multiple items. Take note, however, that (strange as it may seem) with some host DAWs, this might not actually save you any CPU. You'll need to check to see whether this is the case with yours.

Tutorial 11.2: Using Bypass with FX Parameter Envelopes

In this example, we'll make some modifications to our *Mud Sliding* project so that the slapback delay is applied to the harmonica for only a portion of the song, as shown in Figure 11.5. Depending on which options your DAW makes available to you, you should choose one or the other of the two methods shown in the figure.

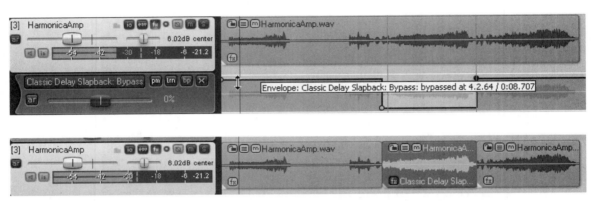

Figure 11.5 Two ways of achieving the same result. The first example (top) shows a bypass envelope being used to ensure that an effect is applied only to a portion of a track (that portion where the envelope has been lowered, less than a third of the track). The second example (bottom) shows the same item with no envelope but instead split into three separate items. The audio effect has been added to only the second of these items, which has also been assigned a different color.

1. Open the project file Mud 110 (or, if you are using parameter modulation, Mud111) and save it as Mud112.

2. If the room microphone track is not already muted, mute it. It is not required for this exercise.

3a. Create a bypass envelope for the slapback delay on the harmonica amp so that the effect is applied only from approx 1 min 23 sec to 2 min 12 sec. Your DAW probably will recognize the special nature of toggle parameters like bypass and automatically create a transition with a square, right-angled shape (see Figure 11.5). If it fails to do this, you will need to select this shape manually.

OR

3b.   Split the harmonica amp media item at approx 1 min 23 sec and 2 min 12 sec and move the slapback delay plug-in from the track's FX bin to the FX bin for this media item.

4.   Save the file.

Wet/Dry Mix Automation

One mixing technique quite often used by some engineers (myself included) is to vary slightly the wet/dry mix of some of the effects at different parts of the song. This can cause subtle variations that can help to maintain the listener's interest, even if she is not always consciously aware that such changes are taking place.

Many effects, especially delay-based effects, have their own wet/dry controls that can be used for this purpose. Others do not. Where this is the case, you can use a bus to house the effect and then automate the output level of this bus. If you are doing this with several different effects (possibly spread over several different tracks), this method can create a lot of screen clutter. A handy feature of some DAWs (including Ableton Live and REAPER) is that they add their own native wet/dry mixer to every effect. Where this feature is available, it can make life considerably easier.

Tutorial 11.3: Wet/Dry FX Mix Automation

In this example, we'll make some modifications to our *Mud Sliding* project so that after the slapback delay is cut from the harmonica, the amount of reverb applied to the kick and the snare will be gradually increased until the end of the song. This should help to build a sense of power and urgency.

1.   Open the project file Mud 112 and save it as Mud113.

2.   Select the snare track and open the interface for the reverb plug-in in this track.

3a.   If your DAW has its own wet/dry control that it adds to the interface of every plug-in, set this to 60% wet for this plug-in and adjust the reverb plug-in's own wet and dry output faders to achieve the desired amount of reverb. Add an automation envelope for the DAW's wet/dry mixer, fading this up toward 80% for the last part of the song, as shown in Figure 11.6.

OR

3b.   If your DAW does not add a wet/dry control of its own to every plug-in, add two envelopes for the reverb plug-in, one for the dry output level and one for the wet output level. Use the envelopes to gradually increase the wet level from the point shown in Figure 11.6 and to decrease the dry level from the same point.

4.   Repeat what you did at Step 3 for the kick track.

5.   Save the file.

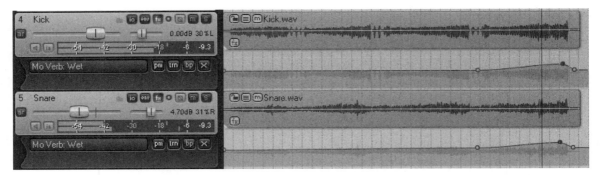

Figure 11.6 This shows the use of automation envelopes to increase the amount of the wet signal (late reverb) added to a kick and a snare toward the end of a song.

Creating and Managing Envelopes: A Summary

Not so many years ago, when audio software programs first gave us the ability to create and use envelopes to automate FX parameters, we all dropped our jaws and gazed at our CRT computer screens in amazement. Today, however, such features are quite rightly regarded as commonplace. Automation (including FX parameter automation) might be one of the most important of your mixing tools, but no less important are the workflow and productivity issues associated with its implementation.

By this I mean that it is not enough for the raw functionality of being able to create and use automation envelopes to be included in a host DAW's feature set. It is also important that the method of implementation of these features is as flexible, simple, powerful, and user-friendly as possible. Otherwise, you might fairly conclude at times that for the time and trouble involved, it just isn't worth it. The process of creating envelopes can be cumbersome and clumsy. Defining exactly the accurate transitions that we want can be finicky and frustrating. Making changes and corrections can be awkward and prone to error. This is one important area where, sadly, not all DAWs are equal.

When you are looking at spending perhaps $500 or more on a host DAW (if you have not already done so), you would be well advised to take the time to research its automation capabilities, limitations, strengths, and weaknesses to evaluate how effectively it can deliver your requirements in this area. Table 11.3 summarizes the issues that I would recommend anyone who needs to use FX parameter automation include in their initial checklist.

Of course, some people will want to make more use of FX parameter automation than others. Personally, I use it extensively, especially to make subtle changes that are intended to add a more natural and human feel to a mix. Others may barely use this feature at all. The greater the use you make of FX parameter automation, the more important these questions will be for you.

Table 11.3 Key Characteristics and Features of DAW Simple Envelope Automation

Item	Comment
Automation modes	This is one of those areas where different DAWs use different terms to describe what is essentially the same thing. As an absolute minimum standard, you should expect to be able to use automation to record and play back fader movements as an alternative to creating your envelopes by hand. If you use any record method of creating automation envelopes, then the option of being able to switch to some form of touch or latch mode is also likely to be important for you. This enables you to replay your automated envelopes at the same time as you tweak the parameter controls to make further changes. Changes are recorded (overwriting the original envelope) only at those places that you choose; the rest of the original envelope remains intact. This is obviously preferable to having to record the entire envelope from scratch all over again.
Record/write precision	When you record parameter changes to an automation envelope, the parameter data actually changes (however minutely) many times a second. However, it is most unlikely that you would want to actually record this number of discrete envelope points. Some sort of option that allows you to specify the degree of precision you require will prevent this from happening.
Freehand draw	Traditionally, the required method of creating automation curves by hand is to click on the curve and then drag the points up, down, left, or right with the mouse. Quite often this method will still serve you well, but it is also likely that there will be many occasions when being able to click, drag, and sweep the mouse to draw your envelope curve in some sort of pencil mode will be both quicker and easier.
Reduce points	Even after using an option to specify recording or freehand draw precision, you may still end up with too many and too cluttered points. A quick and easy way to reduce the number of points without having to delete each one manually will resolve this. Figure 11.7 shows an example where a horizontal fader is used to reduce the number of points exactly as required. As the fader is moved farther to the left, more points are removed.
FX automation on items	Assuming that your DAW allows you to use automation with individual media items as well as complete tracks, you should also be able to use FX parameter envelopes on entire tracks or individual items as you wish.
FX bypass	This has already been discussed. The ability to create an FX bypass envelope for any plug-in is very useful.
FX wet/dry mix	This, too, has been discussed. Being able to add a single wet/dry mix envelope to any FX plug-in can in many cases make FX parameter automation quicker, easier, and clutter free.

(Continued)

Item	Comment
Fade shapes	After every envelope point, the automation curve will fade up or down to the next one. Typically, you should be able to choose from a number of shapes, such as linear (straight line); Bezier curve; smooth curve; fast start, slow end curve; slow start, fast end curve; and so on (see Figure 11.9). The option of square, right-angled transition is also important when you are automating any toggle parameters, such as enable/disable or bypass, which can only ever have one of two states.
Envelope display	Where you have several envelopes on one track, the screen clutter this creates can make working with and editing individual automation envelopes extremely difficult. This issue can be resolved if your DAW makes flexible display options available to you. You need to be able to easily show or hide any or all envelopes as you wish, and in different permutations at different times. Ideally, you should also be given the option to display individual envelopes either in their own separate lanes or imposed upon the media item. Figure 11.8 illustrates this point. A separate lane is useful when you are editing an envelope. However, to minimize screen clutter, it can also be useful to be able to move the envelope over to the media item itself when you have finished making your edits.
Envelope bypass	Don't confuse this with FX bypass. An envelope bypass toggle allows you to compare how your mix sounds with and without the envelope applied.
Raise/lower envelope	I lost count years ago of how many times after carefully crafting an envelope I have found that I needed to raise or lower the entire envelope slightly. Some quick and easy means of doing this is essential, as indeed it also is for raising or lowering an entire *portion* of the envelope (see Figure 11.10).
Precision editing	Adjusting envelope points to get them exactly right can be a very effective way of wasting hours. At the best of times it requires care, concentration, a steady hand—and software with good editing techniques. Absolute essentials here include being able to use some sort of booster key (such as Control) while clicking and dragging for precision editing of envelope points (so that large movements of the mouse result in only small movements of the point) and being able to access some sort of dialog box for typing in actual values if you prefer.
Horiz/vertical lock	Another essential editing technique is to easily be able to restrict a point's movement (when editing it) to vertical only or horizontal only if you wish (as an alternative to freely dragging it). This is another technique for which some booster key (or key combination) needs to be available when clicking and dragging the mouse.
General editing	Look out for other editing features, such as easily and without fuss being able to delete points and selections of points, clear the entire envelope, and delete an envelope.

Item	Comment
Cut/copy with media	This one is self-explanatory, really. You need to have an option to include automation envelopes with any media items being cut or copied and pasted.
Lock/unlock envelopes	It is very easy to click and drag by accident, thereby inadvertently moving an envelope point or shifting an entire envelope or envelope segment. Having an option to lock envelopes can prevent this from occurring—with an unlock option also available for when you want to change your mind.

Of course, automation is not the only thing that matters, and it may well be that overall you prefer a DAW with less than ideal automation implementation because of its strengths in other areas. That's fair enough. If you do, you will at least be aware of some of the improvements you should be asking for!

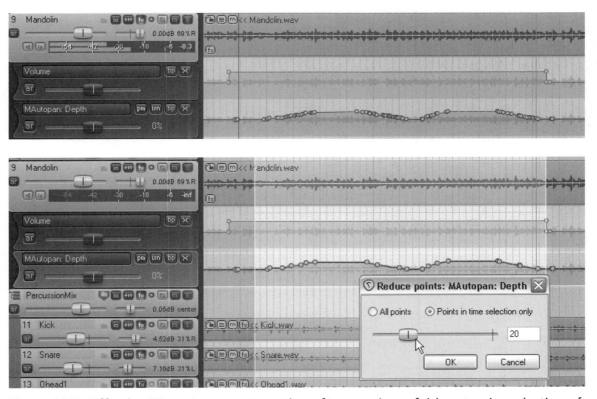

Figure 11.7 Effective FX parameter automation often requires a fairly extensive selection of editing options and features. Shown here is automation of a parameter (MAutopan Depth), recorded from fader movements. Notice the very large number of points on this envelope in the top picture. This many points can make editing the envelope (by perhaps adjusting some points) a difficult and onerous task. Fortunately, the program includes a Reduce Points feature (bottom picture) that can quickly and easily be used to strip out superfluous envelope points.

Figure 11.8   Editing envelopes can be a tedious and slow process. That's why you should get to know which display options your DAW makes available. In the first of the three examples here (top), a single track includes four automation envelopes, all superimposed on the media item. This sort of arrangement makes envelope editing very difficult. The second (middle) example shows each envelope displayed in a separate lane. This clear, uncluttered interface makes editing much easier, but it uses a lot of screen real estate. You might prefer a compromise option similar to the third (bottom) example. In this case, those envelopes on which we are currently working are displayed in their own lanes, while the others are parked on the media item itself.

Figure 11.9   Shown here are examples of some of the shapes you should be able to select for transition from one envelope point to the next.

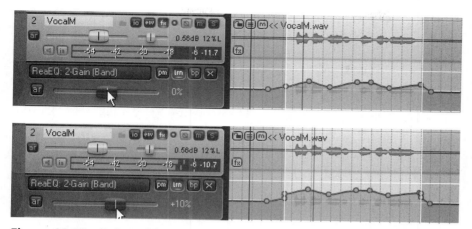

Figure 11.10   Being able to adjust entire sections of an envelope quickly and easily is an important aspect of envelope editing. In the example shown here, it is as simple as selecting the required portion (top) and then using a fader to raise or lower that entire section (bottom).

Project Files Log

If you have completed all of the examples and tutorials in this chapter, you should have created the following files:

> **Preparation:** Foggy110, Mud110, Whiskey110
>
> **Tutorial 11.1:** Whiskey111
>
> **Checkpoint 11.1:** Foggy111
>
> **Tutorial 11.2:** Mud112
>
> **Tutorial 11.3:** Mud113

Your complete project file log should now be as follows:

> Alone00, Alone70, Alone76, Alone80, Alone88, Alone90, Alone91 Alone92, Alone93, Alone94, Alone95, Alone96, Alone97, Alone99, Alone99P
>
> AudioExperiment21, Impulse85
>
> Foggy00, Foggy41, Foggy42, Foggy43, Foggy44, Foggy50, Foggy52, Foggy53, Foggy60, Foggy61, Foggy62, Foggy64, Foggy66, Foggy69, Foggy70, Foggy73, Foggy75, Foggy80, Foggy83, Foggy92, Foggy98, Foggy100, Foggy101, Foggy103, Foggy110, Foggy111

Lying00, Lying23, Lying43, Lying50, Lying51, Lying52, Lying54, Lying60, Lying61, Lying62, Lying80, Lying81

Mud00, Mud40, Mud41, Mud60, Mud63, Mud65, Mud70, Mud74, Mud80, Mud86, Mud86a, Mud87, Mud110, Mud112, Mud113

Whiskey00, Whiskey22, Whiskey30, Whiskey31, Whiskey32, Whiskey33, Whiskey60, Whiskey65, Whiskey67, Whiskey68, Whiskey70, Whiskey71, Whiskey72, Whiskey76, Whiskey80, Whiskey82, Whiskey84, Whiskey87, Whiskey110, Whiskey111

12 Making Space: Stereo Enhancement

This chapter is devoted to one particular family of plug-ins that can be used to enhance or simulate the stereo qualities of your tracks, submixes, and mixes. As you will see in the examples that follow, different stereo and pseudo-stereo effects use different methods of achieving these ends. Some of them can even be added to a track that was recorded in mono to make it sound like a stereo item.

We'll be looking at some examples of these and trying them out on some of the tracks in our sample projects, before discovering that you can often have more control and flexibility over how you apply stereo enhancement to your tracks simply by using one or more of a number of the effects with which you are by now already familiar, rather than employing custom stereo enhancement tools.

Introduction

Stereo effect plug-ins work in a variety of ways. Typically, they start from the premise that the output of a track is usually delivered using two channels—left and right. This is the case whether we are dealing with a mono track, a stereo track, a submix, or a full mix. This can be demonstrated simply by adjusting any track's pan control to determine the relative strength of the signal that is sent to the two speakers. In this case, the content of both left and right channels will be identical; only the *strength* of each signal is determined by the pan control.

An in-depth discussion of recording techniques is outside the scope of this book, but if you want to capture a genuine stereo effect from an instrument, then the way to do so is to record using two microphones. Stereo effect plug-ins aim to achieve their results artificially by modifying the audio signal so that when it is split into its two channels, each is in some way made different from the other, with one of the two being pushed somewhat to the left and the other somewhat to the right. It is important that you understand that this can only work if each of the two channels *is* different in some way. Simply pushing two identical audio signals left and right will not achieve this—it will only affect the overall volume of the audio and the relative balance between the two speakers (in a similar way to that which would be achieved using a simple pan control). We'll work through an example that demonstrates this later.

Some of the more commonly used methods employed by various stereo effects are:

- **Using delay.** Delay-based stereo effects add different amounts of delay to each of the two channels (or delay to one but not the other) and then pan the two channels apart. The parameter controls for this kind of stereo effect are largely similar to those you would find in delay plug-ins.

- **Phase inversion.** This is in some ways the most interesting method. The effect is achieved by simply reversing the phase of one of the two channels. On receiving this sound, the brain interprets these two signals as originating from a stereo source.

- **Making EQ adjustments.** By equalizing left and right channels differently, it is again possible to create the illusion of a stereo source.

- **Stereo enhancement.** This type of effect only works on existing stereo tracks and busses, not on mono ones. It can be used to adjust, for example, the balance and rotation of left and right channels and to push the mix farther apart.

This chapter is divided into the following sections:

- Using delay-based stereo effects

- Using phase inversion stereo effects

- Creating your own stereo effects

- Enhancing stereo in a mix

- Bonus stereo effects plug-ins

Preparation

Throughout this chapter you will be working with the sample projects *Foggy Desperation*, *Mud Sliding*, and *Now Is the Time for Whiskey*. The preparation required should take you only a few minutes.

Preparation: Preparing the Project Files

In each case, the only preparation needed will be to open the specified version of each project and then save it to the new name required for these tutorials. We will be picking up the projects from various earlier stages and taking them from there. They will not necessarily be the latest versions of these projects.

1. Open the file Alone90 that you created earlier and immediately save it as Alone120.

2. Open the file Mud111 that you created earlier and immediately save it as Mud120.

3. Open the file Whiskey111 that you created earlier and immediately save it as Whiskey120.

Delay-Based Stereo Effects

In this example, we will be using the mda Stereo plug-in (see Figure 12.1) to create a stereo effect on a mono item. This plug-in is included in the mda VST Effects package; download details are included in Table 1.2 in Chapter 1.

Figure 12.1   The mda Stereo Simulator plug-in. Its controls include delay and modulation, as well as width, balance, and rate.

Tutorial 12.1: Using a Delay-Based Stereo Plug-In

In this first example, we will be using the mda Stereo plug-in on one of the tracks in the *Alone Again* project.

1.   Open the project file Alone120 and save it as Alone121.

2.   Remove any existing effects from both tracks. Pan both tracks dead center. Play the song.

3.   Into the FX bin of the rhythm guitar track, insert the mda Stereo plug-in and the JS LOSER/gfxGoniometer plug-in. Unless you are using REAPER, you will need to insert ReaJS and then load the JS goniometer into there.

4.   With the stereo plug-in set to bypass, play the song. Notice the visual feedback on the goniometer.

5.   Now engage the stereo plug-in. There really can be no preconceived notion here of what is a right or wrong group of settings, other than to say in this case to leave the balance at 0. This will ensure that the left and right signals will be of approximately equal strength.

6.   Experiment with the other controls until you find the effect you want. The rhythm guitar should sound as if it is wrapped around the lead, almost like two rhythm guitars, in fact. You may wish to also adjust the relative volume of the two tracks. However, a word of caution is needed here. What sounds good when you listen to an instrument on its own might not seem so good when you hear it in the context of an overall mix.

7. As you save the file, notice the very different visual feedback that you are now getting from the goniometer.

Phase Inversion Stereo Effects

In this example, we will be using the JS IX/StereoPhaseInvert plug-in (see Figure 12.2) to create a different stereo effect on the same mono item as before. This plug-in is included on the DVD that accompanies this book.

Figure 12.2   The JS: IX/StereoPhaseInvert plug-in. This is about as simple as it gets—it has only one control.

Tutorial 12.2: Using a Phase Inversion Stereo Plug-In

1. Open the project file Alone121 and save it as Alone122.

2. Pan both tracks dead center. Play the song.

3. In the FX bin of the rhythm guitar track, set the existing mda Stereo plug-in to bypass. After this plug-in (but before the goniometer), insert the JS IX/Stereo-PhaseInvert plug-in. Unless you are using REAPER, you will need to first insert ReaJS and then load the JS plug-in into there.

4. With the phase invert plug-in set to bypass, play the song. Notice the visual feedback on the goniometer.

5. Now engage the phase invert plug-in. Select the drop-down list and select the mode Invert Left.

6. Notice how the goniometer display has changed.

7. Try this experiment. Engage the mda stereo plug-in as well as the phase invert plug-in. Decide for yourself which of the various options you prefer.

8. As you save the file, notice the very different visual feedback that you are again getting from the goniometer.

Figure 12.3 shows how the goniometer visually depicts the sound of your rhythm guitar track in three of the scenarios that you have explored in these two tutorials.

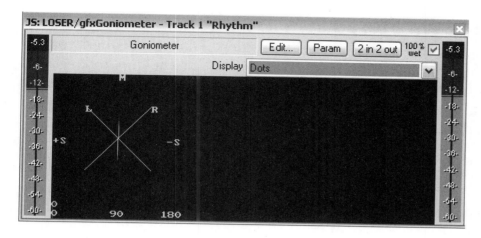

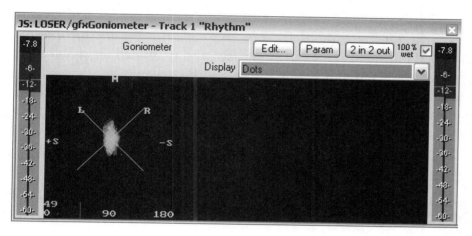

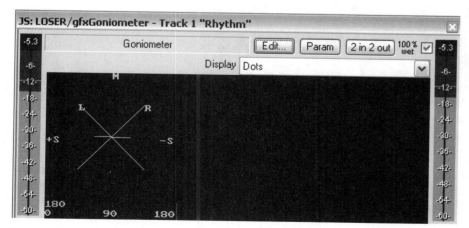

Figure 12.3   A picture paints a thousand words. Shown here is the goniometer display for our rhythm guitar track dry (top), with delay-based stereo enhancement (center), and with one channel's phase inverted (bottom).

Creating Your Own Stereo Effects

Hopefully, you might find this the most interesting section of this chapter. In it, you will explore various ways in which you can apply a number of techniques to create for yourself a stereo environment from a mono track. What's really interesting is that these are all types of effects that you already know how to use. Up until now, you just haven't had occasion to put them together in this way.

If you think about it for a moment, you might be able to figure out that these various stereo effects in reality do little more than create a parallel FX processing chain and process each channel in a different way. This might be less than obvious at first because it is all done behind the scenes. In this section, you can have a go at doing it for yourself. If you like, set yourself the mental goal of trying to create something close to the kind of sound you might have achieved if the part had been recorded with two microphones.

Some of the effects that you have already used do in fact have this parallel processing capability built into them. This includes, for example, ReaDelay, which lets you create two (or more) delay taps, each with different settings and each panned differently. Others include the Kjaerhus Classic EQ plug-in (see Figure 12.4), with its option to EQ both left and right channels independently of each other. Download details for the Kjaerhus freeware VST plug-ins are included in Table 1.2 in Chapter 1.

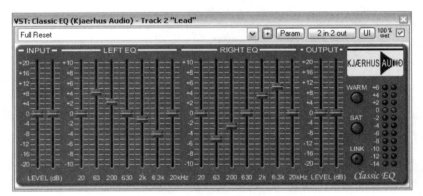

Figure 12.4   The Kjaerhus Classic EQ plug-in lets you pan left and right channels independently—just make sure you disable the Link toggle.

If you wish to experiment with the use of one or both of these plug-ins on a single track (such as the rhythm or lead guitar in the *Alone Again* project), please do so. When you've finished, there's also a tutorial for you to try.

Tutorial 12.3: Using a Delay-Based Stereo Plug-In

In this next example, we will be using a number of different techniques, including equalization, delay, and panning, to create a stereo environment for what initially will be a mono track.

1.   Open the project file Alone122 and save it as Alone123.

2.   Remove all existing stereo effects from the rhythm track. Leave the goniometer there. Add also a goniometer to the master's FX bin.

3.   We are going to set up a parallel FX chain to create a stereo environment for the rhythm guitar. As on the other occasions when we have used parallel FX processing, this can be done (depending on your host DAW's feature set) either by channel splitting, duplicating the track, or using a bus. This exercise assumes that you will be duplicating a track, but you can adapt the instructions to suit one of the other methods if you prefer.

4.   Create a duplicate of the rhythm guitar track and solo just these two tracks. Pan one 70% left and the other 70% right. This next step is important for your understanding of what's happening here.

5.   Play the song. Check what you are hearing with headphones. Observe the output of the goniometer in the master. You should rapidly conclude that duplicating and panning a track by itself will not create any stereo effect. All it affects is the volume of the audio material.

6.   Now add a six-band parametric EQ to both your rhythm guitar tracks. Next, you will need to create mirror image settings on the two EQ instances so that the changes you make to the EQ on each track pretty much compensate for each other. Figure 12.5 illustrates this.

7.   Now as you play the song, you should begin to find that wraparound effect we discovered in Tutorial 12.1. Use your ears to check this with headphones and your eyes to check the goniometer in the master.

8.   Save the file.

9.   Now experiment some more. Add a simple delay effect to the FX bin of one (but only one) of the rhythm guitar tracks. Set a delay time of no more than 15 ms and no less than 7 ms.

10. Save the file.

Enhancing a Stereo Track, Bus, or Mix

In this section you'll experiment with adding stereo enhancement to a bus (a drum submix) and to an overall project mix. Hopefully, you will discover that this is often one of those areas where by using a deft and gentle touch, you can obtain impressive results fairly easily.

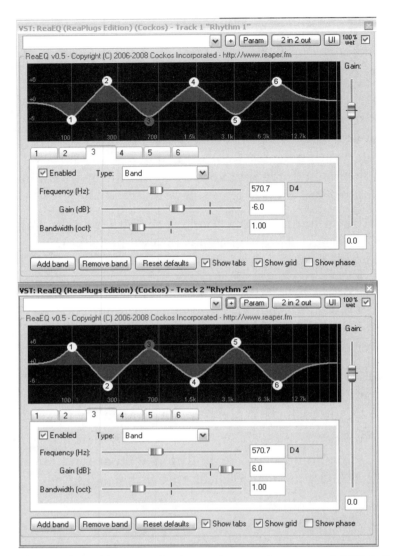

Figure 12.5 The two rhythm guitar tracks, panned 70% left and 70% right, respectively, are equalized so that the changes effectively compensate for each other. The actual settings shown are illustrative only, not a model. You should determine for yourself how many bands you want to use and which frequencies to adjust.

Tutorial 12.4: Adding Stereo Enhancement to a Submix

You can use stereo enhancement with any instrument or vocal submix that you wish, but in practice, more interesting results are likely to be obtainable when the mix includes a variety of very different-sounding tracks, such as a drums submix.

1. Open the project file Mud120 and save it as Mud124. If the RoomMic track is not already muted, mute it.

2. If the three percussion tracks (kick, snare, and perc overhead) have not already been sent to a submix, create this submix now. The output of each of these three tracks should be routed to this submix instead of the master. Of course, any existing sends to a reverb bus should be left as they are.

3. Add an instance of the JS plugin SStillwell/stereowidth to the FX bin for this submix (see Figure 12.6). Unless you are using REAPER, you will need to insert the ReaJS plug-in as a VST plug-in and then load the stereowidth plug-in there.

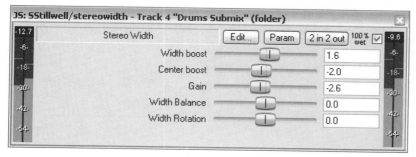

Figure 12.6 The JS SStillwell/stereowidth plug-in included on your DVD can be used to enhance the stereo image of a submix.

4. It should be noticeable how increasing the width boost level and reducing the center boost level will alter the stereo characteristics of the component parts of this submix. Experiment also with the balance and rotation controls. Notice how the latter seems to change the position of the entire drum kit.

5. You should notice that a little stereo enhancement here can add punch and zest to the submix. Too much may make it seem disjointed and clumsy. You'll probably find that settings no more severe than those shown in Figure 12.6 are quite effective. You may need also to adjust one or more of the individual track volume faders within the submix.

6. Save the file when you're finished.

Work with Your Pan Settings Stereo enhancement plug-ins are not (and cannot function as) a lazy substitute for getting the pan settings for your various tracks right in the first place. Their strength lies in their ability to augment and enhance good panning, not to cover up bad work. This applies equally whether you are working with a submix, a stereo bus, or the master track.

Adding Stereo Enhancement to the Whole Mix We'll take a closer look at how you might wish to use audio effects on the master track (for your overall mix) in Chapter 15, "Multiband Compressors, Mastering Limiters, and More," but for now it will do no harm to experiment with adding a touch of stereo enhancement in your master track.

Open the file Whiskey120 and save it as Whiskey124. If you like, use the JS LOSER/ StereoField plug-in (see Figure 12.7). By all means, push the controls out to their limits to see what they will do to the song, but you are likely to be happier with fairly conservative settings, such as those shown in Figure 12.7.

Figure 12.7   The JS LOSER/StereoField plug-in included on your DVD can be used to polish the stereo image of a mix or submix.

Bonus Plug-Ins (Overview)

The DVD supplied with this book includes a number of JS plug-ins designed to assist you with stereo enhancement (including some that you have used in this chapter). Spend some time exploring these for yourself.

Table 12.1 summarizes these. However, I do need to make a brief disclaimer. At the time of writing this, the contents of the ReaJS package still had to be finalized. It is possible that I may have included an item or two in this list that ended up not being included with the package.

Table 12.1 Summary of JS Track, Bus, and Similar Plug-Ins

Name	Description
IX/StereoPhaseInvert	A simple phase invert effect that works by inverting the phase of either channel.
Liteon/pseudostereo	Creates a simulated stereo effect using delay.
LOSER/stereo	A ridiculously easy to use effects plug-in that adds delay to one channel to create a simulated stereo effect.
LOSER/stereoEnhancer	This effect uses the principles of equalization to enhance the stereo effect on an existing stereo track or bus by adding width at specified frequencies.
LOSER/stereoField	This stereo field manipulation effect can be used to adjust the balance or rotation of an existing stereo track or bus.
SStillwell/stereowidth	Another stereo field manipulation effect that can be used to rotate or adjust the stereo balance of an existing stereo track, bus, or mix or to boost the stereo imaging.

Project Files Log

If you have completed all of the examples and tutorials in this chapter, you should have created the following files:

Preparation: Alone120, Mud120, Whiskey120

Tutorial 12.1: Alone121

Tutorial 12.2: Alone122

Tutorial 12.3: Alone123

Tutorial 12.4: Mud124, Whiskey124

Your complete project file log should now be as follows:

Alone00, Alone70, Alone76, Alone80, Alone88, Alone90, Alone91 Alone92, Alone93, Alone94, Alone95, Alone96, Alone97, Alone99, Alone99P, Alone120, Alone121, Alone122, Alone123

AudioExperiment21, Impulse85

Foggy00, Foggy41, Foggy42, Foggy43, Foggy44, Foggy50, Foggy52, Foggy53, Foggy60, Foggy61, Foggy62, Foggy64, Foggy66, Foggy69, Foggy70, Foggy73, Foggy75, Foggy80, Foggy83, Foggy92, Foggy98, Foggy100, Foggy101, Foggy103, Foggy110, Foggy111

Lying00, Lying23, Lying43, Lying50, Lying51, Lying52, Lying54, Lying60, Lying61, Lying62, Lying80, Lying81

Mud00, Mud40, Mud41, Mud60, Mud63, Mud65, Mud70, Mud74, Mud80, Mud86, Mud86a, Mud87, Mud110, Mud112, Mud113, Mud120, Mud124

Whiskey00, Whiskey22, Whiskey30, Whiskey31, Whiskey32, Whiskey33, Whiskey60, Whiskey65, Whiskey67, Whiskey68, Whiskey70, Whiskey71, Whiskey72, Whiskey76, Whiskey80, Whiskey82, Whiskey84, Whiskey87, Whiskey110, Whiskey111, Whiskey120, Whiskey124

13 The Chain Gang: Serial FX Processing

In several earlier chapters, we more than touched on the subject of using a serial effects chain on a track or media item. A serial effects chain is what you get when you place two or more effects (such as EQ and compression) on the same track, one after the other. In this chapter, you will have the opportunity to consolidate what you have already learned, as well as pick up a few more tricks. The emphasis is much more on how the effects work *together* than on the individual effects themselves.

Introduction

In this chapter, you will be taking what you have learned up to now about such effects as noise gates, equalization, compression, delay, and so on and then going back to completely dry tracks and building your effects chains from scratch, starting with a clean slate. The tutorials include examples of building effects chains for vocals, snare and kick, and guitar, but the same principles should apply to the use of effects with any instrument.

This chapter is divided into the following sections:

- Guiding principles for serial effects chains

- Case study 1: the vocals

- Case study 2: the snare and the kick

- Case study 3: the guitar

- Case study 4: the submix

Preparation

Throughout this chapter, you will be working with the sample projects *Foggy Desperation, Mud Sliding,* and *Now Is the Time for Whiskey.* The preparation required should take you only a few minutes.

Preparation: Preparing the Project Files

In each case, the only preparation needed will be to open the specified version of each project and then save it to the new name required for these tutorials. In every case, the version to be opened will be one of the first examples of these projects, originating in Chapter 3 or 4.

1. Open the file Foggy40 that you created earlier and immediately save it as Foggy130.

2. Open the file Mud40 that you created earlier and immediately save it as Mud130.

3. Open the file Whiskey30 that you created earlier and immediately save it as Whiskey130.

Guiding Principles

There are no hard-and-fast rules that can tell you when you should and when you should not use audio effects on a track. Indeed, if there were, then life would become quite boring. However, there *are* a number of guiding principles, questions that you can ask yourself before you start deciding which effects (if any) to use and how to use them. In some cases, the issues behind the various questions may share a certain amount of common ground, but each also has its own specific purpose.

■   What issues are there in this track that I could and should fix before thinking about using any audio effects as such? For example, rather than using a compressor to tame the occasional rogue peak or a multiband compressor to fix the odd sibilant sound (both of which might possibly cause collateral damage!), should I be using a volume envelope?

■   What are my "big picture" goals for this track? For example, do I want it to blend softly into the background of the mix, or do I want it out there and up front—or something in between?

■   How busy or sparse is the overall arrangement? Am I going to be looking at making this instrument fill out more room, or am I going to be struggling to make space for it—or something in between?

■   What other instruments or voices are there that are overtly competing with this track's core frequencies?

■   What word or words would describe the way I want this part to sound overall—for example, full, warm, bright, haunting, worrying, powerful, punchy, soft, intimate . . . ?

■   What do I need to do to achieve this sound? Would I be better using a serial or a parallel FX chain? Which effects do I need, and in which order should I place them? What effects have I used that I would actually be better without?

Because there are no rules, neither is there a guarantee that this list is exhaustive. If you find yourself adding more questions to it, it probably means you're thinking along the right lines.

Determining FX Order   You have already seen in several of the earlier tutorials how the order in which you place effects within a track's FX chain will affect the way the track will sound. Changing the order is likely to change the sound to a lesser or greater extent. Of course, there are no hard-and-fast rules, but there is one over-riding principle that you should keep in mind.

The later an effect appears in the chain, the more likely it is that its impact will be more prominent when the material is played. For example, if you add, say, a touch of delay at the beginning of a chain, following up with perhaps equalization and compression, then in all probability, in the end the delay will be less obvious. That is not to say, of course, that it will not necessarily have done the job required of it. Placing the compression last will attenuate the song's dynamics after the delay and EQ have been applied. On the other hand, reverse the FX order, and the chances are that you will create a brighter, fresher sound. The tutorials that follow will, among other things, demonstrate this principle.

Serial FX Chains on Vocals

This first tutorial will explore some of the different ways in which equalization, compression, and delay can be chained together on a vocal track to achieve different results.

Tutorial 13.1: Exploring a Simple Vocal FX Chain

This exercise uses ReaEQ, ReaDelay, and ReaComp to create the necessary effects. You can, of course, substitute other equivalent plug-ins of your choice if you wish. To help you through this first consolidation tutorial, the instructions will be quite detailed and specific.

1. Open the project file Foggy130 and save it as Foggy131.

2. For the sake of this exercise, mute the vocal harmony track for the time being.

3. Play the song. You might notice that the lead vocal sounds a little thin, almost as if it is fighting to be heard in the mix. If you cast your mind back over some of the earlier tutorials, you might recall how delay can help fill out a thin track, equalization can help boost its warmth and presence, and compression can help lift the quieter passages.

4. Add an instance of ReaDelay to the lead vocal, with settings similar to those shown in Figure 13.1. Later, of course, you can change these if you wish.

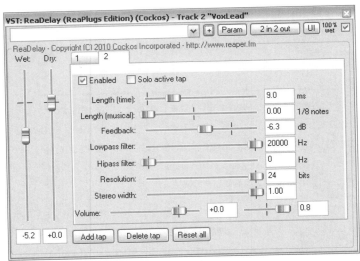

Figure 13.1 Suggested settings for one of the ReaDelay taps used in Tutorial 13.1. The other tap should be panned to −0.8 (bottom-right corner), and the delay time changed to 6.0 ms.

5.   After the ReaDelay, add an instance of ReaEQ with settings approximately as shown in Figure 13.2.

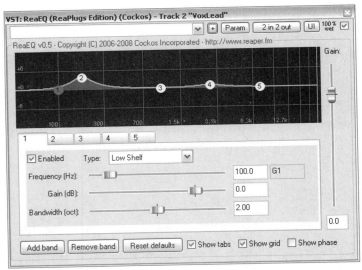

Figure 13.2 Suggested EQ settings for use in Tutorial 13.1.

6.   After the ReaEQ, add an instance of ReaComp with settings approximately as shown in Figure 13.3. Notice that the amount of compression being applied is quite gentle.

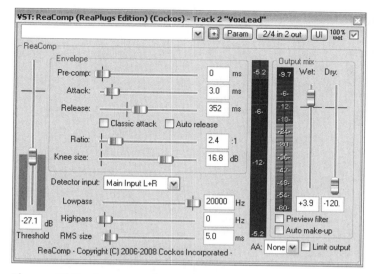

Figure 13.3 Suggested compressor settings for use in Tutorial 13.1—but adjust the threshold level to suit your own track's volume.

7.   Play the song. The vocal should now sound fatter and fuller, with more warmth, finished off with a smoothing of some of its dynamics. Save the file.

8.   Now change the FX order to compressor, delay, equalizer. Leave all of the FX parameter settings as they were. You should notice an apparent increase in the amount of expression and vitality in the vocal.

9.   Change the order again to compressor, equalizer, delay. Not only does the vocal retain the extra expression and vitality, but the delay should also be discernible, albeit quite subtly.

10.   Which is best? You decide! There's no simple correct answer to questions like this. It all depends on where you want to take this mix.

11.   Unmute the vocal harmony. Use some fairly heavy compression on this track so that it sits back in the mix.

12.   Save the file when finished.

Using Mixer Snapshots   The use of mixer snapshots (if your DAW includes this functionality) can be a tremendous boost to both flexibility and productivity when you are building and evaluating alternate effects chains. If your host software includes this feature, take full advantage of it. It enables you to jump from one entire chain to another (to compare how they sound) with usually just a single click (see Figure 13.4).

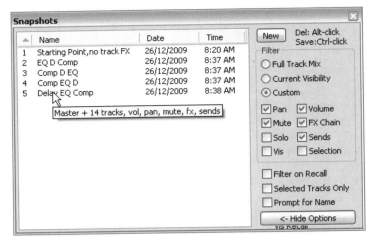

Figure 13.4   If your DAW supports mixer snapshots, use them to help you to evaluate various alternate effects strategies. In the example shown here, one click is all that is needed to select a different scenario.

Serial FX Chains on Snare and Kick

As you draw closer to the end of this book, you'll be given less detail in the tutorial instructions and more opportunity to apply what you have learned for yourself. The more time you are prepared to spend doing this, the easier and more successfully you will find yourself able to apply these principles to your own projects.

Tutorial 13.2: Exploring Simple Percussion FX Chains

If you need to, refer back to the earlier chapters of the book where the various topics required for this exercise were covered in detail. In particular, you should find Chapters 2, 4, 5, 6, and 8 especially interesting. At least equally important as revising this material, however, is the fact that you will need to develop the confidence to trust your ears.

1.   Open the project file Foggy131 and save it as Foggy132.

2.   Construct an effects chain to include a noise gate, reverb, equalizer, and compressor (but not necessarily in that order) to really help bring out the best sound from the kick and snare track in this project. Be prepared to experiment and evaluate strategies for ordering the effects. Be prepared, if you think it helps, to use more than one instance of any plug-in.

3.   Save your work when you're finished.

Serial FX Chains on Guitars

By now you may be getting a little tired of repeatedly reading the line, "There are no hard-and-fast rules, only guiding principles." Nevertheless, that fact does need repeating, not least because those principles will vary so widely in differing circumstances. For example, applied to our drum mix (Tutorial 13.2), those principles will generally offer you a sound basis for working with your mix. There are a number of well-established techniques you can use to brighten up a drum mix (which is not to say that you should be afraid to experiment).

With other instrument groups (such as guitars, for example), this may be less likely to be the case. There are so many different ways in which you might wish to enhance the expression of your guitars that you might want to approach the task with a greater willingness to experiment from the outset.

Tutorial 13.3: Exploring Simple Guitar FX Chains

In this exercise, give yourself a free hand to use effects creatively with your three guitar tracks to create an interesting sound that blends in with the mix and complements the musical style of the song. By and large, the trick is to create subtle differences that will give each of the tracks its own subtle distinction that nonetheless fits in with the overall mix.

If you need to, refer back to the earlier chapters of the book where the various topics required for this exercise were covered in detail. In particular, you should find Chapters 2, 4, 5, 6, 7, and 9 especially interesting.

1.   Open the file Foggy132 and save it as Foggy133. If the vocal harmony track is still muted from a previous exercise, then you should unmute it.

2.   Explore ways in which you can create simple yet effective effects chains on the three guitar tracks and the guitars submix. The example shown in Figure 13.5 points to one possible outcome, but don't just jump in and follow that. Try something for yourself first.

3.   When you have done this, use a single reverb bus to add a touch of reverb to the guitar mix and the vocal tracks. Pay attention to the level of the different sends to this bus.

4.   Make any necessary late adjustments to track and bus volume faders and possibly pan faders.

5.   Save the work when you're finished.

Notice something else about Figure 13.5. You can see that each of the guitar tracks in this example has its own serial effects chain. However, if you consider the guitars as a group rather than as just individual instruments, you can see that when these separate serial effects chains are considered as applied to the guitar mix, you can also see them as being applied in parallel together. By this I mean that because the instruments are so closely related, you cannot really just consider each of these tracks in isolation. You really have to view them as a group.

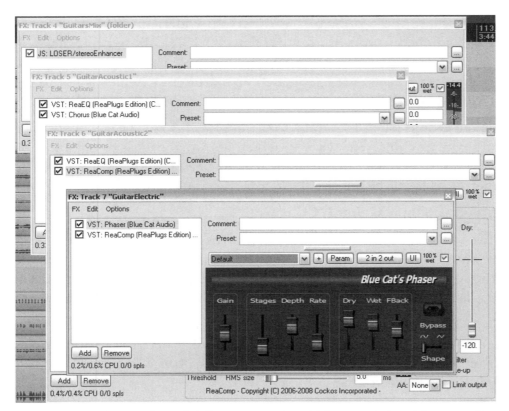

Figure 13.5   The number of different ways in which you might wish to combine effects on guitar tracks is almost limitless, especially when, as here, you have three individual tracks and a submix. The permutation shown here illustrates one possible outcome. The selection of effects used in this example is not necessarily any better or any worse than any other selection that you might come up with for yourself—just different.

Checkpoint

Review both the files Whiskey130 and Mud130. Save each as Whiskey133and Mud133, respectively. Identify at least one track in each project that you consider especially challenging. For example, this might be a female vocal or a slide guitar.

Keeping in mind that more isn't always best, devise a suitable serial effects chain for each of your selected tracks. Save your work when you're finished.

Project Files Log

If you have completed all of the examples and tutorials in this chapter, you should have created the following files:

Preparation: Foggy130, Mud130, Whiskey130

Tutorial 13.1: Foggy131

Tutorial 13.2: Foggy132

Tutorial 13.3: Foggy133

Checkpoint: Mud133, Whiskey133

Your complete project file log should now be as follows:

Alone00, Alone70, Alone76, Alone80, Alone88, Alone90, Alone91 Alone92, Alone93, Alone94, Alone95, Alone96, Alone97, Alone99, Alone99P, Alone120, Alone121, Alone122, Alone123

AudioExperiment21, Impulse85

Foggy00, Foggy41, Foggy42, Foggy43, Foggy44, Foggy50, Foggy52, Foggy53, Foggy60, Foggy61, Foggy62, Foggy64, Foggy66, Foggy69, Foggy70, Foggy73, Foggy75, Foggy80, Foggy83, Foggy92, Foggy98, Foggy100, Foggy101, Foggy103, Foggy110, Foggy111, Foggy130, Foggy131, Foggy132, Foggy133

Lying00, Lying23, Lying43, Lying50, Lying51, Lying52, Lying54, Lying60, Lying61, Lying62, Lying80, Lying81

Mud00, Mud40, Mud41, Mud60, Mud63, Mud65, Mud70, Mud74, Mud80, Mud86, Mud86a, Mud87, Mud110, Mud112, Mud113, Mud120, Mud124, Mud130, Mud133

Whiskey00, Whiskey22, Whiskey30, Whiskey31, Whiskey32, Whiskey33, Whiskey60, Whiskey65, Whiskey67, Whiskey68, Whiskey70, Whiskey71, Whiskey72, Whiskey76, Whiskey80, Whiskey82, Whiskey84, Whiskey87, Whiskey110, Whiskey111, Whiskey120, Whiskey124, Whiskey130, Whiskey133

14 Chaining the Chain Gangs: Parallel FX Processing

You have used parallel effects in a number of the various tutorials and exercises that you have already completed. For example, Chapter 6 introduced you to parallel compression, and Chapter 8 took you through some examples that included the use of parallel effects to create haunting reverb effects. In this chapter you'll be shown some slightly more complex examples and introduced to a couple more handy techniques. These are:

- Exploring panning options within parallel effects chains

- Using parallel effects chaining to create separate wet and dry audio streams and then mixing these together

Introduction

As you become more experienced (and more adventurous), you are likely to discover any number of situations in which the use of parallel effects chains can add body and color to a mix. Two examples come to mind immediately. These are:

- To add body and interest to an otherwise thin arrangement

- To bring out and emphasize particular vocal or instrumental qualities

This chapter will step you through an example of each of these. As before, you should view the example as no more than an illustration of the use of particular techniques, not as a suggested model for what you should (or should not) do with any particular type of instrument.

Preparation

Throughout this chapter you will be working with the sample projects *Foggy Desperation, Alone Again,* and *Now Is the Time for Whiskey.* The preparation required should take you only a few minutes.

Preparation: Preparing the Project Files

In each case, the only preparation needed will be to open the specified version of each project and then save it to the new name required for these tutorials. In both cases, the version to be opened will not be the most recent but will be an earlier one, stripped of some effects so that you can build the examples from scratch.

1. Open the file Alone70 that you created earlier and immediately save it as Alone140.

2. Open the file Foggy84 that you created earlier and immediately save it as Foggy140.

Guiding Principles

The guiding principles detailed in the context of serial effects chains in Chapter 13 will also serve you well when you are thinking about building parallel effects chains. In addition, keep these factors in mind:

■ You might recall that near the beginning of this journey (in Chapter 2), we took time out to explore the important roles that panning and space play in mixing. It is no coincidence that as we near our journey's end, this theme comes into focus again. Parallel effects chains are often (but not always) more successful when you make generous use of left-right panning. The farther apart the different chains are panned, the more clearly each separate chain will be distinguishable in the mix. The closer together they are, the more they will be merged.

■ A commonly used technique with parallel effects chains is for them to be used as a means of employing various effects to emphasize different frequencies within an instrument's overall frequency response. Tutorial 14.1 will include an example of this.

■ Quite possibly, you will find situations in which numerous long and complex effects chains can produce stunning results, but as a general rule, be careful not to overdo it. Being too ambitious can result in an instrument sounding too confused and overly busy.

Parallel FX Chains with a Sparse Arrangement

This example will take a project with only two tracks and explore different ways of creating a full and interesting mix, largely aided by the application of parallel effects chains. Keeping a set of headphones at hand will make it easier for you to fully appreciate the impact of the various changes that are made throughout the tutorial; some of these are quite subtle.

Tutorial 14.1: Exploring the Use of Parallel Effects Chains

This exercise uses ReaEQ, ReaComp, Kjaerhus Classic Delay, Kjaerhus Classic Flange, and the JS LOSER/Exciter to create the necessary effects. You can, of course, substitute other equivalent plug-ins of your choice if you wish. The instructions are quite detailed.

Start by following them to the letter and then go back and make any exploratory changes that you wish at the completion of the tutorial.

1.   Open the project file Alone140 and save it as Alone141.

2.   If you are able to specify a pan law for this project, specify a pan law of −3.0 dB. If your DAW does not allow you to do this but instead uses a different pan law, you will need to adjust the levels of your volume faders accordingly. Just trust your ears!

3.   This project should at this point include just two tracks—a rhythm guitar and a lead guitar. If either track includes any audio effects, remove them. If the master track includes any effects other than the utility limiter, set them to bypass. If there is no limiter there, add the JS Utility limiter and specify a maximum volume setting of −1.0 dB. This is simply a precaution against clipping.

4.   Duplicate the lead guitar track twice, so that you now have three lead guitar tracks. We are going to use this to create three parallel effects chains. Direct these three tracks to a lead guitar submix, so that the output of all three tracks goes directly only to the submix and not to the master. The output of the submix will, of course, go directly to the master.

5.   Duplicate the rhythm guitar track, so that you now have two rhythm guitar tracks. We are going to use this to create two parallel effects chains. Direct these two tracks to a rhythm guitar submix, so that the output of both tracks goes directly only to the submix and not to the master. The output of the submix will, of course, go directly to the master.

6.   Pan the tracks and busses as follows: rhythm guitar 1, 35% left; rhythm guitar 2, 35% right; rhythm guitar submix, center; lead guitar 1, 75% left; lead guitar 2, center; lead guitar 3, 75% right; lead guitar submix, center. This creates a "wraparound" effect—see the top example shown in Figure 14.1.

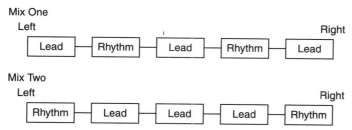

Figure 14.1   This diagram represents the different panning models used in Tutorial 14.1 for Mix 1 (top) and Mix 2 (bottom).

7.   We are now going to apply different effects to different frequency bands on the lead guitar. The exact plug-in settings used here are not the main point; the technique is. Start with the suggested settings; you can adjust them later if you like.

8. Add an EQ plug-in and a delay plug-in to the lead guitar 1 track. Adjust the EQ settings so as to roll off much of the bottom end and boost the top. The critical delay setting is the time, which should be around 50 ms. An example of settings that you could use is shown in Figure 14.2.

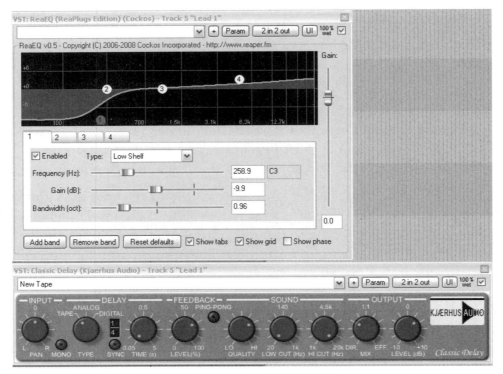

Figure 14.2 Suggested possible plug-in settings for your lead guitar 1 track in Tutorial 14.1.

9. Copy these plug-ins to the lead guitar 3 track. Increase the delay time on this track to about 100 ms.

10. Now add EQ and a flange effect to the lead guitar 2 track. The EQ should be adjusted to boost the warmth while rolling off some top end. Select flange settings of your choice. An example of settings that you could use is shown in Figure 14.3.

11. Solo the lead guitar submix bus and play the song, adjusting the faders and possibly FX parameters until you are satisfied with the overall sound. You will probably need to lower the volume faders on lead guitars 1 and 3 to about −3.5 dB or −4.0 dB and that on lead guitar 2 to about −7.0 dB or −8.0 dB.

12. Use a compressor in the lead guitar submix to tame the louder peaks.

13. Use the JS Delay-Sustain plug-in on rhythm guitar 1 and EQ on rhythm guitar 2. The object of this exercise is to introduce a clearly audible distinction between these two tracks. Figure 14.4 shows one example of possible settings. Use this as a guide, but be prepared to use different settings if you prefer.

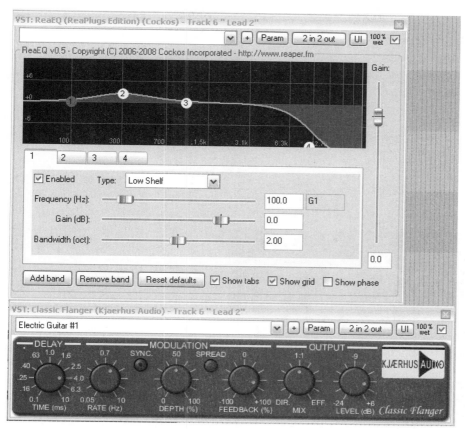

Figure 14.3   Suggested possible plug-in settings for your lead guitar 2 track in Tutorial 14.1.

14.   If you think it needs it, add a compressor to the rhythm guitar's submix bus. Also consider whether you might want to use one of the JS Exciter plug-ins in this bus to brighten the instrument's overall sound.

15.   If necessary, adjust the volume faders for the rhythm guitar tracks and submix. The default level of 0.0 dB will probably not be too far wide of the mark.

16.   If your DAW allows you to create mixer snapshots, do so now (call it Mix 1) and save the file.

17.   Now change the pan settings as follows: lead guitar 1, 35% left; lead guitar 2, 35% right; rhythm guitar 1, 60% left; rhythm guitar 2, 60% right. You will also need to fade down the volume controls on the lead guitar submix, probably by about 5 dB. Save this as another mixer snapshot (Mix 2) and save the file.

18.   Play the song, comparing the two mixes. When you do this, be sure to check in mono as well as stereo. The first should sound fuller with the instruments discernible but well integrated. Mix 2 should give you a greater emphasis on the two instruments. These are just two of a considerable number of different

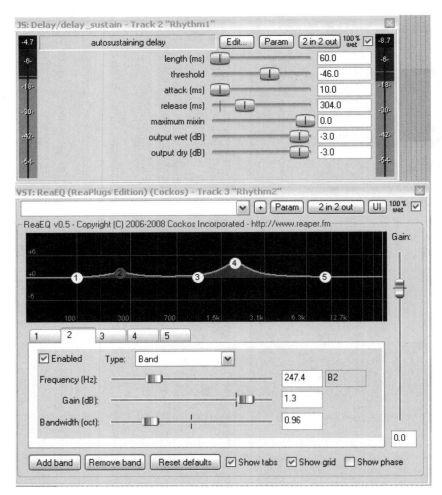

Figure 14.4 Suggested possible EQ settings for your two rhythm guitar tracks in Tutorial 14.1.

scenarios you could create just for this simple arrangement. Which is better? You decide!

19.   Save the file.

Parallel FX Chains on a Lead Vocal

In this tutorial you will explore one example of how parallel effects can be used on a lead vocal. We've already touched on some examples of using parallel effects on a vocal track in earlier chapters (for example, in Tutorial 8.4). This tutorial develops the idea somewhat further.

Figure 14.5 illustrates what you are about to do to your lead vocal in the *Foggy Desperation* song. Used in this way, parallel effects are applied to each of two side channels (panned left and right) and then mixed back in with the original dry material (panned center).

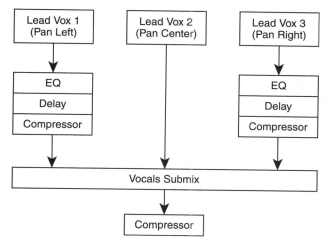

Figure 14.5 This flowchart illustrates how we are going to apply parallel effects chains to a lead vocal. The diagram shows only the lead vocal, not the vocal harmony track.

Tutorial 14.2: Using a Parallel Effects Chain on a Lead Vocal

This exercise uses the plug-ins ReaEQ, ReaComp, and ReaDelay to create the necessary effects. You can, of course, substitute other equivalent plug-ins of your choice if you wish. The instructions are quite detailed. Start by following them to the letter, and then go back and make any exploratory changes that you wish at the completion of the tutorial.

1.   Open the project file Foggy140 and save it as Foggy142.

2.   Remove all the existing effects from the lead vocal track. Also remove the send from this track to the reverb bus that was added in Chapter 8. We are going to start with a clean slate.

3.   Create two duplicates of this track. We are going to create a parallel effects chain.

4.   Make sure that all three lead vocal tracks and the vox harmony track are directed to the vocals submix, so that the output of these individual tracks does not also go directly to the master.

5.   For the time being, set the volume of all three lead vocal tracks to about −5.0 dB.

6.   Pan lead vocal 1 about 50% left, lead vocal 2 dead center, and lead vocal 3 about 50% right.

7.   Add an equalizer to each of the tracks lead vocal 1 and lead vocal 3 (but not lead vocal 2). Adjust the various EQ parameters so that each of these brings out a different aspect of the voice. Figure 14.6 shows an example of this.

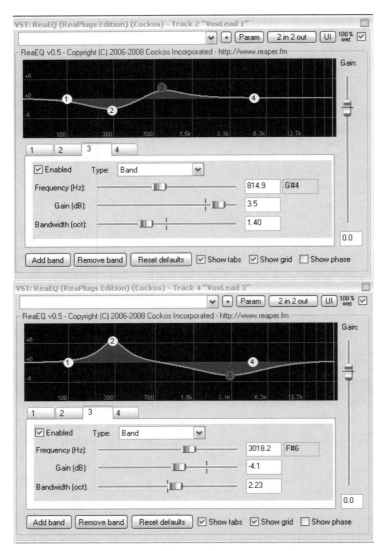

Figure 14.6 An example of possible EQ settings for lead vocal tracks 1 (top) and 3 (bottom), respectively. The point is to shape the frequency curves of both tracks differently.

8. Add an instance of delay after each of the EQ plug-ins on lead vocals 1 and 3. Be fairly conservative in how you use this effect, with different delay times for both tracks. Figure 14.7 illustrates one possible solution that you could use here.

9. Add a compressor after each of these delay plug-ins. Compress these two tracks fairly heavily and then raise the output gain signal to compensate. Figure 14.8 illustrates the kind of compression you should be trying to achieve. In this example, the gain reduction can be as much as -10 dB or so.

10. The overall vocal submix bus will now probably benefit from some very gentle compression.

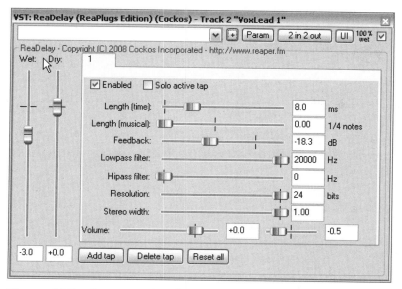

Figure 14.7   An example of possible delay settings for the track lead vocal 1. Use similar settings for the delay on lead vocal 3, but with a greater delay time (about 12 or 14 ms) and a pan setting (bottom right) of +0.5.

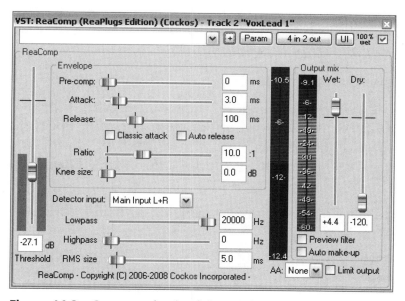

Figure 14.8   Compress both of the tracks lead vocal 1 and lead vocal 3 quite heavily, but do not use compression on lead vocal 2.

11.   To add some reverb to your lead vocals, either create a send from the vocal submix bus to the reverb bus or create separate sends from each of the three lead vocal tracks. The amount of reverb you will need to add will be quite modest.

12.   As you play the song, you may need to make some adjustments to the volume levels of the lead vocal tracks and the harmony vocal track.

13.   Save the file. If you wish, continue to tweak the FX parameters.

Don't Overdo It!   The creative use of parallel effects chains can produce really interesting sounds and achieve great results. However, resist the temptation to overdo it. Effects should be used to add life, variety, definition, interest, and even surprises to your mixes—not to create a confused cacophony!

Project Files Log

If you have completed all of the examples and tutorials in this chapter, you should have created the following files:

Preparation: Alone140, Foggy140

Tutorial 14.1: Alone141

Tutorial 14.2: Foggy142

Checkpoint: Mud133, Whiskey133

Your complete project file log should now be as follows:

Alone00, Alone70, Alone76, Alone80, Alone88, Alone90, Alone91 Alone92, Alone93, Alone94, Alone95, Alone96, Alone97, Alone99, Alone99P, Alone120, Alone121, Alone122, Alone123, Alone140, Alone 141

AudioExperiment21, Impulse85

Foggy00, Foggy41, Foggy42, Foggy43, Foggy44, Foggy50, Foggy52, Foggy53, Foggy60, Foggy61, Foggy62, Foggy64, Foggy66, Foggy69, Foggy70, Foggy73, Foggy75, Foggy80, Foggy83, Foggy92, Foggy98, Foggy100, Foggy101, Foggy103, Foggy110, Foggy111, Foggy130, Foggy131, Foggy132, Foggy133, Foggy140, Foggy142

Lying00, Lying23, Lying43, Lying50, Lying51, Lying52, Lying54, Lying60, Lying61, Lying62, Lying80, Lying81

Mud00, Mud40, Mud41, Mud60, Mud63, Mud65, Mud70, Mud74, Mud80, Mud86, Mud86a, Mud87, Mud110, Mud112, Mud113, Mud120, Mud124, Mud130, Mud133

Whiskey00, Whiskey22, Whiskey30, Whiskey31, Whiskey32, Whiskey33, Whiskey60, Whiskey65, Whiskey67, Whiskey68, Whiskey70, Whiskey71, Whiskey72, Whiskey76, Whiskey80, Whiskey82, Whiskey84, Whiskey87, Whiskey110, Whiskey111, Whiskey120, Whiskey124, Whiskey130, Whiskey133

15 Multiband Compressors, Mastering Limiters, and More

This chapter will take a look at some of the ways in which you can use audio effects in the master track's FX bin to help create a more polished and integrated mix. This process should not be mistaken for mastering. Mastering involves a lot more than simply adding a few effects to a project's master track. Other considerations include (but are not limited to):

- Ensuring a consistency of sound across an entire collection of songs. This includes ensuring not only an evenness of perceived volume between the various songs in the collection, but also an overall level appropriate for the musical genre.

- Making the collection ready for CD duplication and/or Internet distribution.

These matters go beyond the scope of this book. If you are thinking of doing your own mastering, then you will certainly need to understand how to use the various effects covered in this chapter, but you will also need to know a lot more. A good book, such as *Mastering Music at Home* (Course Technology PTR, 2007) by Mitch Gallagher, would be a good next step.

Introduction

When you get to the final stage of your project, you essentially have two options:

- Use the services of a professional mastering engineer to finish the project. If you are not trained and competent in the science and art of mastering, this is the path you should take.

- Finish it yourself. It might appear at first that I am contradicting what I wrote at the very beginning of this chapter, but this need not be the case. For example, the recording might not be intended for public or commercial release. It might be a pre-demo that you wish to present to other members of your band or a hobby project that you just want to share with a few friends and family.

This being the case, this chapter is divided into the following sections. Before you read this list, however, jump past it to the paragraph immediately below it. Read that next, then read the list, then read that paragraph again.

- Reviewing your project

- Getting the volume peaks right

- Premastering: making your project ready for mastering

- Preparing your own final mix

- Equalizing the mix

- Adding reverb to the mix

- Compressing the mix

- Adding stereo enhancement

- Using an exciter or high-frequency stimulator

- Limiting and maximizing the mix

- Dithering and noise shaping

Notice, in particular, that this list includes a number of effects, such as equalization, compression, reverb, and stereo enhancement. However, you should not set out with the mindset that you will necessarily want or need to use all of these effects. In this chapter, you'll be exploring all of these for learning purposes, but in the real world, when you are working with your own material, you should use these items in your mix only if they are clearly going to make your music sound better. Don't start out with the mindset that you should use all or most of these effects just because they are there.

Preparation

Throughout this chapter you will be working with the sample projects *Foggy Desperation* and *Now Is the Time for Whiskey*. The preparation required should take you only a few minutes.

Preparation: Preparing the Project Files

In each case, the only preparation needed will be to open the specified version of each project and then save it to the new name required for these tutorials. The version to be opened will not necessarily be the most recent, but it will be a version that is suitable for use in this chapter.

1. Open the file Foggy142 that you created earlier and immediately save it as Foggy150.

2. Open the file Mud124 that you created earlier and save it as Mud150.

3. Open the file Whiskey120 that you created earlier and immediately save it as Whiskey150.

Reviewing Your Project

The track master is most definitely *not* the place for fixing problems and errors in your mix. Before you even think about doing anything with your master track, you should review your project to make sure it is ready. The issues in Table 15.1 are iterative; this means that you may have to go back and forth between the various issues in order to resolve them. The order is not sacred. Tackle these issues in whichever sequence makes the best sense to you.

Table 15.1 Track and Project Issues for Review

Name	Description
Left right balance	Unless there is something very unusual about your production (and it is possible that there might be), check that the perceived volume of both left and right speakers is about equal throughout the song.
Individual track panning	Does every instrument and voice have as much space as it needs in the mix?
Individual track levels	Does the relative volume of the different parts sound about right? Is anything jumping out too much or being buried in the mix?
Individual track sounds	Does that guitar sound a tad too muddy, or the fiddle too shrill? Problems like this need to be fixed individually at the track level, not in the overall mix settings.
Use of audio effects	Did you perhaps get carried away with that delay, chorus, or reverb? Should you pull one or more of your effects down a touch? Or (from my experience less likely but not impossible) are there any other effects that could usefully be added? Are there any existing ones in use that should be taken away?
Arrangement	Is the overall arrangement too sparse, too busy, or about right? Should you consider holding some parts back for a build, or are there places where you should think about fattening up a too-thin mix?
Mix volume	Is the overall volume of the mix about where it should be for this stage of the mixing process? This question is the topic of the next section.
Different environments	If possible, check how your mix sounds in as many different situations as you conveniently can. Test it in stereo and in mono, on your studio speakers, on your computer's budget speakers, in your car, on your iPod . . . anywhere and everywhere you conveniently can.

Most of these topics are issues that do not really require any further comment from me. They have already been discussed, often more than once, at various places and in different contexts throughout this book. The question of getting the mix volume right, however, does require further discussion.

Getting the Volume Peaks Right

This is yet another area where the optimum outcome will in part depend on the musical genre and on your production goals, but in general you should check your mix for the odd peak that despite all your best efforts just jumps out of the mix too much. This might be caused by a particular burst of emotion by a singer, a single note plucked on a guitar, the crash of a cymbal, or any of a number of other things.

Figure 15.1 shows two especially useful features of Cakewalk's SONAR that can be used to help you here. Turning on the master waveform preview option and enabling the peak indicators feature makes it easier to identify potential problem areas.

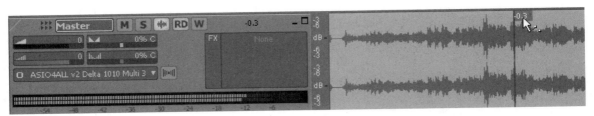

Figure 15.1   If your DAW supports master track waveform preview and peak marker indicators (as does SONAR, shown here), you should enable these features.

If you don't address these rogue peaks, then you will be unable to raise the volume of your mix to a suitable level in readiness for mastering without clipping. Usually the best way to fix the problem is to use volume envelopes. Identify the track or tracks responsible for the problem and simply lower the track volume at these points as required (see Figure 15.2).

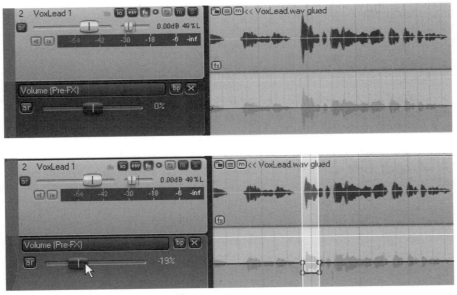

Figure 15.2   Even at this late stage (and especially at this late stage), check your individual tracks for any excessive peaks (top) that can be pulled back using a volume envelope (bottom).

Premastering

If you are using the services of a mastering engineer, then you should talk to that person as early in the production process as possible in order to discover exactly what you should and should not do in getting your material ready for mastering. If anything you are told differs from what follows in the next two paragraphs, then obviously you should be guided by that.

That said, it is likely that your mastering engineer will prefer to be presented with a series of stereo audio files (one for each song), in each case with as clean a mix as possible. Make a note of the format that your engineer requires, along with such specifications as bit depth and sampling rate.

In all probability, if you use any so-called mastering effects (such as a compressor, a high-frequency stimulator, a stereo imager, or a limiter) in your mixing down, then you will be making the engineer's job harder, not easier. However, one aspect that you may need to attend to is the overall volume of your mix. To obtain a consistent reference point, set the master track's volume fader to 0 dB and leave it there. If the mix is too quiet at that level, then it may be difficult to master. Again, this is a question that you should put to your engineer, but you might well be advised to use something like the JS Utility/Volume plug-in to lift the overall volume of your mix so that it peaks quite close to 0.0 dB, perhaps between −2.0 dB and −3.0 dB.

Preparing Your Own Final Mix

In this section we will work through the various audio effects, some of which you might wish to use in preparing your final mix.

Begin by setting the volume fader on the master track at 0 dB. If your mix appears to be on the quiet side (peaking below about −6.0 dB), you might wish to consider using something like the JS Utility limiter as the first item in the master track's FX bin. Keep in mind, however, that it is possible that other effects you might add to this chain could also increase the volume of the mix; therefore, you might need to be flexible about this.

The tutorial at the end of this section will help you tie these pieces together.

Master FX Order   The order of the various effects in this section represents a fairly sensible order in which to use any of these effects that you wish to apply to a master track. Many of the same issues that were discussed in Chapter 13, when we looked at serial effects chains on individual tracks, also apply here. For example, if you find the need to use a high-frequency stimulator to add a little sparkle to your mix, then you are likely to want to place this near the end of your chain. Otherwise, its impact can be weakened by effects that might come after it, such as compression or reverb.

Notice, however, that your maximizer/limiter and dithering or noise shaping (if used) should always be placed at the very end of the chain, as the last steps in the mixing process.

Equalization

By now you should know quite a lot about equalization—at least I'm going to assume you do. Let's just focus here on equalization as it might be applied to a final mix. What you're really trying to achieve here is a good tonal balance for the overall blend of voices and instruments. You really should, however, be thinking of minor tweaks and adjustments, not savage surgery. Remember that any changes you make here will be applied to *everything* in the mix. As an analogy, you might be inclined to add a dash of salt to a bowl of nuts to help bring out their qualities, or perhaps a sprinkling of sugar on fruit to sweeten it just that little bit. But I suspect that you'd want to be very careful about adding sugar or salt to a bowl of fruit and nuts mixed together!

Use an analyzer such as Voxengo Span (see Figure 15.3) to analyze the frequency response of your mix. It might even help to compare this to the frequency response of someone else's mix of a different song of the same genre and see which you like.

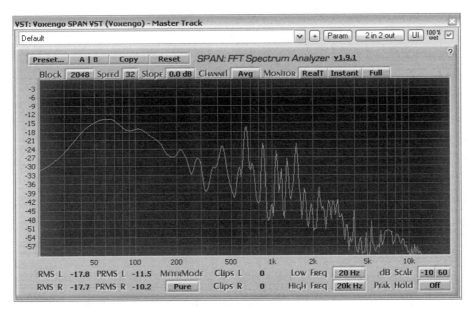

Figure 15.3   Voxengo Span is a good-quality freeware frequency analysis plug-in that gives you a good degree of control over how the information is displayed. Download details can be found in Table 1.2 in Chapter 1.

Possible uses of equalization at this stage include rolling off any possible bottom-end rumble; attenuating the midrange a little if your mix sounds too muddy, honky, or abrasive; adding a small gain around 100 Hz or 200 Hz if the mix needs more warmth;

and or adding a small amount of gain above 10,000 Hz or so to give the overall mix a little air. Figure 15.4 shows an example of this.

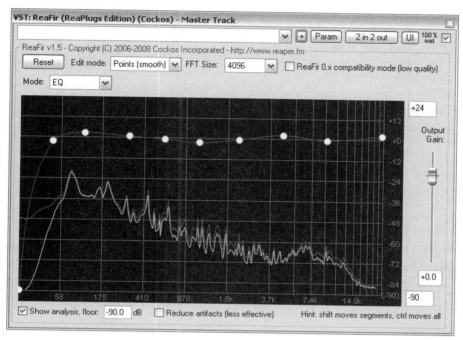

Figure 15.4   An example of how equalization might be applied to a final mix. The line connecting the white dots shows the EQ curve. The brighter of the two jagged lines shows the frequency response post-EQ. The fainter of these two lines shows the frequency response pre-EQ. Note that this is an illustrative example, not a model.

Linear Phase or Parametric (Program) EQ?   In Chapter 4, the subject of linear phase EQ (as opposed to normal program parametric EQ) was introduced, along with the observation that many sound engineers prefer to use linear phase EQ on their master tracks. The example shown in Figure 15.4 is of a liner phase EQ.

That said, two important points need to be revisited. The first is that unless your DAW supports PDC (*plug-in delay compensation*), using linear phase EQ might introduce latency issues. The second point is that you should always let your ears be your judge. The best one to use is the one that sounds best to you.

Reverb

We already discussed this extensively in Chapter 8. This is most definitely *not* the time or the place to create your Grand Canyon reverb effect. For the most part, you should try to avoid the need to use reverb in the track master. At most, you might find that the gentlest touch with the most conservative of settings might help to bind the mix together.

Multiband Compression

You might recall that you used a multiband compressor in Chapter 6 (Tutorial 6.8). A multiband compressor exhibits all of the characteristics of an ordinary compressor, with one very important additional feature: It allows you to specify different settings for different frequency ranges. If you are wondering why you might wish to do this, then here are two facts to consider:

- Different sections of your mix tend to focus on and around different frequencies. By compressing different bands differently, you may be able to enhance the special characteristics (such as warmth, presence, or sparkle) of each individual band.

- One quick look at a spectral analysis graph of any of your projects will show that some frequency bands generate more volume than others. It can make perfect sense to want to use different threshold settings for different frequencies.

Even more so with multiband compression than with simple compression, it really does pay to be gentle. The mix to which you are applying this effect is by now built up from an extraordinarily complex weaving together of diverse parts. Remember the fruit-and-nut analogy that I made when talking about using equalization with a mix? Well, you need to be at least twice as careful when you are dealing with multiband compression.

For me, a multiband compressor needs to allow you to define (at least within reason) as many or as few bands as you like and to be able to define the boundaries between each band as you wish. This is one of those areas where different sound engineers hold differing opinions. Some prefer to use only three bands when working on a master track, some four, and others five. As is so often the case, musical genre will have its part to play, but by and large I prefer to use a four-band compressor (see Figure 15.5).

I've said several times throughout this book, "There are no rules, only laws." Well, that's true, but when it comes to multiband compression and mixes, the laws are so unforgiving that you could just about take this next statement as a rule: *Use only low compression ratios when you are using compression on a final mix.* Even a ratio of 2:1 will almost certainly be too high. Somewhere between 1.1:1 and 1.5:1 is the area where you should be looking.

Speaking of ratios, some multiband compressors actually allow you to specify ratios *below* 1:1. Tread with extreme caution here. A ratio below 1:1 turns a compressor into an upward expander. This is another subject that was covered in Chapter 6. It's possible that you may wish to do this—for example, if you are presented with the mixdown of a song in the form of an over-compressed stereo wave file and then asked to rescue it. It's also possible that you might want to do something really weird and unconventional with your song. Otherwise, the best advice I can give is to stay well way from using a multiband compressor as an upward expander.

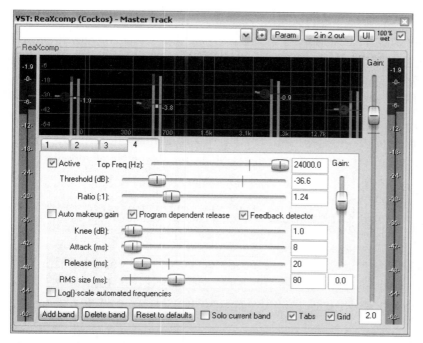

Figure 15.5   Shown here is ReaXcomp, used as a four-band compressor. Notice the options to add or remove bands and to play the mix with any band soloed.

It's also helpful if you use a multiband compressor that lets you solo any band to which you wish to pay particular attention. Apart from anything else, this makes it easier for your ears to tell you where to set the boundaries between the different bands.

Stereo Enhancement

There's not a great deal that needs to be added here about stereo enhancement and stereo imaging plug-ins. As you learned in Chapter 12, use them carefully and gently if at all. Too much stereo enhancement can unglue a mix, making it sound uncomfortable or even worrying. On this general topic, though, there is another point worth making. A good habit to get into is to check your mix from time to time in mono as well as stereo. Most DAW hosts include a toggle switch or button for this purpose on the master track. To understand why this matters, let's take a moment to reflect on the nature of mono and stereo.

With mono, of course, if you are using two speakers, exactly the same signal will come out from both speakers. You might just as well use only one speaker. This is the case, for example, with AM radio.

Stereo, of course, is different. Any material panned 100% left or 100% right will be heard from only the one speaker. In practice, of course, most of your material will be panned somewhere in between these two extremes, and hence it will seem to originate from a point somewhere between the two speakers. The key words here are *will seem*. If you have only the two speakers, how can a signal possibly originate from somewhere in between the two? The answer is that it cannot! Stereo is in fact an *illusion*, and the various elements that go into creating that illusion won't necessarily blend comfortably with each other when they are mixed together into a single mono signal.

The mathematics that lies behind the illusion of stereo is actually quite complex, and there would be little point in getting bogged down in it here. This is another one of those areas where some people will wish to understand the theory (because they find it interesting), while others will just want to know what works. I'll give you a brief overview; if you want to pursue the topic in depth, you'll need to Google away!

The two components of a stereo signal (left and right) are commonly referred to as A and B, respectively. The signal that you hear coming from your speakers is made up of A and B. That's simple enough, but from here on in it starts to get a bit tricky. The stereo illusion is brought about by the *differences* between the two signals. If you like, think of this as A − B. As you have seen in some of the plug-ins you used in Chapter 12, this illusion can be created in a number of ways, including variations in time (delay) and EQ filtering.

When a stereo mix is heard in mono (as, for example, happens with AM radio or monophonic television), the two signals A and B are simply added together, and the same summed signal is sent to both speakers. What you are getting now is A + B. Think about the implications of this for a moment. Various techniques have been used to make two signals sound different—and then they are added back together again! If your instincts are causing you to feel a little uncomfortable at this point, then you should trust them. This is because those same techniques that are used to produce the stereo effects that we love to hear so much are also likely to create problems when the signal is converted to mono. They can make a mix sound muddy or dull, for example. In some circumstances, they could even create phasing problems that might make an instrument all but disappear altogether. Little wonder, therefore, that it makes sense to check regularly to ensure that your mix will sound good in both stereo and mono.

High-Frequency Stimulators

In Tutorial 10.2 (Chapter 10), you used an exciter (high-frequency stimulator) to brighten up a guitar mix that otherwise may have sounded slightly dull. In the same way, you might wish to use an exciter on your master track to brighten up your mix a little. When used in a final mix, however, you only want the effect applied to the ultra-high frequencies (see Figure 15.6).

You might wonder why you would wish to do this when perhaps an equalizer could do the job. The simple answer is that you can use an ordinary equalizer if you wish, with a single high-shelf filter. However, an exciter is easy to use and can give you greater

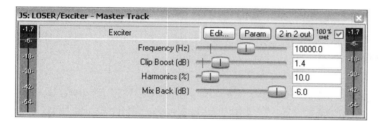

Figure 15.6   An exciter can be used to add a touch of air to a final mix. To do this, you should set it to work only on frequencies of 10,000 Hz (or even higher) and over.

precision, largely due to its additional parameters, such as (in this case) additional faders to allow you to also adjust separately the level of the high harmonics.

Master Limiters/Maximizers

You have already encountered several examples of the use of a simple utility limiter. Up until now, the main use you have had for limiters is simply to prevent clipping. A mastering limiter is more sophisticated than this. It prevents clipping, but it also does much more than this. It also can be used to work like a compressor, lifting the volume during quieter parts of the song so that the overall volume of the song is lifted up toward whatever limit is set (usually at or just below 0 dB) without going over it. Because it raises the level of the output in this way, it is often called a *maximizer*.

Figure 15.7 shows the JS LOSER/masterLimiter, which is included on your DVD. You can see that it has more controls than a simple limiter does. It is no coincidence that you will recognize some of these (such as attack and release) as also being present in a compressor; their function is similar. Table 15.2 summarizes the parameter controls that you should typically expect to find in a master limiter or maximizer. As with other types of audio effects (compressors and noise gates, for example), you are likely to find that not all maximizers will have exactly the same parameter controls.

Figure 15.7   A maximizer can be used to boost the volume level of your final mix without clipping.

Table 15.2 Summary of Master Limiter Controls

Name	Description
Threshold	This determines the level at which the limiter is engaged. The more you move this control farther to the left (specifying a lower threshold level), the greater the range within which the signal is increased will be.
Look ahead	This enables the limiter to anticipate any sudden surges in volume that may be coming and to deal with them more smoothly, so as not to create too sudden or harsh a limiting effect.
Attack	This works in a similar way to the attack control of a compressor. If in doubt, a lower setting is safer than a higher one.
Hold	This is similar to the hold control on other plug-ins; it can be used to apply the limiter to the audio signal for a specified period after the signal falls back below threshold level. Again, if in doubt, use a cautious, low setting.
Release	Again, this serves a similar function to the release control on various other plug-ins. You can use it to determine a period of time over which the limiter will be gradually released when the signal falls back below the threshold level. A setting of about 150 ms to 300 ms can help create a smoother transition.
Auto release	An auto release (or program-dependent release) option will delegate to the software the job of working out the optimum release times for you. Where this control is present, start with it engaged and see whether it gives you the results you want.
Reduction	This is not actually a control but an indicator. Usually this takes the form of some sort of graphic display. In the example shown in Figure 15.7, it is a fader. It indicates at any point in time the amount of attenuation that the maximizer/limiter is applying to the final signal. It may seem strange to talk of attenuating a maximized signal. Think of it this way: The value shown here is the number of decibels by which the final signal would have exceeded 0.0 dB and clipped had a limit not been imposed.

Misusing a maximizer will do more harm to your mix than anything else. The single most important control to get right is the threshold. The optimum setting will vary with different musical genres. The more you pull the threshold to the left, the more the output will be pumped up, and the more the dynamics will be squeezed out of your song. You have to know your musical genre, know what you are aiming to achieve, know how to use the maximizer, and know how to trust your ears.

Dithering and Noise Shaping

Finally, we'll take a look at a dithering and noise shaping plug-in, although with many DAWs you will not need to use one. It's there just in case you do. Here's an example of when you might. Let's assume that you will be preparing your mix for distribution on audio CD. To be produced in this format, your mix must ultimately be rendered as a 16-bit wave file. You will, of course, need to consult your DAW's documentation for information about how to do this.

When you are rendering down from a higher bit depth (such as 24-bit or 32-bit) to 16-bit, there is inevitably some loss of audio precision. In a few words, dithering and noise shaping are two similar techniques that can be employed to minimize the impact of this and to help you produce the best possible quality outcome. This is yet another of those areas where we could get lost in the technical minutiae for hours. All I intend to say here is that these techniques are two methods of achieving essentially the same end. Think of it like this.

When you render from 24-bit to 16-bit without the use of either of these techniques, the last 8 bits just get chopped off the end of each and every single piece of digital data as it is converted. This can result in a rough and grainy sound, especially at lower frequency levels. Dithering and noise shaping do their job by actually adding some very quiet background noise—"good" noise, if you like—back into the processed data to mask this.

So if this is so good, why do I say you quite possibly won't need a dithering or noise shaping plug-in? The answer is that these features are very often built into the audio engine itself. Somewhere among your settings and preferences, there may be an option to specify that when you come to finally render your mix down to 16-bit, you want to engage the DAW's dithering or noise shaping capabilities. Consult your DAW's documentation. If I'm wrong and there is no built-in option, then you should use a plug-in such as the JS utility provided on your DVD (see Figure 15.8).

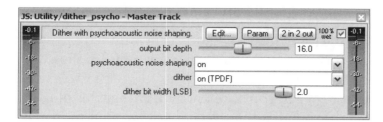

Figure 15.8 The JS: Utility/dither_psycho plug-in. It's there if you need it, but check what features your host DAW has to offer first.

This brings us to a final question: If both options are available, which should you use, dithering or noise shaping—or maybe both? I'm not going to attempt to answer that one, other than to say that if your audio engineering and mixing capabilities have reached a pinnacle where the most critical factor in determining the final quality of your mix is whether you choose to use dithering or noise shaping, then you are indeed worthy of much praise and acclamation.

This is one of those subjects on which different people hold equally strong and equally sincere different views. If you wish to pursue this topic further, hop on to any audio forum and join in the debate. Or you could just test the various options for yourself and see whether your ears really notice any difference.

Tutorial

Congratulations, you have reached the final tutorial! The step-by-step example that follows will guide you through the process of using audio effects on your master track. There is a lot contained in this exercise. Don't be surprised if it takes you a couple of hours or more to complete it. Be patient and don't cut corners if you want to get the best from it!

Tutorial 15.1: Using Effects in the Master Track

In this first example, we will be using the *Foggy Desperation* project. In the checkpoint that follows this tutorial, you will have the opportunity to work with some of the other sample projects.

1. Open the project file Foggy150 and save it as Foggy151.

2. Review this project in accordance with the suggestions made in Table 15.1. Make any changes you think are necessary.

3. In your master FX bin, set the JS Utility limiter (if it is still there from an earlier exercise) to bypass. You won't be using this for your final mix, but it can be useful to leave it there for now in case you want to use it to prevent clipping.

4. If the master FX chain does not already include the JS Utility Volume plug-in, load it as the first item in this FX bin (via ReaJS if necessary). Play the song. Adjust the plug-in's volume fader to ensure the song peaks at about −3.0 dB to −5.0 dB.

5. Next add your preferred master track EQ plug-in. Experiment with settings similar to those shown in Figure 15.4. Note that if you are using ReaFir (as shown in Figure 15.4), you will need to select EQ mode. You can create your EQ curve by clicking and dragging on the graph. When you have finished, engage this plug-in only if you think it is improving the sound of the mix. Otherwise, set it to bypass.

6. After the EQ, add a reverb plug-in, such as Mo'Verb. For the purpose of this exercise, choose a preset such as Insert − Natural Hall and then fade both ER and wet levels down to about −20 dB or −35 dB each and the dry level up to 0 dB. Check this with your headphones. If you find a level where the reverb is barely (if at all) discernible but helps to bind the mix together, then you should leave the reverb engaged. Otherwise, set it to bypass.

7. Now add a multiband compressor after the reverb. The example uses ReaXcomp, but of course you can use any other. This example assumes that you are using

four bands. Depending on which software you are using, take whatever steps are necessary to end up with four bands.

8. Select and solo Band 1. Set a ratio of about 1.2:1 and a threshold level that engages the compressor gently. If auto make-up gain is available, turn this option off. If auto (program-dependent) release is available, turn this option on. Adjust the upper frequency for this band (see Figure 15.9 if you are using ReaXcomp) so that you are satisfied that you are catching just the bass frequencies here. This will probably be around 100 Hz to 120 Hz.

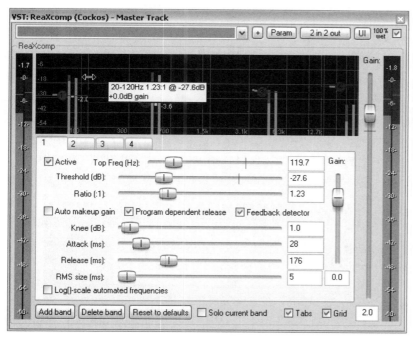

Figure 15.9 You can adjust the boundaries of each ReaXcomp band by clicking and dragging on the vertical lines on the graph.

9. Repeat this process for the other three bands. Be slow and careful. In Figure 15.9, the upper boundaries of Bands 2 and 3 are set at about 1,200 Hz and 12,000 Hz, respectively.

10. Select Band 2 and add about 1.0 to 1.5 dB gain. Notice how this warms the mix a little.

11. Still on Band 2, lower the threshold to about −50 dB and raise the gain to about +8 or 9 dB. Notice how this makes the mix much muddier. Restore these settings to what they were after Step 10.

12. Make such subtle changes to the gain levels (up or down) for Bands 3 and 4 as to achieve a more balanced sound. You might or might not consider such

changes necessary. In Figure 15.9, although it's not obvious, I have taken about 0.6 dB off the Band 3 gain. Check the mix in mono and then again in stereo.

13.   If you wish to experiment with a stereo enhancer, such as JS SStillwell/stereo-width, then do so. If you do, check the mono mix regularly. As you increase the stereo width boost relative to the center boost more and more, you may notice in stereo that the mix actually starts to come apart, with different parts of different instruments appearing to come from all over the place. Check it in mono, and you will find that you have made it muddier.

14.   If you can find some fairly gentle settings for this plug-in that make the mix better, then leave it there. Otherwise, remove this from your FX bin altogether.

15.   Now add an exciter, as shown in Figure 15.6. Use the levels shown there as a guide. If you find that you can use this plug-in to add a little air to your mix, then you should do so.

16.   Finally, add a master limiter to the FX bin. Start with fairly conservative settings, such as those shown in Figure 15.7. Now fade the threshold slowly farther and farther left. As you lower the threshold, the volume will be pumped up more and more. Soon you will see your master's VU meter just about stuck at about −0.1 dB as the song is belted out at a constant volume. This is what I mean by ruining a mix!

17.   Fade the threshold back to the right until the sound seems right to you. This is likely to be (for this song) somewhere between −2.0 dB and −4.0 dB. See the upcoming "How Loud Is Loud Enough?" note.

18.   Save the song.

19.   Individually set all of your plug-ins to bypass. You should notice a dramatic difference in the sound.

20.   Be prepared to make any adjustments to these plug-in parameters in order to create a cleaner, fuller, fresher sound. Learn by doing! This is another area where mixer snapshots, if available, can be very useful.

21.   Save the file again when you're finished.

How Loud Is Loud Enough?   The question of just how loud your mix should be is not an easy one to answer. At its peak, it will never, of course, exceed the limit that you set, but the more heavily compressed and maximized the mix is, the more often it will hit that peak and hence sound louder. Getting it right comes with experience and with understanding the musical genre. For the example in Tutorial 15.1, you would be likely to aim for an output with maximum volume jumping around briskly generally in the range of −6.0 dB to −0.1 dB.

Checkpoint

Give yourself a complete license to do what you want in this exercise. Explore in turn each of the two projects Mud150 (saved as Mud151) and Whiskey 150 (saved as Whiskey 151) to see what you can do to them with the considered use of audio effects in the master FX bin.

Bonus Mixing Plug-Ins (Overview)

The DVD supplied with this book includes a number of plug-ins (including some that we have encountered briefly in earlier chapters) that can be useful when you are polishing a final mix. These include those listed in Table 15.3.

Table 15.3 Summary of Some Useful JS Mixing Plug-Ins

Name	Description
Liteon/pseudostereo	A stereo enhancer.
LOSER/Compciter	A combined compressor and high-frequency exciter.
LOSER/Exciter	A high-frequency stimulator.
LOSER/masterLimiter	A limiter whose features (including attack, release, and hold) make it suitable for use on the master track.
LOSER/SP1Limiter	A less sophisticated master limiter.
LOSER/stereoEnhancer	A stereo enhancer.
LOSER/StereoField	A stereo imager used to manipulate the stereo field of a mix. Controls include rotate and width. Rotation can be used to balance the relative left-right total levels in a mix without moving existing instruments away from the center. However, this can also upset the artistic balance and depth of the mix.
SStillwell/louderizer	Simply makes the mix louder.
SStillwell/mastertom	A program-dependent compressor especially suited to high-energy music.
SStillwell/realoud	Another way to make your mix louder.
SStillwell/lstereowidth	A combined stereo enhancer and stereo image manipulator.
SStillwell/width	A subtractive stereo enhancer, very easy to use.
Utility/dither_pscho	A dithering utility used when rendering to 16-bit from a higher bit depth.

Project Files Log

If you have completed all of the examples and tutorials in this chapter, you should have created the following files:

Preparation: Foggy150, Muddy150, Whiskey150

Tutorial 15.1: Foggy151

Checkpoint: Mud151, Whiskey151

Your complete project file log should now be as follows:

Alone00, Alone70, Alone76, Alone80, Alone88, Alone90, Alone91 Alone92, Alone93, Alone94, Alone95, Alone96, Alone97, Alone99, Alone99P, Alone120, Alone121, Alone122, Alone123, Alone140, Alone 141

AudioExperiment21, Impulse85

Foggy00, Foggy41, Foggy42, Foggy43, Foggy44, Foggy50, Foggy52, Foggy53, Foggy60, Foggy61, Foggy62, Foggy64, Foggy66, Foggy69, Foggy70, Foggy73, Foggy75, Foggy80, Foggy83, Foggy92, Foggy98, Foggy100, Foggy101, Foggy103, Foggy110, Foggy111, Foggy130, Foggy131, Foggy132, Foggy133, Foggy140, Foggy142, Foggy150, Foggy151

Lying00, Lying23, Lying43, Lying50, Lying51, Lying52, Lying54, Lying60, Lying61, Lying62, Lying80, Lying81

Mud00, Mud40, Mud41, Mud60, Mud63, Mud65, Mud70, Mud74, Mud80, Mud86, Mud86a, Mud87, Mud110, Mud112, Mud113, Mud120, Mud124, Mud130, Mud133, Mud150, Mud151

Whiskey00, Whiskey22, Whiskey30, Whiskey31, Whiskey32, Whiskey33, Whiskey60, Whiskey65, Whiskey67, Whiskey68, Whiskey70, Whiskey71, Whiskey72, Whiskey76, Whiskey80, Whiskey82, Whiskey84, Whiskey87, Whiskey110, Whiskey111, Whiskey120, Whiskey124, Whiskey130, Whiskey133, Whiskey150, Whiskey151

16 Where To From Here?

Three hundred or so pages ago, we started out on a journey of discovery not only to explore the main types of audio effects that are available for you to use with your recording projects, but also to understand how they work and how you can use them to your advantage. I hope that you have found the journey as enjoyable as I have and that you have learned much along the way.

If you glance through this chapter, you'll see two tables containing what at first might look rather like a glossary. You might be tempted to just skip over this. Don't. Those tables contain a summary of many of the most important issues that you will need to get a grip on in your use of audio effects. Taking a little time now to read through them and apply what they have to say can save you hours (and more) of frustration long into the future. Good luck!

Introduction

The only question that remains is that of how we should mark the end of this journey. For me, it makes sense to do so by getting down to identifying and discussing those nuts-and-bolts issues that will make it as quick and easy as possible for you to work with your DAW to get the very best out of your audio effects.

It isn't enough just to have a beautiful collection of plug-ins installed and buried away inside your computer. The more you have, the more important it is to know what's there and to be able to keep track of them. If the truth is told, most of us have more effects on our computers than we can recall from memory. This gives rise to two final questions that we need to consider—plug-in *management* and plug-in *interface*.

- By *plug-in management,* I mean the different tools, tricks, and techniques that your DAW makes available to you to organize your plug-ins so that any item you want to use will be readily available at your fingertips pretty much the moment you want to use it.

- By *plug-in interface,* I am referring to the way in which your host DAW works with you and with your plug-ins—especially third-party ones—to get the job done quickly, easily, efficiently, and enjoyably.

Of course, there will be gray areas—issues that don't necessarily fit entirely into one of these categories or the other. I'll squeeze them into the picture as best I can when they arise. What's more, not every host DAW will include in its feature set every single item listed in the two tables that follow. Your job is to find out exactly which of these features your DAW host does support and to learn how you can best use them.

Plug-In Management

Plug-in management is essentially about you having control over how your plug-ins are organized, both on your hard drive and when working within your host DAW. To put it at its simplest, if you can't keep track of what you've got, you won't be able to use it. Table 16.1 lists some of the most useful features that can help you manage your plug-ins. Some of them have already been discussed; many have not.

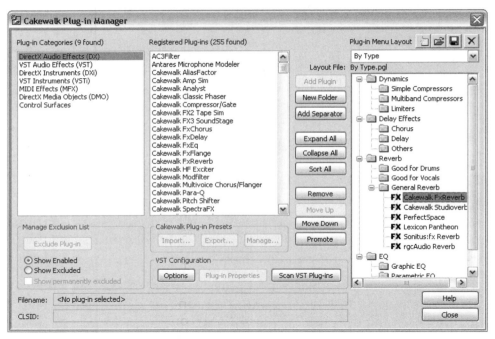

Figure 16.1   SONAR's Plug-In Manager lets you organize and group your plug-ins not just any which way you want, but also every which way you want. You can create as many groups and subgroups as you want, include the same plug-in with as many groups as you like, and rename them as you wish. Groups are automatically converted into menu trees—and with a couple of clicks, you can switch from one entire menu tree to another.

Plug-In Interface

The third-party plug-ins that you use with your DAW will most likely originate from a wide variety of sources. Each designer will have a preferred way of going about the job and a personal set of ideas on what makes a good interface. Every DAW handles its FX plug-in interface in ways that are to some extent unique. Every individual user has a

Table 16.1 Useful Plug-In Management Features to Look for in a DAW

Name	Description
Plug-in format recognition	Which of the different plug-in formats (for example, VST, DX, RTAS, AU) you are able to use will in the first instance be determined by your computer's operating system (such as Windows or Mac OS). However, it may also be further limited by the capabilities of your DAW program. Check which formats it can and cannot use.
Multiple plug-in folders	Before you can use any third-party plug-ins with your DAW, you need to install them on your hard drive. Outside of your DAW there will be several important management tasks that you will want to make as easy as possible, such as installing and uninstalling plug-ins, updating them, adding and removing files, accessing their documentation, and so on. The more flexible your host is in re-cognizing plug-ins from your operating system, the better. Some, for example, insist that they all must be installed in a single direc-tory. Others give you the flexibility to work within your operating system in whatever ways you like.
Creating plug-in groups	Typically, the default order for listing plug-ins within your DAW when you want to select and add one to a track's FX bin is simple alphabetical name order. This usually isn't very helpful. You need to be able to group them as you wish—for example, to group all your EQ plug-ins together, all your dynamics plug-ins together, and so on. SONAR's Plug-In Manager (see Figure 16.1) is a good example of plug-in management.
Searchable FX browser	Having your FX organized into groups won't always be enough when you wish to explore your effects library or to find a particular effect. Being able to search the list to find a particular effect or to list all effects with a particular character string in their name can be a great benefit.
Change default plug-in names	By default, your host DAW will assign to any and every plug-in the name supplied to it by the plug-in itself. For some plug-ins you will wish to change this name (used by default on your plug-in menus) to something more useful and which better reflects its purpose. For example, you might wish to change *SIR* to *Impulse Reverb*.
Track templates	Track templates allow you to store an entire track (or group of tracks) along with various audio effects and other settings. They lend them-selves to many applications, but one that really stands out is parallel FX processing. Once created and stored, an entire track template can be recalled into a project with just a couple of mouse clicks.
FX chains	An FX chain differs from a track template in that it stores only a track's plug-in chain (with, of course, the parameter settings). This can then be recalled into the FX bin of any existing track or media item in any project, again with just a couple of clicks. You'll find countless uses for these. For example, over time you may develop

(Continued)

Name	Description
	three or four favorite techniques for working with, say, female vocals. Simply create three or four different FX chains and recall any of them at will.
Preset management	As well as being able to access and use any presets supplied with a plug-in, take the time to learn how your DAW lets you create, manage, and retrieve your own presets. This can be a huge timesaver.
Mixer snapshots	Being able to take (and recall) mixer snapshots on the fly will make it so much easier for you to be imaginative, creative, and experimental in the use you make of plug-ins. This was discussed in several of the tutorials.
Undoable parameter changes	Check whether your DAW supports the ability to undo changes that you make to FX parameter values in much the same way as you can undo actions within the host DAW itself. The option to turn this feature on and off is also handy; this enables you to ensure that once you have your FX settings right, you can return to other aspects of your project (such as panning and volume levels) where you can tweak and undo to your heart's content without disturbing your FX parameter settings.
FX processing options	Especially if your computer uses multiple processors, check to see whether your DAW settings can be managed to make the most efficient use of your hardware when processing effects.
Plug-in compatibility options	Making a particular plug-in work with a particular host DAW can at times be a challenge. This is not really surprising. In most cases, the third-party plug-ins that you are using were not written with your particular host in mind. The ability to tweak your DAW's behavior to enable it to meet the idiosyncratic needs of those plug-ins that it finds difficult can be a great help here. Figure 16.2 shows an example of this, REAPER's VST Plug-Ins Settings page.
Plug-in run mode	The problem of crashes caused by compatibility issues between a plug-in and a DAW host is an all too common one. One way of at best avoiding and at worst reducing the inconvenience that this can cause is to have an option to specify for individual plug-ins whether you would like them to be hosted and run within the same process as the DAW itself or whether you would like them firewalled and run as separate processes. The latter option may be more resource intensive, but it is also likely to make your DAW more stable when it is confronted with a possible "rogue" plug-in.
Project file recovery mode	No matter what precautions you take, you must expect that there may still be times when a difficult plug-in will cause your DAW to crash. In some cases, this can even be triggered by simply inserting the plug-in into a track's FX bin. This is one more reason why saving a project often makes good sense. It is also important that you read up on your DAW's project recovery mode (it should have one), which will enable you to reopen the project with its plug-ins omitted, set to bypass, or set offline.

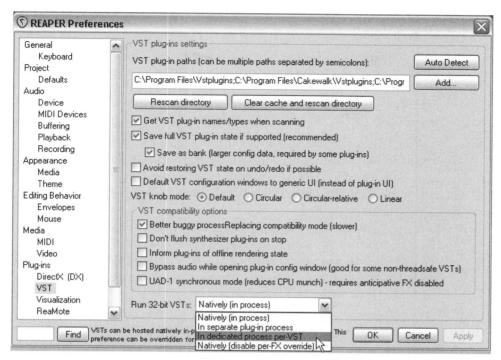

Figure 16.2   REAPER's VST plug-ins management options. Take the trouble to understand your host DAW's plug-in management options, what they do, and how you should best use them.

preferred method of working that another individual might not like. Put all that together, and how on earth are you supposed to come up with a plug-in interface that pleases most of the people most of the time?

The answer is, in part at least, by providing plenty of options that everybody can customize to suit their own needs. Another large part of the answer is to keep the basic interface as clean and simple as possible. Table 16.2 summarizes some of the issues involved. Remember that not every DAW can boast all of these features. Your next task is to find out which of these items you do have available, which are important to you, and how you can apply them. Don't attach any importance to the order in which these items are listed; what matters most is how important each of these features is to you.

Table 16.2 Useful Plug-In Interface Features to Look for in a DAW

Name	Description
FX parameter automation	For me, this is one of the most important of the many plug-in interface issues. That's why there is a whole chapter devoted to this topic, Chapter 11.

(Continued)

Name	Description
Access to FX	Ideally, you want to be able to manage both individual effects and complete FX chains as quickly and easily as possible. It helps if they can be accessed from both the main track view and the mixer view.
FX window display options	For me, this is very important. There may be times when you will want the FX windows displayed to automatically follow your track selection, so that as you move from one track to another, that track's FX are automatically displayed and opened. Other times, you may want to keep just one FX window at a time open, so that as you open one, any others are automatically closed. Then at other times, you might wish to keep as many open as you want. Check to see whether your DAW preferences and settings include options for you to select these and, indeed, other possible scenarios.
Rename FX instances	We've already discussed this—a few times, in fact. It can help you to keep in control of what you are doing to be able to rename a particular instance of (for example) an EQ plug-in to something like "Warmer vocal" or "Brighter guitar."
Cut/copy/paste FX	Make sure you are fully conversant with your DAW's technique for copying or moving a plug-in from one track to another (including any drag-and-drop method and/or shortcut keys)—including copying FX, complete with their settings, from one project to another.
Change FX order	Find (and use) the easiest and quickest method for changing the order of plug-ins within a track's FX bin. Usually, this is simply drag and drop.
Automatable bypass toggle	This has already been discussed. A simple bypass toggle for each individual effect that can be automated can be a very useful tool.
Other FX bypass options	The ability to use FX bypass toggles with individual tracks and items, busses, the master, and the entire project will help you to make wet/dry comparisons when you are evaluating your effects.
Automatable wet/ dry mix	This, too, has already been discussed. A wet/dry mix control added to plug-ins can make it quick and easy for you to tweak your effects, as well as being potentially a handy automation envelope.
Keyboard control	If you're used to keyboard navigation, then the option to pass keyboard control to plug-ins when they have focus will serve you well. This, for example, might allow you to use Tab and Shift+Tab to jump between parameters.
Show FX controls in mixer	Every effect will have some controls that you'll likely need to adjust more than others. For a compressor, for example, these are likely to include threshold and ratio. Being able to add these to your DAW's mixer and/or track control area (see Figure 16.3) can be tremendously useful. It gets even better if these controls are

Name	Description
	also saved with your track templates and FX chains (see Table 16.1).
Control surface implementation	The use of a control surface to adjust FX parameters with its physical knobs, buttons, and rotary and fader controls can potentially make life a lot easier than having to depend on a mouse all the time. However, any benefits that this brings will rapidly diminish if every time you switch from one plug-in to another, you have to spend five minutes reassigning the physical controls to the various FX parameters. Check to see whether your DAW makes it possible for you to assign these controls intelligently, so that you only have to set up the controls once for each type of plug-in. The control surface can then be told to automatically apply its controls to whichever plug-in has focus at any time.
Render/freeze/ unfreeze	Audio effects can be rather CPU intensive. The option of destructively rendering your effects onto a track can free up CPU. The ability to freeze a track with its effects in place will produce a similar result but is more useful than simple rendering if it comes with the option to unfreeze (restoring the track to its former status) if you later need to change your mind.

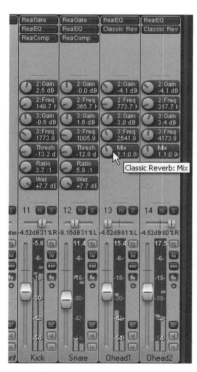

Figure 16.3 Adding FX parameter controls directly to a track's control panel in either mixer view (shown here) or the main track/arrangement view or both can give you faster and easier precision control over those items that are most likely to need tweaking.

Index

A

Abbey Road Studios, 218
Ableton Live, 2
    reverb presets, 194
    VST effects, storing, 8
    wet/dry mix automation with, 267
accordions
    frequency bands for, 74
    frequency range of, 43
acoustic environment, 38–39
acoustic guitars. *See* guitars
AIF files, 122
aliasing and bandwidth, 83
Alone Again file, 14
alto sax
    frequency bands for, 75
    frequency range of, 42
amplitude, 27
amplitude program, mixer snapshots
    with, 34–35
Arrange window, 5
Arrangement view, 5
atmosphere, delay creating, 58–62
attack. *See also* noise gates
    and compressors, 130–131
    in dynamic parameter modulation,
      265
    master limiter control, 318
AU format, 9
audio effects. *See also* chained audio
      effects; specific effects
    combining, 62–65
    reviewing project for, 309
    types of, 49–62
    window display options, 330
audio items, 5
audio shaping graph in dynamic
      parameter modulation, 265
audio signal flow, 65–66
    noise gates and, 105
    sidechain gating and, 114
auto make-up. *See* compressors
auto-pan, 242–244
auto release master limiter control, 318
automation, 257–273. *See also* dynamic
      parameter modulation; wet/dry
      automation
    bypass automation, 259, 264–267,
      269
    cut/copy with, 271
    display of envelope, 270
    editing, 270, 272
    envelope bypass toggle, 270
    EQ changes, automating, 260–262

    fade shapes for, 270
    horizontal/vertical lock, 270
    lock/unlock envelopes, 271
    methods of using, 259
    modes, 269
    noise gates, automation envelopes
      for fine-tuning, 112
    plug-in interface and, 329
    raise/lower envelope process, 270
    record/write precision for, 269
    reduce points for, 269
    simple parameter envelopes,
      258–259, 260–263
    summary of working with, 268–272
auxiliary/aux busses, 10
auxiliary track, 113, 154

B

background noises. *See* noise gates
band filters, 78–82. *See also* high-pass
      filters; high-shelf filters; low-pass
      filters
    band-pass filters, 80–81
    bell filters, 78
    with compression, 141–142
    DVD, bonus plug-ins on, 99
    low-shelf filters, 80
    notch filters, 80–81
band-pass filters, 80–81
bandwidth, 82–84
    octaves, bandwidths expressed in, 83
    Q values, bandwidths expressed in,
      83
    tutorial on, 84–86
banjoes, frequency range of, 42
bass guitars
    EQ changes for, 87
    frequency bands for, 74
    frequency range of, 42
bass trombone, frequency range of, 42
bassoon, frequency range of, 42
bell filters, 78
bleeds, noise gates and, 101, 110–112
Blue Cat
    Audio Flanger, 217–218, 220–221,
      236
    Audio Phaser, 236
    Audio Stereo Chorus plug-in,
      178–179
    Freeware Bundle, 17
Boss DM-2 delay, 165
brass instruments
    frequency range of, 42
    frequencys banks of, 74

busses
    effects busses, 9–10
    reverb bus, using, 197–198
bypass automation, 259, 264–267, 269
    plug-in interface options, 330

C

Cakewalk. *See also* SONAR; Sonitus
      compressor
    FX2 Tape Sim, 253
    vocal strip plug-in, 252
carrier track, 226
cellos, frequency range of, 42
chained audio effects, 64–65. *See also*
      serial effects
    channel strips and, 251–252
    guidelines for placing effects in
      guitar FX chain, 235
    guitar effects, 234–237
    parallel chained FX, 236–237
    and plug-in management, 327–328
    reverb effects chains, 211–213
chamber reverb, 198–199
channel effects, 241
channel splitting, 22
channel strips, 251–252
chorus, 176–180
    DVD, effects on, 237
    flanging compared, 218–219
    LFO shapes for, 178
    parameters, summary of, 177
    plug-ins, summary of, 181–182
    stereo chorus, 178
    tutorial for using, 178–179
Christian Borss's HybridReverb2
      plug-in, 209–211
clarinets, frequency range of, 42
clipping, 27
clock, defined, 6
comb filtering, 219
combining audio effects, 62–65
compatibility of plug-ins, 328
compression zones, 146–147
compressors, 121–161. *See also*
      multiband compression;
      ReaComp; Sonitus compressor
    attack, 130–131
    auto make-up, 138
      tutorial for using, 148–149
    auto release control, 137–138
    band filters with, 141–142
    chaining effects with, 64–65
    de-essers, compressors as, 245,
      246–247